Addiction, Representation and the Experimental Novel, 1985–2015

Addiction, Representation and the Experimental Novel, 1985–2015

Heath A. Diehl

ANTHEM PRESS

Anthem Press
An imprint of Wimbledon Publishing Company
www.anthempress.com

This edition first published in UK and USA 2022
by ANTHEM PRESS
75–76 Blackfriars Road, London SE1 8HA, UK
or PO Box 9779, London SW19 7ZG, UK
and
244 Madison Ave #116, New York, NY 10016, USA

First published in the UK and USA by Anthem Press in 2021

Copyright © Heath A. Diehl 2022

The author asserts the moral right to be identified as the author of this work.

All rights reserved. Without limiting the rights under copyright reserved above,
no part of this publication may be reproduced, stored or introduced into
a retrieval system, or transmitted, in any form or by any means
(electronic, mechanical, photocopying, recording or otherwise),
without the prior written permission of both the copyright
owner and the above publisher of this book.

British Library Cataloguing-in-Publication Data
A catalogue record for this book is available from the British Library.

ISBN-13: 978-1-83998-566-9 (Pbk)
ISBN-10: 1-83998-566-6 (Pbk)

Cover image: Cyrsiam / Shutterstock.com

This title is also available as an e-book.

For Gary and the kids
Again
Always

Story is the heartbeat of humanity and humanity gets really dark when the wrong stories are leading the people.
—Lauren Gunderson, *The Revolutionists*, p. 16

CONTENTS

Introduction	1
1. Bearing Witness: *Leaving Las Vegas* (1990)	19
2. Betraying: *Dope* (2006)	47
3. Gaslighting: *The Girl on the Train* (2015)	67
4. Transgressing: *Less Than Zero* (1985)	93
5. Disorienting: *The Orange Eats Creeps* (2010)	115
Conclusion	137
Bibliography	149
Index	161

INTRODUCTION

> One can feel obliged to look at [representations] that record great cruelties and crimes. One should feel obliged to think about what it means to look at them.
> —Susan Sontag, *Regarding the Pain of Others*[1]

At least since the advent of Modernism, which Thomas B. Gilmore, in his book *Equivocal Spirits: Alcoholism and Drinking in Twentieth-Century Literature* (1987), regards as a period of widespread cultural addiction,[2] the addict[3] has densely populated the history of the Western novel, stumbling blindly through its pages often as an object of scorn and derision to be looked at and pitied, but rarely to be understood in her/his/their complexity and treated with compassion. Indeed, pity has long constituted the default emotion assigned to the addict by Western writers, a not unsurprising trend given the etymological origins of the

---

[1] Susan Sontag, *Regarding the Pain of Others* (New York: Farrar, Straus and Giroux, 2003), 95.
[2] Thomas B. Gilmore, *Equivocal Spirits: Alcoholism and Drinking in Twentieth-Century Literature* (Chapel Hill: University of North Carolina Press, 1987), 16.
[3] Throughout this volume, I purposefully make use of the contested and ideologically problematic term "addict" when referring to the set of tropes and cultural narratives that comprise the social identity of someone with a substance use disorder. I do so as a means of keeping that problematic legacy—a legacy that I seek to unsettle in this volume—at the forefront of my mind and the minds of my readers. The phrase "substance use disorder" refers to the medical condition that has long been dubbed simply "addiction." I use this phrase not only for accuracy's sake (i.e., this is the terminology employed in the most recent, fifth edition of the *Diagnostic and Statistical Manual of Mental Disorders*), but also as a subtle but persistent means of reminding my readers that "addiction" is first and primarily a medical condition—a fact that too often is undermined by the narratives of weak will and loose morality that have dominated discussions of substance use disorders for more than two centuries. Finally, I use the term "addiction" as an umbrella category to denote the entire set of lived experiences that is precipitated and framed by, but not exhaustively constitutive of, the medical condition now known as a "substance use disorder."

term "addiction" in the Latin *addictiō*, which denotes "the binding of a person to another as a servant, adherent, or disciple."[4] Commonly regarded as a form of psycho-physical enslavement to a controlled or/and an illicit substance, addiction persistently has been represented within the novel, and, more broadly, within myriad forms of Western cultural representation, not as a disease (despite the wealth of scientific evidence that insists it is precisely that), but as a self-imposed moral quandary that shackles a person to a drug by way of a weak will.

When viewed through the lens of pity, any suffering, but particularly suffering that is perceived as self-imposed, as addiction commonly is, always and only reads as a spectacle of degradation, whether emotional, financial, moral, physical or/and psychological. Here, I employ the term "spectacle" in a manner similar to Emily Roxworthy, who, in *The Spectacle of Japanese American Trauma: Racial Performativity and World War II* (2008), defines the term as "the staging of an event and arrangement of an audience that rewards passive consumption and deters engaged witnessing, most often through what twenty-first-century Americans increasingly recognize as a strategy of 'shock and awe.'"[5] Stated differently, Roxworthy suggests that trauma, by default, is framed within Western modes of representation by extreme, albeit not necessarily exaggerated, pathos: for example, the presentation of a worst case outlier as representative of the whole.[6] This approach to representing trauma locates the reader in a position of passive consumption, and elicits from that reader an emotional response—perhaps pleasure (i.e., scopophilia) or fear (i.e., scopophobia)—but disallows an active witnessing whereby the addict (i.e., the subject of the representation, or, in the parlance of the novel, the protagonist) becomes something other than an object-to-be-codified and consumed.

Charles Jackson's *The Lost Weekend* (1944)[7] stands as an exemplar of these trends in the Modern addiction novel, introducing a character into the Western imaginary that is degraded in myriad ways by his alcoholism and, as result, that is cast as an object-to-be-pitied. For Jackson's protagonist, Don Birnam, "The drink [is] everything."[8] He repeatedly lies to his kind, albeit enabling, brother,

---

[4] "addiction, n." *OED Online*, December 2018, Oxford University Press, http://www.oed.com.ezproxy.bgsu.edu/view/Entry/2179?redirectedFrom=addiction (accessed January 10, 2019).

[5] Emily Roxworthy, *The Spectacle of Japanese American Trauma: Racial Performativity and World War II* (Honolulu: University of Hawai'i Press, 2008), 8.

[6] For a thoughtful examination of this tactic as it is expressed in the genre of reality television, see chapter 2, "Welcome (Again) to the Circus: Resurrecting the Freak Show and the Inebriate Asylum in A&E's *Intervention*," of my book *Wasted: Performing Addiction in America* (London: Routledge, 2016).

[7] Charles Jackson, *The Lost Weekend* (New York: Vintage Books, 2013).

[8] Ibid., 19.

Wick, as a means of facilitating his never-ending quest to drink, and he takes great pride—even pleasure—in this ability to be a "crafty sly masquerader."[9] Through such deceptions, Birnam undermines the sense of familial responsibility that drives Wick's altruistic actions and thereby divorces himself from the very kinship structures that might inject a semblance of order and compassion into his otherwise chaotic existence. And it is not just family with whom Birnam plays the crafty sly masquerader. He also commits fraud and petty theft against strangers in the hopes of securing a few more dollars to bankroll his addiction, actions that mark him as not merely deceitful but criminal.

Of course, like most alcoholic characters across the history of Western literary representation, Birnam does not just exhibit sociopathic characteristics but also repeatedly proves himself a narcissist, comprised of equal parts self-aggrandizement and self-loathing. He locates himself, for example, within the celebrated literary pantheon of such talented, but tormented, figures as "Poe and Keats, Byron, Dowson, Chatterton,"[10] despite the fact that he has failed to achieve even a modicum of recognition, let alone fame, for his own writing. At the same time, Birnam experiences disgust, shame and self-loathing on virtually every page of the novel, and acknowledges how tired and hopeless he feels in the face of alcoholism, "that interminable process and recurring cycle."[11] To no avail, he engages in self-reproach, "Why did he *ever* do it, why was he *always* doing it over and over again?,"[12] the indeterminacy of the pronoun "it" acting as a stand-in for the unspeakable addiction that at once torments and thrills him. And all of Birnam's internal conflict is set against the backdrop of a deeper, and, for the United States of the 1940s, an even more shocking secret that Birnam has battled for his entire existence: homosexuality. His visit to the sanitarium late in the novel is perceived simultaneously as scandalous and as an affirmation—indeed, an etiology—of the addiction that torments him. In the end, what Jackson manages to create is a profoundly insular and claustrophobic diegetic world in which readers often feel trapped within, and, indeed, enslaved by, the mind of a man who is doggedly pursuing self-destruction. The extreme pathos of Birnam's torment assaults readers with a form of trauma that is both painful to look at and impossible to ignore. In short, a spectacle of degradation.

The degraded nature of Jackson's protagonist is underscored by the relationship that the text forges between character, subject matter and readers—a relationship that undermines the expectations that readers typically have for

---

[9] Ibid., 47.
[10] Ibid., 17.
[11] Ibid., 222.
[12] Ibid., 43.

protagonists within literary realism. In conventional examples of literary realism, a tradition on which *The Lost Weekend* borrows quite heavily in terms of narrative structure and world building, the protagonist functions as both the center of attention and readers' foothold within the diegetic world. That the protagonist character exists as the focal point of the narrative encourages the reader to "redefine every aspect of the plot in terms of its effect on the protagonist, along with a penchant to believe the protagonist, a willingness to take the protagonist as the text's ultimate author."[13] Read this way, the protagonist becomes a point of identification through which readers can bridge the gaps between the extra-diegetic and the diegetic worlds and enter into what Rick Altman, in *A Theory of Narrative* (2008), terms "a participatory present [in which the reader shares] the protagonist's position."[14] This is not to suggest that readers and the protagonist are one, as the term "identification" only ever connotes a sense of connection, or a "fellow feeling," between two or more entities; but it is to suggest that the protagonist is a crucial tool for providing readers access to the diegetic world and for facilitating those readers' understanding of and emotional investment in the narrative that unfolds.

In *The Lost Weekend*, by contrast, the character of Don Birnam most certainly exists as the focus of the narrative to the point that, as I note above, the diegetic world eventually is contracted to encompass only the span of his claustrophobic, and increasingly delusional, interiority. But rather than drawing readers in and providing a tool through which those readers can better understand and be more invested in both character and narrative, Jackson repeatedly (albeit implicitly) emphasizes the stark contrasts between his protagonist and his readers, thereby identifying Birnam not as a point of identification, but as a point of differentiation. The near-constant emphasis on pathos and degradation, rather than eliciting the readers' sympathy and cementing a compassionate bond between character and readers, has a distancing effect, producing within readers feelings of equal parts disgust and contempt. Within this dynamic, the addict character becomes a symbol of radical alterity akin to the displays of human oddities in the freak shows and museums of the nineteenth century: or, to rework a statement that performance artist and cultural critic Coco Fusco has made regarding the silhouette work of US artist Kara Walker, *The Lost Weekend* becomes a statement regarding sober readers' scopophobic fascination with abject imagery of addicts.[15] As such, the self-loathing that Birnam expresses particularly with regard to his unpublished

---

[13] Rick Altman, *A Theory of Narrative* (New York: Columbia University Press, 2008), 181.
[14] Ibid., 183.
[15] Coco Fusco, *The Bodies That Were Not Ours: And Other Writings* (London: Routledge, 2001), 38.

manuscript, *In a Glass*—"who would ever want to read a novel about a [...] drunk!"—registers as a kind of metafictive commentary on the worth (or, more aptly, lack thereof) of Jackson's own protagonist.

This literary tradition not only presents Western readers with a very limited and narrow view of the lived experiences of addiction but also prescribes for those readers a similarly limited and narrow vantage point from which to engage with such representations. Repeatedly coerced into accepting the addict character's degraded state as both pitiful and as a consequence of her/his/their moral failure, Western readers always and only are "obliged to look at [representations] that record great cruelties and crimes" but not "think about what it means to look at them."[16] Stated differently, Western addiction fiction encourages its readers to locate themselves in a position of privilege vis-à-vis that addict character—that is, to regard the addict as somehow disadvantaged, even if that misfortune is "deserved" because presumably "self-inflicted," and therefore to see the self/reader as somehow a more fortunate, morally superior being. This is, of course, one of the most common operations of pity as a relational dynamic; indeed, in *Literature of Pity* (2014), David Punter acknowledges that, in the vernacular, the term "pity" typically is used "in relation to third parties," especially those who are (or, are perceived to be) disadvantaged, and he goes on to explain that as a result of such expressions of pity, "we might be accused [...] of condescension, of being patronizing, of extending rather than ameliorating a position of privilege."[17] In other words, pity places readers at a remove from the addict character, encouraging a dispassionate, but not entirely emotionless, response to that character and her/his/their experiences and opening readers up to patronization, condescension and paternalism.

Unfortunately, *The Lost Weekend* is not an anomaly in the trajectory of Western literary history; in fact, during the two-plus-year period when I was actively researching and refining the scope of the current volume, I read nearly three hundred novels about addiction from across myriad subgenres and national traditions, and more often than not, this narrative pattern and character trope stood as the default modus operandi for representing who addicts are and how they navigate the world with a substance use disorder. My research spanned over a hundred years of literary production, with the earliest novel read being Robert Louis Stevenson's *The Strange Case of Dr. Jekyll and Mr. Hyde*, which was originally published in 1886, and the most recent being Julian Barnes's *The Only Story*, which was published in 2018. Yet, whether reading Oscar Wilde's *The Picture of Dorian Gray* (Ireland, 1890), Jacqueline Susann's

---

[16] Sontag, *Regarding the Pain of Others*, 95.
[17] David Punter, *Literature of Pity* (Edinburgh: Edinburg University Press, 2014), 1.

Valley of the Dolls (United States, 1966), Stephen King's *The Shining* (United States, 1977), Luke Davies's *Candy: A Novel of Love and Addiction* (Australia, 1977), Jay McInerney's *Bright Lights, Big City* (United States, 1984), Irvine Welsh's *Trainspotting* (Scotland, 1993), Mian Mian's *Candy* (Japan, 2003), Chris Abani's *GraceLand* (Kenya, 2004), Essam Youssef's *A 1/4 Gram* (Egypt, 2008), Isabel Allende's *Maya's Notebook* (Chile, 2013), or James Hannaham's *Delicious Foods* (United States, 2016), Western readers repeatedly have experienced the addict as a morally toxic and self-destructive force bent on destroying the very institutions, practices and ideologies that historically have connoted reason, order and civilization. Across gender lines, ethnic/racial heritages, national traditions, generational cohorts and literary subgenres, such novels, and countless others, concern themselves not with who addicts are and with how addicts navigate the world with a substance use disorder, but rather with how addiction is perceived and, more so, censured from the standpoint of sobriety, and they ultimately illustrate how deeply entrenched these shared misunderstandings of addiction are in the Western novel, and, indeed, in the broader Western cultural imaginary.

By about six months into my reading for this project, I had reached a point where my interest in addiction fiction had not simply waned, but had dramatically plummeted due to what I perceived as the dearth of meaningful and substantive representations of addiction. I was at times frustrated, and at other times enraged, at the lack of compassion that I witnessed with respect to how the lived experiences of addiction were being represented within the pages of the Western novel, and the condescending way that I, as a reader, was being positioned in relation to those representations. Why, I wondered, was the reach of Puritanism so expansive, encompassing vast swaths of time and location to systematically degrade and fix the addict within one of two destinies: death or shame-filled remission? Why were moral superiority and disgust the only emotions that I, as a reader, was permitted to feel in relation to the addict? Where were the novels, I wondered, that allowed, even encouraged, me "to imagine the experiences of others and to participate in their sufferings,"[18] not in an assimilative or appropriative manner, but in a way that reveals a sensitivity to suffering, a passion for social justice and a commitment to action, three key preconditions to compassion, according to Kathleen Woodward?[19]

---

[18] Martha C. Nussbaum, "Compassion: The Basic Social Emotion," *Social Philosophy and Policy* 13, no. 1 (1996): 27–58 (50).

[19] Kathleen Woodward, "Calculating Compassion," in *Compassion: The Culture and Politics of an Emotion*, ed. Lauren Berlant (New York: Routledge, 2004), 59–86 (68).

At the half-year mark, I experienced—quite unexpectedly—a resurgence of interest in addiction fiction when I read Paula Hawkins's *The Girl on the Train* (2015), interestingly enough not as research for the current volume, but in preparation to teach an Honors Seminar course on the topic of "Exploring the *Dark Places* of Domestic Noir." After six months of reading thousands of pages in which addicts figured as little more than spectacles of degradation whose shame and, often, horrific deaths only ever served as kudos for readers' sobriety, *The Girl on the Train* was a revelation: a text whose chief concern at once appears to be challenging, rather than recapitulating or reifying, "the conventional wisdom and values"[20] surrounding the lived experiences of addiction, especially as that wisdom and those values are represented in literary works like *The Lost Weekend*. The challenge that Hawkins's novel poses to more conventional works of addiction fiction derives chiefly from the ways in which the author manipulates readers' expectations regarding narrativity, genre and spectatorship. Once I had identified what enabled Hawkins's novel to stand out from the morass of novels like *The Lost Weekend*, I began reading in earnest once again, but this time my energies were concentrated on locating other novels that, whether explicitly or implicitly, refused to remain within the formal, generic or/and ideological boundaries established in Western addiction fiction.

Experimentation in the novel principally manifests itself in acts of formal risk-taking and subversion; however, in the current volume, I depart from common understandings regarding the degree to which authors must deviate from prevailing narrative expectations in order for that author's work to be classified as *experimental*. In *Experimental Fiction: An Introduction for Readers and Writers* (2014), for instance, Julie Armstrong suggests that this type of writing, whose aim, she argues, is "not necessarily to tell a story,"[21] is always and only decidedly anti-realist, as "traditional realism" is "considered to be too restricting to express some writers' thoughts and ideas."[22] For me, Armstrong's view of experimental fiction is itself too restrictive, in that it seems to recognize as constitutive of that body of literature only those works of postmodern fiction that so violate traditional narrative expectations—and so adamantly refuse to provide readers with even a modicum of "rules" for the reading experience—that those works only ever frustrate and confound readers. Within this dynamic, the text remains shrouded in ambiguity, if not outright

---

[20] Martha C. Nussbaum, *Cultivating Humanity: A Classical Defense of Reform in Liberal Education* (Cambridge, MA: Harvard University Press, 1998), 99.
[21] Julie Armstrong, *Experimental Fiction: An Introduction for Readers and Writers* (London: Bloomsbury Academic, 2014), 7.
[22] Ibid., 2.

perplexity and chaos, resisting even the most active and informed attempts by readers to wrest meaning from it. Given this definition of *experimental fiction*, only a single novel examined within this study (i.e., Grace Krilanovich's *The Orange Eats Creeps*, 2010) would even meet Armstrong's criteria.

In the current volume, my view of *experimental fiction* is more liberal, or inclusive, than Armstrong's, thereby rendering the scope of this study more expansive and, I would argue, the findings much richer than they might otherwise be. While I agree with Armstrong that "experimental fiction departs from conventional expectations or Aristotelian principles,"[23] and that such works "make more and new, sometimes baffling, demands on the reader,"[24] I include within that body of writing a much broader and more diverse collection of approaches to narrativity than Armstrong and her ilk likely would. To be sure, in my research, I opted to read many realistic texts, acknowledging, as Catherine Belsey writes in her seminal text *Critical Practice* (1980), that "the movement of classic realist narrative towards closure ensures the reinstatement of order, *sometimes a new order*, sometimes the old restored, but always intelligible because familiar."[25] In fact, I even included in the final Table of Contents several texts—among them John O'Brien's *Leaving Las Vegas* (1990), Sara Gran's *Dope* (2006) and Hawkins's *The Girl on the Train*—whose narratives initially might seem to align fairly closely with the formal and ideological mandates of classic realism. Yet, I argue that all of these works are experimental because of the unique and often unexpected ways in which they position readers vis-à-vis both addict characters and narrative action. These novels, and the two others that I examine within the subsequent chapters, do not necessarily demand that readers "suspend their *autopilot* expectations" in toto, as would be the case for the kinds of novels under study in Armstrong's book, but they do require readers to "discover *new* ways of seeing"[26] that enable them to regard addict characters and their lived experiences in more critical and compassionate ways than the Western novel historically has encouraged its readers to do.

The chapters of this study are not ordered chronologically; rather, the argument that I chart throughout the body of this volume proceeds by degrees from least to most experimental ways of seeing. The novels included in this study challenge readers to bear witness to addiction without the requisite framework of pathos inherited long ago from realism. They gaslight readers, feeding them false information as a means of calling into question some of readers'

---

[23] Ibid., 5.
[24] Ibid., 6.
[25] Catherine Belsey, *Critical Practice* (London: Routledge, 1980), 75 (emphasis added).
[26] Armstrong, *Experimental Fiction*, 7.

most deeply held preconceptions regarding the lived experiences of addiction. They variously undermine, rework and transgress generic boundaries, and, in so doing, invite readers to inhabit (albeit temporarily) a world in which addiction is not emblematic of moral sickness and the addict need not be maligned in order to be understood. And, finally, they invent entirely new, and as such often disorienting, worlds which operate according to unfamiliar, even confounding, rules, thereby encouraging their authors and their readers to imagine the possibilities of a world in which the addict is not always and only a monstrous abjection.

As the above explanation makes clear, the current volume is principally concerned with the myriad ways in which writers create and, of equal import, readers engage with addiction fiction. Methodologically speaking, this book marks a return—if, indeed, there ever was a departure within the field of English studies—to the type of reader-response theory advanced, from roughly the 1970s forward, by such thinkers as Wayne Booth, Stanley Fish, Wolfgang Iser and Louise M. Rosenblatt.[27] While reader-response theory, broadly defined, constitutes a somewhat amorphous field of literary criticism—one that is explicated in a very nuanced and precise manner by Robert C. Holub in *Reception Theory: A Critical Introduction* (1984)[28]—the many related, but distinct, critical approaches that are housed under its umbrella do share some key foundational assumptions that serve as a guiding force for my work in the pages that follow. The current study begins with the assumption that meaning belongs to a text, is both "circumscribed by [a text]" and "traceable

---

[27] It is important to note that a return to Reader-Response Criticism in the contemporary moment is not a de facto regression given that theoretical schools of thought (like historical periods) do not simply and conclusively "end" when their popularity has waned, or/and when they have been replaced by another flavor-of-the-month; instead, the influence of such theories bleeds over into succeeding periods and schools of thought, continuing to shape the direction and course of scholarship within a field of study sometimes long after their heydays have passed. Within the field of English studies, many of the foundational principles of Reader-Response Criticism continue to influence the ways in which a wide variety of critics—from postmodernists to cultural critics to feminist scholars and historicists, to name only a few—enter into and engage with texts. In large part thanks to identity politics and postmodern theory, we in English studies have, since the 1970s, become increasingly more attuned to the significant ways that our histories, our experiences and our presumptions come to bear on our interpretive processes. Regardless of the specific critical framework that we might employ to wrest meaning from a literary text, most English studies scholars in the current moment would, I suspect, concur that meaning-making begins in the distinct reading process that a unique critic brings to a specific text in a given historical moment, an assumption that we inherit directly from Reader-Response critics.

[28] Robert C. Holub, *Reception Theory: A Critical Introduction* (London: Methuen, 1984).

to it,"²⁹ and that, within this dynamic, readers become "flawed but reverential seeker[s] after the truths [...] preserved in literary art."³⁰

Each of the five body chapters of this volume takes as its proper object a contemporary Western novel about the lived experiences of addiction and proceeds under the assumption that those texts are endowed by their creators with a set of meanings that are available to those who possess the literary competence to access them.³¹ However, while the current volume refuses to ignore some of the key intellectual legacies bequeathed to contemporary readers by the New Criticism of the mid-twentieth century, neither does it shackle readers to the author's intentions or/and an objective text that is meaningful independent of the reading experience. Instead, I regard these novels as what Umberto Eco has termed "open texts"—that is, as texts "that not only [call] for the cooperation of [their] own reader, but also [want] this reader to make a series of interpretive choices which even though not infinite are, however, more than one."³² In so doing, I recognize that "meaning is never a fixed essence inherent in the text but is always constructed by the reader, the result of a 'circulation' between social formation, reader and text."³³

Throughout the pages of this volume, I follow the lead of Jane P. Tompkins, who, in the Introduction to *Reader-Response Criticism: From Formalism to*

---

²⁹ Jane P. Tompkins, "An Introduction to Reader-Response Criticism," in *Reader-Response Criticism: From Formalism to Post-Structuralism*, ed. Tompkins (Baltimore, MD: Johns Hopkins University Press, 1980), ix–xxvi (xv).

³⁰ Ibid., xiii.

³¹ My use of the phrase "literary competence" here is a nod to the work of Jonathan Culler, in which the literary critic regards "literary competence" as "the possession or 'mastery' of the literary conventions which are required, in addition to linguistic competence, for either the writing or reading of literature" (Shea, "Culler, Jonathan Dwight" 283). In his essay "Literary Competence," Culler explains this concept in greater detail, noting: "When a speaker of a language hears a phonetic sequence, he is able to give it meaning because he brings to the act of communication an amazing repertoire of conscious and unconscious knowledge [...]. [W]hen the sequence of words is treated *as a literary work*[,] [...] [t]he work has structure and meaning because it is read in a particular way, because these potential properties, latent in the object itself, are actualized by the theory of discourse applied in the act of reading" (101–2). See Victor Shea, "Culler, Jonathan Dwight," in *Encyclopedia of Contemporary Literary Theory: Approaches, Scholars, Terms*, ed. Irene Rima Makaryk (Toronto: University of Toronto Press, 1993), 283–84; and Jonathan Culler, "Literary Competence," in *Reader-Response Criticism: From Formalism to Post-Structuralism*, ed. Jane P. Tompkins (Baltimore, MD: Johns Hopkins University Press, 1980), 101–17.

³² Umberto Eco, *The Role of the Reader: Explorations in the Semiotics of Texts* (Bloomington: Indiana University Press, 1979), 4.

³³ Belsey, *Critical Practice*, 69.

Post-Structuralism (1980), suggests that "texts are written by readers, not read, since [...] the formal features of the text [...] and the reader's interpretive strategies are mutually interdependent."[34] Tompkins goes on to explain that "a [text] cannot be understood apart from its results. Its 'effects,' psychological and otherwise, are essential to any accurate description of its meaning, since that meaning has no effective existence outside of its realization in the mind of a reader."[35] Within these pages, I regard myself as a reader whose principal charge is to engage actively and compassionately in the interpretive process—a process informed as much by my own literary competence as by the sociohistorical situatedness of the text—in order to understand how the novels under study contribute to, challenge and at times undermine ongoing conversations about who addicts are and how it feels to navigate the diegetic *and* extra-diegetic worlds with a substance use disorder.

For each of the novels included in the Table of Contents, I have identified one primary narrative technique, or device, that is at work in that text and that, in some way, challenges the generic, thematic or/and topical conventions that have predominated within Western representations of addiction over the past two centuries. In effect, the current volume undertakes the important and timely project of unfixing the addict. In this respect, to "fix" the addict is not to insist on sobriety or death as an always and already—an understanding that conflates the term *fix* with the denotation *repair* and perpetuates a treatment model of addiction in which the addict will only ever exist as a problem-to-be-solved.[36] Instead, by isolating these techniques and analyzing their operations within not only the chosen literary texts but also the social formations that have affixed the addict to a limiting and harmful set of representations, I seek to reveal the ways in which these experimental novels unhinge the addict's *image* within the popular Western imaginary, offering a more diverse collection of representations, as well as more possible responses to the representations than simply the defaults of moral superiority or/and disgust. In short, through unconventional approaches to narrativity and narrative voice, the novels that I discuss within this book challenge readers both to acknowledge and to attempt to understand the addict's humanity, and, in so doing, these works open up an opportunity for readers to recover their own.

---

[34] Tompkins, "An Introduction to Reader-Response Criticism," xxii.
[35] Ibid., ix.
[36] This terminology and concept borrow heavily on much of the work done in the field of disability studies around the medical model of disability. For a thoughtful overview of this concept, see Colin Cameron, "The Medical Model," in *Disability Studies: A Student's Guide*, ed. Cameron (Los Angeles, CA: Sage, 2014), 98–100.

In *Cultivating Humanity: A Classical Defense of Reform in Liberal Education* (1998), Martha C. Nussbaum suggests that "the literary imagination develops compassion," often simply by "asking [readers] to confront—and for a time to be—those whom we do not usually like to meet,"[37] certainly an apt description of the addict in Western literary history. Nussbaum's discussion of the ways in which literary texts can help to facilitate a poetics of compassion, particularly with regard to those individuals whom readers may be inclined (or, coerced) to see "as invisible, their prospects as unrelated to one's own,"[38] offers a compelling framework through which to begin my own investigation into the texts I have chosen to discuss in this book, aligning in interesting and productive ways with some of the core tenets of Reader-Response Criticism. As with Reader-Response Criticism, Nussbaum's theory of compassionate reading focuses its attention on the spectator who, as a precondition to exercising compassion, must acknowledge "that another person, in some ways similar to oneself, has suffered some significant pain or misfortune in a way for which that person is not, or not fully, to blame."[39] This is a particularly difficult obstacle to overcome with respect to the topic of addiction, given the predominance of addict blaming that occurs across Western cultures, and yet it is precisely the place where compassion must begin since, as Dr. Adi Jaffe explains in *Psychology Today*, "blame and shame come from a place of judgment, which has no place in a helping effort."[40]

By contrast, to read with compassion is to read not from a place of judgment, but rather for a place of attempted understanding, which is perhaps why Nussbaum regards compassion as "essential for civic responsibility."[41] Reading for the purpose of understanding demands that readers confront the addict on the addict's own terms, no matter how challenging or even "offensive" those terms may be, while also and simultaneously recognizing the presuppositions about addiction (and even about what constitutes "offensiveness") that they, as readers, bring to the reading experience and how those presuppositions potentially compromise their ability to understand. Reading for the purpose of understanding further challenges readers to acknowledge "a sense of their own vulnerability to misfortune [...] to entertain the thought that this suffering person might be them."[42] This attitude, too, is particularly difficult for some to adopt in relation to addicts precisely because addiction is

---

[37] Nussbaum, *Cultivating Humanity*, 99.
[38] Ibid., 92.
[39] Ibid., 90–91.
[40] Adi Jaffe, "Want to Beat Addiction? Stop Blaming Addicts," *Psychology Today*, April 23, 2018, https://www.psychologytoday.com/us/blog/all-about-addiction/201804/want-beat-addiction-stop-blaming-addicts (accessed January 24, 2019).
[41] Nussbaum, *Cultivating Humanity*, 99.
[42] Ibid., 91.

widely (and erroneously) perceived to be a disease of the will, rather than of the body and the mind, and, as children of the Enlightenment, twenty-first-century Western audiences want to believe that they possess a greater sense of control—including self-control—than they actually do. This is particularly true with respect to Westerners' vulnerabilities to a substance use disorder. But in order to read compassionately, we must transgress (if only momentarily) the seemingly indelible lines of demarcation between them and us, between Other and self,[43] and accept that no one, including the self, is invulnerable to misfortune and suffering. When we do so, compassionate reading potentially can foster compassionate action, which Nussbaum suggests is driven principally by the Golden Rule, or the thought "that might have been me, and that is how I should want to be treated."[44]

At present, a modest, but substantive, body of scholarship exists within the fields of cultural and literary studies around the topic of addiction; *Addiction, Representation and the Experimental Novel, 1985–2015* builds on and distinguishes itself from this existing scholarship in several noteworthy ways. In the first place, although addiction as a literary subject, as well as a lived experience, elicits—even insists upon—strong emotional responses on the part of those who encounter it, the topic to date has virtually escaped the notice of those critics who seek to uncover the ways in which literature touches, moves and mobilizes readers, as Melissa Gregg and Gregory J. Seigworth describe the central purpose of affect theory.[45] Despite the important role that compassion might (nay, should) play in the practices of writing and reading addiction fiction, the current volume is the first book to work at the intersections of affect theory, addiction and the novel.

Additionally, since the late twentieth century, addiction has become a *de rigeur* topic of study for scholars within the broadly defined, interdisciplinary field of cultural studies, producing such significant texts as Avital Ronell's *Crack Wars: Literature Addiction Mania* (1992), Janet Farrell Brodie and Mark Redfield's *High Anxieties: Cultural Studies in Addiction* (2002) and Anna Alexander and Mark S. Roberts's *high culture: reflections on addiction and modernity* (2003). However, in these previous studies, when literature is discussed at all, it is cast simultaneously as a reflection of the "rituals of human life in communities"[46] and as

---

[43] Ibid., 92.
[44] Ibid., 91.
[45] Melissa Gregg and Gregory J. Seigworth, "An Inventory of Shimmers," *The Affect Theory Reader*, ed. Gregg and Seigworth (Durham, NC: Duke University Press, 2010), 24.
[46] Julie Rivkin and Michael Ryan, "Introduction: 'The Politics of Culture,'" in *Literary Theory: An Anthology*, ed. Rivkin and Ryan (Malden, MA: Blackwell, 1998), 1025–27 (1025).

a site at which various political, social and economic (but not literary) forces converge. Stated differently, the literature seemingly is not, in itself, regarded as a valuable avenue of inquiry for understanding how a group of people talks to themselves about the lived experiences of addiction, but rather is seen, at best, as a mere illustration of larger socioeconomic and politico-cultural conversations about addiction, which, in such inquiries, displace the literary text as the proper object of study. But what is overlooked in such inquiries is how the literature functions *as literature* in order to make meaning about addiction—that is, how literary language, poetic devices and the modes of operation that characterize literary output provide insight into how a culture talks to itself about who addicts are and how it feels to navigate the world with a substance use disorder.

A prime example of this type of study is Jane Lilienfeld and Jeffrey Oxford's *The Languages of Addiction* (1999), which identifies from its opening line the contested terrain of "alcoholism theory" as its proper object. While the essays included in Lilienfeld and Oxford's volume discuss a myriad of literary texts— from Gustav Flaubert's *Madame Bovary* (1856) to Thomas Hardy's *The Mayor of Casterbridge* (1886) to Ernest Hemingway's *The Sun Also Rises* (1926) to Djuna Barnes's *Nightwood* (1936) and James Baldwin's "Sonny's Blues" (1957)—the argument thread running through the volume never strays from the editors' initial statement of purpose: that is, "to use literature as a springboard to a sensitive discussion of alcoholism and drug addiction."[47] Indeed, although Lilienfeld suggests at the close of her introductory chapter that "the questions raised and the intertextual resonances from these divergent texts enlarge the readers' awareness of how one might understand alcoholism and addiction as they are created in literature,"[48] in the end, the focus remains firmly placed on sociocultural discourses, or languages, of addiction, with the fiction serving as mere illustration of what is happening beyond the pages of literary output.

When, on the rare occasion, critics have narrowed their sights to the literature, their inquiries have most frequently concentrated on how the biography of the addict-author lends insight into the operations of the literary texts. Works like Tom Dardis's *The Thirsty Muse: Alcohol and the American Writer* (1989), Frank Hilton's *Baudelaire in Chains: A Portrait of the Artist as a Drug Addict* (2003) and Olivia Laing's *The Trip to Echo Springs: On Writers and Drinking* (2013) perhaps are more accurately classified as *literary history* or even *literary biography* than as literary criticism given that the proper object at the center of

---

[47] Jane Lilienfeld and Jeffrey Oxford, eds., *The Languages of Addiction* (New York: St. Martin's Press, 1999), unpaginated front matter.
[48] Jane Lilienfeld, "Introduction," in *The Languages of Addiction*, ed. Lilienfeld and Jeffrey Oxford (New York: St. Martin's Press, 1999), xxiv.

each study is the lived experiences of the artist and not her/his/their artistic output. This approach, while quite insightful with respect to the psychology of the addict-author, nonetheless tells readers very little about how the literature functions as a repository of cultural knowledge regarding addiction, producing said knowledge precisely through the ways in which it tells stories and the kinds of stories that it ultimately tells, or refuses to tell.

Cara Fabre's *Challenging Addiction in Canadian Literature and Classrooms* (2016) shares with the current volume a deep and profound interest in the ways in which "addiction narratives emerge" from literature and "[inform] our common sense understanding" of the lived experiences of addiction.[49] And, to be sure, literary texts figure much more prominently in the work of Fabre than in the work of Dardis, Hilton and Liang; in fact, the body of Fabre's book is comprised of incisive and nuanced analyses of six contemporary Canadian novels about addiction, including Christy Ann Conlin's *Heave* (2002), Heather O'Neill's *lullabies for little criminals* (2006), Ibi Kaslik's *Skinny* (2004), Kevin Patterson's *Consumption* (1967), Beatrice Culleton Mosionier's *In Search of April Raintree* (1983), and Eden Robinson's *Monkey Beach* (2000). However, Fabre's project differs significantly from the work that I undertake in the current volume, most particularly with respect to methodology and purpose. Fabre undertakes a "discourse analysis"[50] of the aforementioned texts and advances the claim that "the tools of critical pedagogies can be applied to [the] study of addiction narratives" (15) as a means of "teaching destigmatizing understandings of addiction" (23). In this way, literature figures as a bridge spanning "the gap between course content and social interactions" (22), but it is only meaningful as and when it serves to refigure (for student-readers) the ideological tropes of addiction through a lens of social suffering (4).

Susan Zieger, in *Inventing the Addict: Drugs, Race, and Sexuality in Nineteenth-Century British and American Literature* (2008), focuses her readers' attention on the interrelationship between literary texts and sociocultural discursive formations of the addict—a preoccupation that Zieger, Fabre and I share. However, Zieger's work is very narrowly focused on a modest body of largely canonical British and US literary texts from the nineteenth century, including (but not limited to) Harriet Beecher Stowe's *Uncle Tom's Cabin* (1852), Robert Louis Stevenson's *The Strange Case of Dr. Jekyll and Mr. Hyde* (1886) and Bram Stoker's *Dracula* (1897). Moreover, Zieger is principally invested in uncovering the sociocultural mechanisms (of which literature is but one) that "invented" the addict as both a pathological and a fetishized identity. For Zieger, as for

---

[49] Cara Fabre, *Challenging Addiction in Canadian Literature and Classrooms* (Toronto: University of Toronto Press, 2016), 24.
[50] Ibid., 12.

Fabre, the literary texts function as a means to an end, rather than a meaningful end in and of themselves.

Gilmore's *Equivocal Spirits* suggests from its onset that "an author's work [...] and its details"[51] are of primary concern to the critic. Yet, despite the fact that Gilmore "gives priority" to the literature *qua* literature,[52] ultimately his study differs from this project in two significant ways. First, throughout *Equivocal Spirits*, Gilmore places equal emphasis on literary representation and scientific knowledge, assuming that "a mastery of the scientific knowledge of alcoholism [...] is indispensable both as a foundation for studying literary representations of the illness and as a means of accurately appreciating the distinctive contribution that literature makes."[53] As a result, Gilmore's study at times still gives short shrift to the question of "literariness"—that is, "the qualit[ies] which [make] a work literary"[54] and how those qualities function to make meaning about the addict.

A second difference between *Equivocal Spirits* and the current volume concerns the scope of these two projects. Unlike Gilmore, who, as the subtitle of his volume indicates, focuses exclusively on "Alcoholism and Drinking in Twentieth-Century Literature," I am concerned here with a variety of substance use disorders, including alcoholism (i.e., *Leaving Las Vegas* and *The Girl on the Train*), heroin (i.e., *Dope*) and methamphetamine addiction (i.e., *The Orange Eats Creeps*) and polysubstance use disorder (i.e., Bret Easton Ellis's *Less Than Zero*, 1985). To be sure, this approach to addiction fiction initially might appear problematic, in that it seems to uncritically level out differences among specific substance use disorders and individual addicts. On one hand, this is exactly the effect and intent of my approach. Within Western culture, the addict has long been held hostage within an overdetermined, monolithic representational trope that refuses to acknowledge the rich diversity of experiences that actual addicts enjoy in their everyday lives. I acknowledge this problematic representational legacy in the current volume by bringing together a fairly wide range of addict characters and lived experiences under the singular moniker of *the addict*. At the same time, I confront this legacy head-on by analyzing each text separately in its own chapter and, throughout these pages, by highlighting both the similarities and the differences that mark the individual addict characters' experiences. In so doing, I seek simultaneously to reveal and to begin to untangle (or, unfix) the messy, complicated and diverse literary/lived experiences that lurk just beneath the oversimplified surface of *the addict*.

---

[51] Gilmore, *Equivocal Spirits*, 7.
[52] Ibid., 6.
[53] Ibid., 8.
[54] Holub, *Reception Theory*, 17.

At the heart of the current study is the assumption that the novel constitutes a key site at which twenty-first-century Western readers learn about addiction, although such works are not often explicitly (or, expressly) pedagogical in nature. Like Belsey, I assume that "literature as one of the most pervasive uses of language may have an important influence in which people grasp themselves and their relation to the real relations in which they live."[55] In large part, the addiction novel attains this power and authority due to the predominance of traditional literary realism within this vast body of literature; with the documentary-like nature of narrative verisimilitude, the form of realism lends to its representations of addiction, even ones that are grossly inaccurate, an authority that many readers translate as Truth. Fiction also constitutes a key archive of cultural knowledge about addiction because the contemporary novel is widely accessible to individuals across socioeconomic statuses, racial/ethnic backgrounds, abilities and educational levels, at least in developed Western nations where public education, discretionary income and recreational reading are fairly commonplace. I would argue, then, that much of what lay readers know (or, *think* we know) about addiction comes not from empirical evidence or scientific literature, but rather from popular culture artifacts that, thanks to their realistic narrative techniques, are regarded as Truth.

This fact alone would not be problematic, were it not also the fact that while such representations initially might appear quite varied and diverse in terms of both content and form, in actuality the addiction novel is, as I explain above, characterized by a remarkable degree of sameness across time, geography and situation. As this same narrative pattern appears time and again over varied historical moments, geographical locales and sociocultural formations, the stories that it tells about the addict and her/his/their lived experiences only ever gain their power, authority and influence through the twin acts of repetition and recognition. That addiction fiction encompasses a range of both popular and literary genres further extends the scope of its Truth-effects and influence well beyond a single target readership. The ubiquitous nature of such stories ultimately marks them as not simply a representation of extra-diegetic reality, but, for some readers, Reality itself. Stated differently, over time the fiction attains the power to shape its readers' expectations and attitudes about addiction, and, in so doing, also holds sway over our legislation, our available treatment options and even our research agendas, which perhaps explains why the vast majority of existing scholarship regarding addiction fiction has, unlike the current study, focused on canonical Western literature penned largely by cis white males.

---

[55] Belsey, *Critical Practice*, 66.

Tompkins notes that "when discourse is responsible for reality and not merely a reflection of it, then whose discourse prevails makes all the difference,"[56] an important reminder of the power that artists (and critics) wield in their creative endeavors that has remained at the forefront of my mind throughout the researching for and writing of the current volume. Within *Addiction, Representation and the Experimental Novel, 1985–2015*, I have been ever-mindful of the intimate relationships that exist between representation and "reality"—that is, the myriad meaningful ways in which the two entities not only reflect and comment on, but also actively shape each other in the acts of writing, reading and living. I have accepted the obligation to look at the representations of addiction that I discuss in the pages that follow, and I have vigilantly and, I hope, compassionately thought through what it means to look at those representations in this historical moment and from my unique vantage point as an addict scholar.

It would, of course, be naïve to assume that one study of this nature that concerns itself with a mere five novels has the potential to undo the insidious stranglehold that such discourses have had over the Western imaginary at least since the nineteenth century when the addict emerged as a recognizable identity. Yet my chief hope for *Addiction, Representation and the Experimental Novel, 1985–2015*—idealistic though it may be—is that this volume will advance a set of discourses that stand in opposition to the dominant understandings of addiction that have long prevailed in the West. Such discourses would encourage readers to view addiction neither as a disease (although, diagnostically speaking, it is precisely that) nor as a cautionary tale (as the Western novel persistently has made it out to be), but simply and finally as a very human condition worthy of understanding, respect and, of utmost importance, great, great compassion.

---

[56] Tompkins, "An Introduction to Reader-Response Criticism," xxv.

Chapter 1

BEARING WITNESS: *LEAVING LAS VEGAS* (1990)

John O'Brien's *Leaving Las Vegas* (1990) follows as its primary focal character a sort of Everyperson alcoholic named Ben who lives by a single "golden rule that even he no longer has the power to veto: there is nothing that will stop [him] from drinking."[1] "Physically crippled with alcoholism and psychologically afraid of being too far from its source,"[2] Ben opts early in the novel to move from Los Angeles to Las Vegas, "land of anytime alcohol,"[3] where he can engage in a strict, round-the-clock daily drinking regimen that will enable him to "maintain [the] illusion of physical health" and "keep the sickness at bay."[4] The narrative action that ensues from this inciting incident takes readers on a near-continuous tour of dive bars, red-light districts and by-the-hour motel rooms that is punctuated, often seemingly at random, by episodic bouts of fitful sleep, vomiting, erectile dysfunction and blackouts. These narrative events propel Ben along an inexorable path to desolation, physical decay and, in the end, death.

On its surface, the plot of *Leaving Las Vegas* might initially appear to be little more than another, garden-variety tale about the addict's tragic devolution into chronic alcoholism—a narrative trope so common to the addiction novel that the two have long been understood, especially within the context of US arts and letters, to be interchangeable. And, indeed, this is precisely the tradition into which both critics of the novel and O'Brien's own publishing house repeatedly have placed *Leaving Las Vegas*. Writing in 1995, when the novel first went back into print, *Entertainment Weekly*'s Chris Nashawaty describes *Leaving Las Vegas* as "an oddly romantic, bender-to-oblivion book that was more autobiographical than anyone had imagined."[5] The adjective "bender-to-oblivion,"

---

[1] John O'Brien, *Leaving Las Vegas* (New York: Grove Press, 1990), 181.
[2] Ibid., 69.
[3] Ibid., 65.
[4] Ibid., 61.
[5] Chris Nashawaty, "John O'Brien's Bittersweet Departure," *Entertainment Weekly*, November 10, 1995, https://ew.com/article/1995/11/10/john-obriens-bittersweet-departure/ (accessed January 30, 2019).

used here to describe the narrative trajectory of O'Brien's novel, is telling in that it advances an all-too-familiar interpretation of the addict's lived experience that begins in shame—after all, this type of drinking spree typically is accompanied by the complete absence of self-care—and ends in erasure, invisibility and absence. But Nashawaty does not stop there; instead, he goes on to suggest that this novel, written just two years before the author—an alcoholic himself—died by suicide, was "a 189-page suicide note."[6]

The synopsis included on the back cover of the novel also uncritically taps into similarly overdetermined cultural narratives about alcoholics and alcoholism, casting the narrative both as "a *disturbing* and *emotionally wrenching* story of a woman who embraces life and a *man who rejects it*," and as "a compelling story of unconditional love between two disenfranchised and *lost souls*."[7] The verbiage here echoes common attitudes toward addiction: immersed in the "emotionally wrenching" pathos of their own poor choices—namely, rejecting the sanctity of life—addicts are seen, both by self and by others, as morally irredeemable ("lost souls") and, as a result, embark on a crash course with a painful death. The seemingly inevitable equation that is drawn between addiction and moral decay/death is reinforced by the contrast that this author advances between Ben, the alcoholic, and Sera, the prostitute, who ultimately chooses (at least in this interpretation) to embrace, rather than reject, life.

To be sure, the addiction novel is built firmly on the foundation of such contrasts, whether meaning is derived from a contrast between the reformed addict and her/his/their former self (e.g., Tony O'Neill's *Down and Out on Murder Mile*, 2008), between the addict and a morally superior foil (e.g., Mark Lindquist's *The King of Methlehem*, 2007), or between the addict and a recovering addict (e.g., Heather O'Neill's *lullabies for little criminals*); I would argue this narrative trope is so common, in fact, that it has become the default interpretative frame for virtually any work of addiction fiction in which such contrasts potentially can be drawn, even, as in the case of *Leaving Las Vegas*, when those contrasts are directly undermined by textual evidence.

Leaving Las Vegas of necessity acknowledges this representational legacy that the addict character brings to the diegetic world simply through its portrayal of an alcoholic who seemingly is hell bent on self-destruction and, over the novel, never strays from his objective of drinking himself to death. In this respect, O'Brien's novel only marginally deviates, at least plot-wise, from literary forebears—like F. Scott Fitzgerald's *The Beautiful and Damned* (1922), Brian Moore's *Judith Hearne* (1955) and John Cheever's "The Swimmer" (1964)— that shroud the experiences of addiction in a spectacle of degradation. But

---

[6] Ibid.
[7] Emphasis added.

I would argue that O'Brien's referencing of this legacy is not uncritical, and, in fact, might even be intentionally misleading—a means of heightening the readers' awareness of the kinds of preconceptions about addiction that they bring to the reading experience in order to challenge and thereby unsettle those existing preconceptions.

This kind of self-reflexivity is fairly common to representations of hot button topics that carry the weight of deeply entrenched cultural stigmas, like addiction or AIDS. Writing about the NAMES Project AIDS Quilt, cultural critic Marita Sturken explains, "The AIDS epidemic could not have been memorialized in a traditional way because [...] it encompasses highly contested notions of what constitutes normality, moral behavior, and responsibility."[8] Sturken goes on to assert that "part of [the quilt's] power lies in how it retrieves this discourse of morality and responsibility and turns it back on itself: To be moral, say the quilt panels, is to state a name in the face of discrimination; to be responsible, they say, is to care for the dying."[9] To be sure, significant differences exist between addiction and AIDS. While both are classified as *medical conditions*, and while both carry the immense stigma associated with behavior perceived to be reckless and immoral, those behaviors—the former typically perceived as both drug-related and sexual, while the latter typically is perceived as exclusively drug-related—boast of very different cultural histories in the West and, as such, exact very different demands on and portend sometimes very different consequences for their subjects.

These differences notwithstanding, a number of Sturken's observations regarding AIDS and the NAMES Project AIDS Quilt resonate quite strongly with the lived experiences of addiction and the ways in which I see those experiences being represented in O'Brien's novel. *Addiction, Representation, and the Experimental Novel: 1985–2015* is premised on the idea that to represent addiction in a "traditional way" (read classic realism) is to advance a view of those lived experiences that recapitulates their perceived abnormality, immorality and irresponsibility, even in those instances when the addict character is "saved" from the perils of addiction. One need only recall, for instance, the taint of addiction, prostitution and even domestic violence that lingers over Baby at the close of *lullabies for little criminals* (2006) to understand the conservative ideological pull of literary realism. Such representations strip the addict of basic human dignity by replacing her/his/their distinctive, if flawed, identity with a one-size-fits-all cliché that ultimately serves the twin purposes of demeaning and demoralizing the addict.

---

[8] Marita Sturken, *Tangled Memories: The Vietnam War, The AIDS Epidemic, and the Politics of Remembering* (Berkeley: University of California Press, 1997), 219.

[9] Ibid.

By contrast, *Leaving Las Vegas* gives voice to what is perhaps one of the most fundamental of human needs: the desire to be seen without filters and without reference to narratives that the individual had neither a hand in writing nor an investment in retelling. That O'Brien's principal focal character repeatedly expresses a desire to be seen perhaps not as the hero, but certainly as the main character, of his own life story—indeed, that this desire constitutes Ben's primary character arc throughout the novel—of necessity brings a heightened awareness to the readers' role as those who gaze into the diegetic world and observe the lived traumatic experiences of the addict character. Called to bear witness to Ben's alcoholism, the readers ultimately are challenged to read with the intent to understand, to empathize without interjecting pathos and to listen without resorting to easy judgment or simple moralism.

My attribution of witnessing to readers initially might appear problematic given that, particularly within the area of trauma studies, the act of bearing witness most frequently is ascribed to the individual who has experienced a particular trauma. As Gillian Whitlock explains in "Protection," "Testimony bears witness to terrible events; it is the first-person account of collective trauma, suffering, and survival."[10] Understood in this manner, witnessing is an act that first and foremost must be performed by those who have been touched by suffering and, in the aftermath, have the capacity and the access to resources to share that suffering through testimony, as witnessing both presupposes and demands an intimate knowledge of trauma that is always and only borne of first-hand experience. Yet, in that same chapter, Whitlock goes on to acknowledge that "the addressee, spectator, and witness are all of concern in testimonial discourse,"[11] a claim that seems to suggest that within the relational dynamic that is formed in the act of offering testimony, all parties involved are called upon to bear witness, although the form that the witnessing takes will necessarily vary depending on the individual's relationship both to the testimony and to the trauma that precipitates it. Stated differently, the act of bearing (firsthand) witness to an instance of trauma always and already presupposes the presence of a spectator whose charge is to listen; or, as Dori Laub explains in "Truth and Testimony: The Process and the Struggle," the listener "becomes the [...] witness *before* the narrator does."[12]

---

[10] Gillian Whitlock, "Protection," in *We Shall Bear Witness: Life Narratives and Human Rights*, ed. Meg Jensen and Margaretta Jolly (Madison: University of Wisconsin Press, 2014), 87.

[11] Ibid.

[12] Dori Laub, "Truth and Testimony: The Process and the Struggle," in *Trauma: Explorations in Memory*, ed. Cathy Caruth (Baltimore, MD: Johns Hopkins University Press, 1995), 69.

In the current chapter, I regard witnessing in a similar manner. I take as a given that, within the reading experience, the addiction novel constitutes a type of "first-person testimony" that bears witness to the trauma of addiction, even in those instances when the novel is neither narrated in first-person point of view nor influenced by the author's own struggles with addiction. At the same time, I regard readers—whose presence within the dynamic of testifying is presupposed—as another type of witness, one whose role *as witness* historically has been both undervalued and undertheorized perhaps because readers exist at a significant remove from the trauma itself. Given the important role that readers play in the testimonial exchange, I seek in this chapter not only to explicate how readers are called upon to witness the trauma of addiction in *Leaving Las Vegas* but also to articulate how those readers, in the act of witnessing, might begin to challenge more traditional and deeply entrenched representations of addiction.

Taking the Addict's Voice

In order to understand how O'Brien's novel undermines more traditional means of representing addiction, it is first necessary to explain briefly the approach to narrativity that the author adopts. The diegetic action of *Leaving Las Vegas* alternates between two focal characters: Sera, a streetwise prostitute in Las Vegas who, at the beginning of the novel, is on the run from her abusive former lover/pimp, Gamal Fathi; and Ben, an LA-based alcoholic who, by the time readers meet him, is already mired in an addiction-related illness that remains unnamed throughout the novel, but most likely is end stage liver disease. *Leaving Las Vegas* opens with a lengthy chapter—one that spans nearly one-third of the novel—that introduces readers to Sera and provides some character exposition. This chapter of the novel focuses almost exclusively on a single act of violent gang rape that Sera experiences at the hands of three clients, and the immediate aftermath of that event, which includes a multiday convalescence at the blackjack tables while her injuries heal.

Ben eventually is introduced to the reader on page 59 of the slim 189-page novel. His initial chapter, like Sera's, provides readers with exposition to his narrative, although Ben's backstory—and, for that matter, present lived experience—is significantly more fragmentary and erratic given both his reticence as a narrator and the frequent en bloc blackouts that punctuate his memory/experience. The remaining chapters of the novel alternate fairly evenly between the two characters and concentrate on the few, short weeks during which Sera and Ben share an unconventional relationship, one that is at times life-affirming, and at other times quite devastating. Narrated in third-person present, the action of *Leaving Las Vegas* takes on an added urgency and immediacy as it chronicles the brief window of time that spans between Ben's move to Las Vegas and his death.

The alternating, and ultimately overlapping narratives of O'Brien's two focal characters help to illuminate the central dramatic conflict that gives shape to the diegetic action in *Leaving Las Vegas*; this conflict can most readily be discerned by pinpointing the key commonalities that are shared between Sera and Ben. Most significantly, both characters face stigma—Sera for her profession, Ben for his addiction—and both struggle to maintain a sense of identity in the face of the pervasive sociocultural stigmas that persistently threaten to overwrite their self-image. Early in the novel, readers are reminded of the disgust that both prostitution and alcoholism commonly elicit among the US public when Sera casually listens to a call-in radio program hosted by an evangelist named Reverend Phil during a taxi ride through the streets of Las Vegas. When asked to account for all of the "evil" overtaking the city, Reverend Phil responds:

> The only way to fight the evil is to lose it from your mind, Jo. Look away from that devil. Look away from that pornographer. Look away from the robber. Look away from the murderer. The Lord will deal with them. Have faith, Jo, that they will be swept from this city. The drunk, the prostitute, the will not, live not suicides, will be swept away from our clean floor and into the pit to burn.[13]

Here, the Reverend's fire-and-brimstone rhetoric echoes the type of heavy-handed moralism that defined the Temperance movement of the nineteenth and early twentieth centuries and was responsible for signage like "The CHILDREN'S HORROR: 'Daddy' Coming Home DRUNK"[14] and "Drinking Leads to Neglect of Duty, Moral Degradation, and Crime."[15] The Reverend draws a false analogy among a variety of behaviors—some criminal, some not—and then proceeds to advance the sweeping generalization that not only are these behaviors comparable (which they are not), but also they are equally immoral or/and criminal (which, again, they are not).

---

[13] O'Brien, *Leaving Las Vegas*, 29.

[14] "Temperance–History," *Ohio History Connection*, http://www.ohiopix.org/contentdm-search-results/?cdm-keywords=Temperance--History&cdm-mode=all&cdm-field=subjec (accessed January 30, 2019).

[15] "Retirement and the Demon Drink," *The Summerhouse Years*, May 3, 2017, http://thesummerhouseyears.com/retirement-and-the-demon-drink/ (accessed January 30, 2019).

While the equation drawn between prostitution/alcoholism and immorality in the passage cited above is voiced by an agent of organized religion, and therefore perhaps not reflective of the views of the wider population of in the United States, O'Brien does suggest that this kind of thinking enjoys a much greater foothold in contemporary US culture than just the evangelical fringe. To the young men who rape her, for instance, Sera is regarded merely as an object to be fucked and discarded. When Sera refuses one of the men's request for anal sex, the man turns not to Sera but to his friend who arranged the encounter and says, "Jim, you said I could fuck her in the butt,"[16] as if Jim's initial engagement of Sera's services entitles him to dictate how she (as Jim's "property") can and will be used for the duration of the encounter. Similarly, to the cab driver who picks up an obviously battered Sera following the rape, she is the punchline of a joke that only he finds humorous: "'What's the matter, honey, get a delivery at the back door that you weren't expecting?' says the driver, laughing at her discomfort."[17] Neither her tricks nor the cab driver actually see Sera as a human being who experiences pain and who possesses both a voice and a rich interior life; to them, and to countless others within O'Brien's fictional world, Sera is simply "the Prostitute," an oversimplified proxy for an entire class of persons that, thanks to the lingering stronghold that Puritanism continues to exact on US culture, has, for centuries, been profoundly misunderstood both within and beyond the bounds of literary representation.[18]

Ben, too, repeatedly is stripped of his humanity and reminded in various ways that, to those around him, he will always and only be "the Drunk." At a bar in Malibu, for instance, Ben ponders the dramatic shift in attitude toward himself that he has witnessed among both staff and other patrons:

> There was a time when he nurtured his stature as a *regular* in bars all over Los Angeles [...] He enjoyed being called by name, having his drink order predicted, or at least guessed at. But now he is known to those places as a pathetic drunk [...] [H]e must now endure judgment as part of his bar tab. They hate to see him. They roll their eyes. They shake their heads. Serving him has become a moral question for bartenders

---

[16] O'Brien, *Leaving Las Vegas*, 14.
[17] Ibid., 16.
[18] See, for example, Debra A. Castillo, *Easy Women: Sex and Gender in Modern Mexican Fiction* (Minneapolis: University of Minnesota Press, 1998); Laura Hapke, *Girls Who Went Wrong: Prostitutes in American Fiction, 1885–1917* (Bowling Green, OH: Bowling Green State University Popular Press, 1989); Kimberly B. Stratton and Dayna S. Kalleres, eds., *Daughters of Hecate: Women & Magic in the Ancient World* (New York: Oxford University Press, 2014).

that once poured liquor into his glass freely. *On me!* they would exclaim, and marvel at his ability to drink enormous quantities and never give a hint of intoxication. He was a star. Now he is a case.[19]

Ben's verbiage, particularly at the end of the passage, is telling. The contrast between "star" and "case" indicates the degree to which Ben, in the estimation of his fellow bar patrons, has devolved, perhaps both morally and physically, since earlier in the novel one bartender makes a passing reference to Ben's physical degradation.[20] What also is interesting is the presumption that drives the onlookers' invasive judgment, the very public and unapologetic manner in which both bar patrons and bar staff offer their unsolicited condemnation of Ben—a presumption that is not unsimilar to the ways in which Western readers have been indoctrinated to read the addiction novel. To these onlookers, Ben is a moral problem to be solved—not a human being, but a scientific "case" (even a lab rat) from which to draw hasty generalizations regarding who addicts are and how it feels to navigate the world as an alcoholic.

Reclaiming the Addict's Voice

Of course, Ben's "woe is me" ruminations on his treatment at the hands of bar staff and patrons possibly could be explained away as merely a manifestation of the narcissism that is pathologically ascribed to the addict,[21] except for the fact that O'Brien actively implicates his readers in the self-same set of practices that are being described above. To understand how O'Brien implicates readers in these acts of overgeneralization, it first is necessary to examine how Ben is introduced to those readers. While Ben is introduced by name to readers on page 60, those readers initially meet Ben on only the

---

[19] O'Brien, *Leaving Las Vegas*, 98.
[20] Ibid., 94.
[21] Psychoanalysts Richard B. Ulman and Harry Paul, for instance, suggest in their coauthored book that "from a descriptive (rather than judgmental) point of view, our study views an addict as the quintessential narcissist. An addict, who is self-involved and self-absorbed, has little awareness of the presence of other persons or things as independent entities [...] [N]arcissistically disturbed individuals, including an addict, 'understand the environment in which they live only as an extension of their own *narcissistic universe*" (28). Attitudes like this, common across both the soft sciences and, more broadly, Western culture at large, take on added credence when presented under the umbrella of innocuous "description" and even scientific discovery and they are problematic not because they are inaccurate, but because they suggest that addiction is primarily, if not exclusively, an exercise in narcissism, a claim that ignores both the ways in which addiction strips a person of agency and the fact that addiction is, first and foremost, a medical condition.

second page of the novel—a fact of which readers are most likely unaware until nearly three-quarters of the way into *Leaving Las Vegas*.[22] At this early point in O'Brien's novel, Sera is sitting on the curb in front of a 7–11 located on Las Vegas Boulevard, "sucking weak coffee through a hole in the plastic lid of a red and green Styrofoam cup,"[23] when she spies "a staggering drunk, heading east on the near sidewalk, [take] a dive directly in front of her."[24] Worried about this nameless stranger, Sera asks, "You want me to help you?" to which the "staggering drunk" "groans out what sounds like *no* and starts to move."[25] Sera's instinctual response is to "[feel] embarrassed for [the drunk]" and look away—a not uncommon reaction to addiction in the Western world, regardless of whether the addict is a stranger or an intimate. When her gaze returns to the place where the man has face planted onto the cement, Sera discovers that the "[staggering drunk] is gone." As Sera scans the empty street for any sign of the man, she ponders: "There is a bottle in his future—perhaps sooner a glass—elsewhere on the line."[26]

In this scene, Ben appears to function simply as set dressing—that is, as a carefully chosen, albeit nondescript, prop designed to establish setting and mood, but no more significant than the blinding fluorescents of the Strip or the deafening *whirs* and *chings* of the slot machines. In other words, the Ben that readers meet on the second page of *Leaving Las Vegas* is a stock character: namely, the Drunk. As a conventional type that is at once recognizable and knowable to readers because of its frequent repetition across literary history, the stock character lacks the depth and complexity that typically is associated with realistically drawn characters and often exists within the diegetic world merely as a functionary to facilitate the protagonist's growth, development and narrative journey. The town drunk, or the tavern fool, stands as one such stock character that, throughout the history of Western popular culture, has appeared in such instantly recognizable forms as Weasel Craig in Stephen King's *'Salem's Lot* (1975), Otis Campbell in *The Andy Griffith Show* (1960–68) and Margaret (Peggy Pope) in *9 to 5* (1980). At times, this type of stock character serves merely as comic relief at moments of heightened narrative conflict (e.g., Barney Gumble in *The Simpsons,* 1989–present). But more often the town drunk functions as an object lesson in moral virtue, providing his fellow characters,[27] as well as readers, with a cautionary tale about

---

[22] O'Brien, *Leaving Las Vegas*, 139.
[23] Ibid., 3.
[24] Ibid., 4.
[25] Ibid., 5.
[26] Ibid.
[27] It is important to note that the town drunk typically is cast as male—a choice that, historically, has had especially devastating consequences for female addicts in the

the dangers of excess (e.g., Simon Stimson in Thornton Wilder's *Our Town*, 1938). In this capacity, the town drunk serves an important pedagogical role in the exercise of social control, which, as Nancy Armstrong notes in *Desire and Domestic Fiction: A Political History of the Novel* (1987), has been a key function of the Western novel since its earliest origins.[28]

O'Brien encourages readers to pay only passing attention to Ben, the Tavern Fool, in these initial pages of *Leaving Las Vegas* by engaging in a very clever act of narrative sleight of hand. Specifically, O'Brien directs the readers' focus to another focal character, Sera, whom readers assume is the central protagonist of the novel given that she is the first and only named character that O'Brien has introduced. This assumption is reinforced by the fact that Sera is the lens, if not the point of view, through which readers are invited to experience O'Brien's fictional Las Vegas. As the readers' touchstone in the diegetic world, Sera guides their response to the diegetic action. When she looks away from the staggering drunk, presumably filled with disgust by the reckless excess that his actions suggest, readers most likely also feel not simply compelled, but entitled, both to look away and, of greater significance, to judge. Further, from the doubly safe remove of a focal character and third-person limited point of view, readers likely will arrive at the same hastily drawn conclusion regarding Ben as Sera appears to have done—he is Sin City Incarnate—despite the fact that they have only just, and only briefly, met him. That readers share some of Sera's presuppositions about Ben/addiction implicates readers in the problematic machinations of stereotyping and overgeneralization that, for

---

extra-diegetic world, whose experiences simply are not (and, indeed, cannot) be represented within the figure of the generic male addict. Indeed, much research, particularly within the soft and hard sciences, points to significant physiological, sociocultural and behavioral differences between male and female addicts, including: Justin J. Anker and Marilyn E. Carroll, "Females Are More Vulnerable to Drug Abuse Than Males: Evidence from Preclinical Studies and the Role of Ovarian Hormones," in *Biological Basis of Sex Differences in Psychopharmacology*, ed. Jo C. Neill and Jayashri Kulkarni, 73–96 (New York: Springer-Verlag, 2011); Jill B. Becker, Michele L. McClellan, and Beth Glover Reed, "Sex Differences, Gender and Addiction," *Journal of Neuroscience Research* 95, nos. 1–2 (2017): 136–47; Yih-ing Hser, M. Douglas Anglin, and Mary W. Booth, "Sex Differences in Addict Careers: III. Addiction," *American Journal of Drug and Alcohol Abuse* 13, no. 3 (1987): 231–51; and Megan E. Roth, Kelly P. Cosgrove, and Marilyn E. Carroll, "Sex Differences in the Vulnerability to Drug Abuse: A Review of Preclinical Studies," *Neuroscience and Biobehavioral Reviews* 28, no. 6 (2004): 533–46. Despite the wealth of scientific research on this topic, this author is unaware of any investigation that has been undertaken into the ways in which addiction, sex and gender intersect in the literary narratives of female addicts. Such a project is well overdue.

[28] Nancy Armstrong, *Desire and Domestic Fiction: A Political History of the Novel* (Oxford: Oxford University Press, 1987).

over two centuries, have emboldened Westerners to write addicts off as mere wastes of life.

Of course, readers are not made aware of their implication in this machinery until much later in the novel; indeed, it is not until nearly three-quarters of the way into *Leaving Las Vegas* that Sera reveals to Ben, "You know, I saw you last week [...] I saw you fall down on the sidewalk."[29] Throughout *Leaving Las Vegas*, O'Brien makes very clear to his readers that the organization of narrative events is key to understanding the novel. The shift in focal characters, which, as I note above, initially occurs approximately one-third of the way into the narrative, perhaps is the first blatant indication that readers should pay careful attention to the underlying architecture of the narrative, although there are several additional, and more subtle hints to this effect peppered throughout the initial Sera chapter.[30] In any text, a shift in the readers' vantage point provides those readers a clear signal that there is some insight to be gleaned from that shift—some bit of knowledge, or some kernel of wisdom that is only available through the lens of a particular character or/and through a contrast of perspectives. Similarly, when repetition occurs, readers are obliged to consider the import of such echoes with respect to narrative, character or/and theme development. Repeated motifs might point to the central narrative conflict, just as the numerous references to mirrors in *Leaving Las Vegas*[31]—or, in other addiction novels, such as Jay McInerney's *Bright Lights, Big City* (1984) and Steve Earle's *I'll Never Get Out of This World Alive* (2011)—allude to the focal characters' struggles to define themselves in light of social mores that systematically work to stereotype and stigmatize them.

That this reference to Ben's initial stumble into the narrative is placed so late in the novel is quite telling with respect to how *Leaving Las Vegas* regards and addresses its readers. As I suggest above, by permitting readers initially to witness this scene alongside Sera, and by presenting it without much context or any backstory, O'Brien seems to validate any embarrassment, disgust or/and avoidance—common default reactions to alcoholism—that the readers might experience. At the same time, the significant distance that O'Brien interjects between these two scenes, and the intervening narrative action that occurs over those 137 pages, demand that readers reevaluate their initial reactions from a critical remove. The repetition of the opening scene is a signal to readers to pay close attention not only to what is happening within the

---

[29] O'Brien, *Leaving Las Vegas*, 139.
[30] For instance, Sera's narrative feels episodic, despite an underlying chronology, due to the interjection of uncontextualized flashbacks and the interruption of narrative action with again uncontextualized parenthetical asides.
[31] See, for example, pages 9, 44, 49, 84–85, 113, 115 and 175.

diegetic world, but also to how those readers are responding to the action in the extra-diegetic one. It is a reminder that first impressions can be, and often are, not simply erroneous, but potentially quite devastating, especially when the subject of those impressions is part of a historically marginalized and vulnerable group, like addicts. Once this scene is replayed after readers have been invited (to greater or lesser degrees) into Ben's rich interior life and both readers and Sera have come to know Ben as more than just the Tavern Fool, readers should perceive this scene with much greater understanding and compassion. No longer a self-destructive cliché, Ben must, at this late point in the novel, be understood as a complex, flesh-and-blood man with motivations, with needs and with vulnerabilities. This repeated scene functions as a call for readers to listen carefully to Ben's narrative, to pay greater attention to the lived experiences of alcoholism than most Western readers are inclined to do. In short, O'Brien's experimentation with narrative structure serves as a powerful reminder that, as Mark Muller advocates in "The Importance of Taking and Bearing Witness," "What matters most is that the witnesses take voice, find voice, rather than others giving it to them and that having taken voice, the rest of the world listens and learns."[32]

Listening to the Addict

In *Leaving Las Vegas*, O'Brien not only calls on readers to listen to Ben without filters but also insists that those readers see themselves more clearly and honestly as a means of understanding the biases regarding alcoholics and addiction that they bring to the reading experience. One particularly noteworthy scene in this regard occurs shortly after Sera cedes narrative focus and Ben is introduced by name to readers. That morning, as Ben showers and readies himself for yet another day of binge drinking, he experiences a kind of epiphanic moment, although the revelation is more for the readers' sake than Ben's own: "He looks in the mirror and doesn't care that he is an alcoholic. The issue is entirely irrelevant to him. He does all this deliberately, with purpose. Yes, of course I'm an *alc*, he thinks. What about it? It's not what the story is about."[33] The mirror historically has functioned as a symbol of introspection and self-analysis, a topic that I take up in much greater detail in relation to Bret Easton Ellis's *Less Than Zero* (1985) in Chapter 4 of the current volume.

---

[32] Mark Muller, "The Importance of Taking and Bearing Witness: Reflections on Twenty Years as a Human Rights Lawyer," in *We Shall Bear Witness: Life Narratives and Human Rights*, ed. Meg Jensen and Margaretta Jolly (Madison: University of Wisconsin Press, 2014), 258.

[33] O'Brien, *Leaving Las Vegas*, 67–68.

Here, though, the mirror operates ironically. If mirrors traditionally provide both readers and characters a window into characterization and motivation, then here the mirror resists—even rejects—that revelatory impulse, instead issuing readers a challenge to look beneath their seemingly obvious, but ultimately superficial, first impression of Ben. Ben admits to being an alcoholic, but suggests here that such a superficial assessment fails to encompass the complexity of both his lived experiences and his character. At the same time, he refuses to reveal what the story is about, thereby identifying the mirror as a site that simultaneously reveals and conceals.

O'Brien uses the mirror to comment on the all-too-familiar impulse to "see" addicts as two-dimensional caricatures, rather than as richly detailed, complex human beings.[34] O'Brien's indictment of the cultural tendency toward the oversimplification of addicts and addictions is most clearly illustrated in the collapsing of "space" between the readers and the focal addict character in this scene. This collapsing, or narrowing, of space between readers and character is especially noteworthy, and, indeed, experimental, given the point of view through which O'Brien has opted to narrate his tale. Much existing addiction fiction implicitly regards the novel as a site at which the addict character's confession unfolds in the presence of readers, a perhaps not unsurprising phenomenon given the stranglehold that the Twelve Steps and its particular brand of talk therapy has long maintained over the Western addiction industry. This effect most commonly is achieved through the employment of first-person point of view, which casts the reading experience as an intimate tête-à-tête between two parties whereby one party (i.e., the I-narrator) discloses a piece of information about her-/himself/themselves that others (perhaps even the second party) might consider humiliating, shameful or/and prejudicial.[35]

Tama Janowitz's *Slaves of New York* (1986), for instance, foregrounds from its opening lines the kind of self-reflexive, revelatory tone common to both the

---

[34] This attitude might in part find its origins in Alcoholics Anonymous and, more broadly, Twelve Step philosophy, which adamantly rejects the idea of diversity among addicts' lived experiences. As David Foster Wallace very accurately characterizes a Boston AA group in *Infinite Jest* (1996), "Everybody, but everybody Comes In dead-eyed and puke-white and with their face hanging down around their knees and with a well-thumbed firearm-and-ordnance mail-order catalogue kept safe and available at home, map-wise, for when this last desperate resort of hugs and clichés turns out to be just happy horse-shit, for you. You are not unique, they'll say: this initial hopelessness unites every soul in this broad cold salad-bar'd hall" (349). This same idea permeates not only AA meetings (in content and structure) but also the rhetoric of *The Big Book*.

[35] "confession, n." *OED Online*. June 2018. Oxford University Press. http://www.oed.com.ezproxy.bgsu.edu:8080/view/Entry/38779?redirectedFrom=confession (accessed July 24, 2018).

confession and first-person addiction fiction: "After I became a prostitute, I had to deal with penises of every imaginable shape and size. Some large, others quite shriveled and pendulous of testicle."[36] These lines are characterized by a heightened degree of intimacy, manufactured between the I-narrator and the readers in the act of disclosing the speaking subject's colorful work history, which also and simultaneously marks these words as not simply a statement of fact, but an acknowledgement of an experience that some individuals (albeit not this particular I-narrator) most certainly would regard as unseemly. In other words, a confession.

Janowitz's narrator exhibits a similar degree of unabashed frankness with regard to her drug use and addictions: "For myself, I had to choose the most difficult profession available to me; at night I often couldn't sleep, feeling myself adrift in a sea of seminal fluid. It was on these evenings that Bob and I took drugs. He would softly tie up my arm and inject me with a little heroin, or, if none was available, a little something else."[37] Noteworthy in this passage is the unconventional tone that the I-narrator adopts toward the subject matter. The allusion to promiscuous sexual practice is almost poetic, and carries none of the stigma that, within the broader US culture, an admission to prostitution most certainly would. Additionally, the description of heroin use is at first banal—little more remarkable than had the narrator revealed "on these evenings Bob and I had dinner"—before turning intimate. The allusion to a tourniquet, used to render veins more prominent prior to intravenously injecting an illicit substance, here takes on an almost sexual connotation given the narrator's word choice, which alludes both to light bondage (i.e., "softly tie up") and physical penetration (i.e., "inject me"). That these acts are performed by Bob in response to the narrator's restlessness marks the exchange as tender, compassionate—emotions almost entirely unassociated with the kind of codependent, enabling relationship that readers tend to witness between two addict characters. In the end, whether the confession is delivered in a straightforward manner, seemingly lifted verbatim from a transcript of a Narcotics Anonymous meeting, or the confession borders on exhibitionism, spinning the kind of shockingly salacious tale witnessed in *Slaves of New York*, it always and only demands a degree of frankness and intimacy between character and readers uncommon in everyday discourse.

In an interesting twist both on the genre of addiction fiction and on the dynamics of its reception, O'Brien opts for third-person point of view, as opposed to first. Third-person point of view typically locates the readers at a remove from the narrative, placing between the readers and the characters an

---

[36] Tama Janowitz, *Slaves of New York* (New York: Bloomsbury, 1986), 1.
[37] Ibid., 2.

often unnamed and unidentified third-party narrator whose relevance to the diegetic action (if, indeed, there is any) is at best unclear. The narrator mediates the relationship between the readers and the diegetic action, much like the camera lens serves as an intermediary between the spectator and the photographic subject. This "neutral" third party guides the readers through the narrative, carefully selecting and framing those events that are significant to the development of plot, theme and character, all the while remaining in the wings of the action, as invisible and as unobtrusive as possible. Within this dynamic, the readers become voyeurs, looking from afar into a series of events to which those readers at times feel little connection, emotional or otherwise; their sole job is simply to look/read, an observation that is underscored by the etymological roots of the word "voyeur" in the French *voir*, meaning "to see."[38] This method of representing trauma enjoys "a long pedigree";[39] indeed, as Susan Sontag explains in *Regarding the Pain of Others* (2003), "Torment, a canonical subject in art, is often represented [...] as a spectacle, something being watched (or, ignored) by other people."[40]

From the onset of *Leaving Las Vegas*, O'Brien titillates the readers' voyeuristic impulses with respect to representations of pain/injury by crafting a narrative that at once appears to delight in the distance created between readers and the graphically traumatic events that are unfolding on the page. Titled "cherries," the first chapter of O'Brien's novel introduces the readers to an exhausted Sera who "has been walking around now for at least two hours and wants desperately to rest";[41] within a few pages of her introduction, Sera is brutally gang raped at the hands of "three college boys, each wearing numbered jerseys and carrying the ubiquitous Heineken bottles."[42] Tellingly, Sera's gang rape is alluded to in terse prose that describes in an almost clinical voice the set of brutal actions that both precipitate and constitute the rape itself: "[She is] stopped by a blow, catching her full in the face. A flash of colored sparks lead [*Sic*] her into darkness [...] She wakes hurting, her face in a bloody pillow and someone on her back."[43] Here, as elsewhere within the narrative, the rape is never explicitly named, O'Brien opting instead to punctuate the narrative with a series of somewhat generic physical actions that merely trace the contours

---

[38] "voyeur, n." *OED Online*, June 2018, Oxford University Press. http://www.oedo/com.ezproxy.bgsu.edu:8080/view/Entry/224799?rskey=homfrS&result=1 (accessed July 2, 2018).
[39] Susan Sontag, *Regarding the Pain of Others* (New York: Farrar, Straus and Giroux, 2003), 40.
[40] Ibid., 42.
[41] O'Brien, *Leaving Las Vegas*, 3.
[42] Ibid., 12.
[43] Ibid, 15.

of the actual violence and violation that are happening to Sera. Sera's hair is "tugged hard." She is "punch[ed in the face]" and "kicked sharply on the side of her head." There is blood. There is shouting. There is "someone on her back." But never once—save in the coarse dialogue where the "college boys" encourage one another to "Fuck her in the rear!"[44]—does O'Brien's narrator acknowledge the forced anal penetration that Sera really is experiencing during this scene. Here, the clinical narrative voice, in conjunction with the disinterested third party forcibly interjected between readers and character, work to distance the readers from the diegetic action, resisting the pathos and discouraging the kind of heightened emotional investment that such scenes often demand in first-person accounts.[45]

The type of distancing effect that O'Brien fosters in the initial, lengthy chapter of the novel is undermined quite dramatically in the mirror scene mentioned above. The scene opens with a lengthy narrative frame, voiced in third-person present, that orients readers with respect to time, geography, action and character. Through this bit of extended narration, the readers learn that the action takes place at "ten-thirty-one" on a "spring [morning] in Los Angeles."[46] Having accompanied Ben on his "usual"[47] early morning drinking regimen—"Alcohol leads to predictability"[48]—readers understand that Ben was fired from his job the previous week,[49] presumably after months of alcohol-fueled incompetence followed by repeated absences,[50] and now, with his "final paycheck, added to what was left of his once substantial savings,"[51] he intends to drink himself to death. This narrative frame regularly alternates between a more objective style of narration that simply describes from afar the diegetic action (e.g., "In his kitchen he picks up the bottle of vodka"[52]) and a more subjective style of narration that penetrates, to greater or lesser degrees, the consciousness of the focal character and invites the readers, albeit only ever momentarily, to experience the diegetic world from Ben's vantage point.

---

[44] Ibid.
[45] Luke Davies's *Candy: A Novel of Love and Addiction* offers an interesting counterpoint to the narrative voice in *Leaving Las Vegas*, framing drug use and its many effects, including a particularly melodramatic miscarriage, within prose that is dripping with both self-loathing and pathos.
[46] O'Brien, *Leaving Las Vegas*, 65.
[47] Ibid., 61.
[48] Ibid., 62.
[49] Ibid., 65.
[50] Ibid., 66.
[51] Ibid., 66.
[52] Ibid., 67.

In the mirror scene, readers witness this alternation of narrative style unfold in six brief statements. The section begins with a narrative frame that orients readers to setting (i.e., bathroom) and diegetic action (i.e., shaving); through these initial five words (i.e., "He looks in the mirror"), O'Brien "provides the reader with direct access to the kind of information about the external world that the inwardly-oriented monologist could not be expected to verbalize."[53] In the same breath, though, the narrative shifts to a more subjective voice, bringing readers closer to the focal character's consciousness by permitting them access to Ben's self-perception (i.e., "[he] doesn't care that he is an alcoholic"). This voice persists over the coming two sentences, as first Ben's attitude (i.e., "The issue is entirely irrelevant to him") and next his motivation (i.e., "He does all this deliberately") are revealed. Sentence four marks a dramatic shift in narrative style whereby the subjective voice that merely talks *about* Ben's feelings and motivations, dancing around but never fully penetrating his consciousness, is supplanted by direct interior monologue: "Yes, of course I'm an *alc*, he thinks." At this point, the distance between the action that is being taken within the diegetic world—namely, Ben's admission to alcoholism—and the verbalizing of that act are collapsed into a single declarative statement. In the moment of its utterance, this statement merges diegetic and extra-diegetic time, bringing readers and focal character into a shared temporal space. In the final two statements of the quoted passage, the unconventional (and, for some readers, uncomfortable) nature of this shared temporality is exploited through the use of direct address. When Ben questions, "What about it?" and then declares, "It's not what the story is about," the implied subject of his address is O'Brien's readers, a point that is reinforced by the self-reflexive reference to O'Brien's novel (i.e., "the story") that punctuates the final, declarative statement.

Learning from the Addict

This kind of "breaking of the fourth wall," fairly uncommon to and experimental in the context of third-person narration, is experienced as incredibly jarring to readers. The direct acknowledgment of the readers' presence in the diegetic world momentarily shatters many of the conventions of realistic fiction, chief among them the suspension of disbelief that enables readers to imaginatively experience the diegetic action without breaching the thin veil between the characters' and the readers' worlds. As such, this exchange between Ben and O'Brien's readers reworks and refocuses the operations of

---

[53] Vladimir Tumanov, *Mind Reading: Unframed Interior Monologue in European Fiction* (Amsterdam: Rodopi, 1997), 4.

the readers' gaze, thereby disrupting the sanctity and the quietude of the reading experience. Whereas the gaze in addiction fiction typically objectifies the addict and her/his/their addiction as a spectacle of degradation, here readers are indicted as the object of their own gaze. Ben's confrontational tone calls into question the widely held, albeit erroneous, belief that *addict* is an all-consuming identity category that supersedes, even cancels out, any other markers of identification and experience. For readers, who likely see themselves mirrored in Ben's indictment, the statement "It's not what the story is about" functions as a challenge to look inward, issued by an addict character who refuses to be either a lab rat or a case.

O'Brien experiments with point of view throughout *Leaving Las Vegas*, regularly inviting readers to move by degrees closer to (or, further from) Ben's consciousness as a means of encouraging those readers to resist the pull of stereotype and see Ben as he truly is, warts and all. Quite often this invitation is almost imperceptible—a quick change in pronoun, a subtle shift in voice. And readers are never permitted to linger for long in Ben's conscious mind. In fact, most often readers occupy Ben's consciousness only long enough to glimpse some well-hidden aspect of his character, and then the narration shifts back to the unnamed and largely disinterested third-person voice.

During the scene in which Sera invites Ben to move out of the motel and into her home, for instance, the narration reads:

> "What you don't understand is[...]," he begins, wanting to come clean with her, to tell her not to worry about the cost of the room because it will all be handled by his plastic estate; in other words, to tell her that he not only wants to crawl off into a dark motel room, but that he really does want to die there as well. But it is too much, too unkind. This isn't what she wants to hear, and it certainly isn't what he wants to say. No, he's still alive and he wants to be with her. She apparently wants to be with him. So what's the problem? He'll spend some time here; then, when things get really bad, he'll move to a hotel. She'll probably be glad to get rid of him.[54]

While much of this passage is narrated at a critical remove from the focal character, there are several key moments of intimacy shared between Ben and O'Brien's readers that serve as subtle, but significant, reminders of readers' duty to bear witness to the complexity of Ben's lived experiences without interjecting pathos or resorting to easy judgment. Specifically, the moments of greatest intimacy, when readers are able to penetrate Ben's consciousness,

---

[54] O'Brien, *Leaving Las Vegas*, 151.

reveal the deep and profound need that addicts often experience for human connection (e.g., "he's still alive and he wants to be with her [...] So what's the problem?"), despite the widespread cultural narrative that would equate addiction with rabid narcissism and staunch isolationism.

Furthermore, the interrogative "So what's the problem?" directly acknowledges readers' presence in the diegetic world by targeting those readers as the subject of the address; in so doing, O'Brien challenges readers to consider whether Ben's need for intimacy and connection struck them as a "problem" and, if it did so, then why. This question, then, indicts not only O'Brien's readers but also larger cultural narratives that would systematically work to alienate and abject the addict. The passage concludes with a nod to Ben's emotional/psychological vulnerability, voiced in third person but obviously the product of an interior experience that could only ever be Ben's. To claim that Sera will "probably be glad to get rid of him" reveals a fragile ego, one that begs to be comforted through contradiction; the statement further characterizes Ben as a man who, thanks to repeated torment at the hands of a maniacally sober society, is uncertain of his own worth in the world and must therefore reject before he is rejected. Readers bear witness to this impulse in Ben when, as his alcoholism spirals to its inevitable conclusion, he allows himself to be discovered having sex with a prostitute so that Sera will "get rid of him."[55]

The glimpses into Ben's consciousness are precisely about empowering the addict to assert his voice amidst the din of cultural narratives that work to silence and entrap him within overdetermined stereotypes. At the same time, it is important to recognize that these glimpses are momentary and fragmented, an attempt, I would argue, to resist readers' desire to co-opt the addict's experience. Co-optation manifests itself as an exercise of power whereby a more privileged and powerful individual/group will seize the "property" (broadly defined) of a less powerful or/and marginalized group and then use that "property" for its own ends. This "property" can be literal material goods, but it also can be less tangible, but no less valuable items, like lived experience. One might, for example, consider the experiences of coming out and the way in which this rhetoric/practice, so grounded as it is in acts of resistance to Western systems of homo-/transphobia and heterosexism, has, over time, been adopted by groups as wildly diverse as atheists, sex workers and, most ironically, far-right Republicans. Another, more timely example is the co-optation of the rhetoric of the Black Lives Matter movement by largely white, privileged males who, feigning disenfranchisement, insist that "All Lives Matter." In these and other instances, the act of co-optation dramatically alters the

---

[55] Ibid., 185.

meaning of the experience being stolen from the less privileged group, often overwriting and simultaneously negating the lived experiences of abuse, persecution or/and subjugation that initially gave rise to those experiences. In this respect, co-optation stands as the antithesis to understanding.

Given this explanation, it is quite easy to imagine why the lived experiences of addicts might be so frequently subject to the act of co-optation, particularly, although not exclusively, in the West. Addiction poses a direct challenge to the ideals of temperance and restraint that have defined Western civilization since its earliest of origins. To co-opt those experiences is to normalize and affirm the "superiority" of that which those experiences most directly oppose and contradict, which, in the case of addiction, is moderation, sobriety. This is why cultural representations of addiction so commonly demonize the addict—even in those instances when the addict becomes sober.

Blacking Out

O'Brien resists the urge to co-opt the lived experiences of the addict not only through his choice of point of view, but also through the interjection of en bloc blackouts, which render the narrative incomplete, fragmented. While blackouts are alluded to throughout Ben's narrative, the first instance of a blackout that dramatically interrupts the narrative occurs on page 90 of the novel. In the scene that immediately precedes this blackout, Ben has solicited a prostitute and is walking into a motel when "he is struck with a wave of alcohol that has been building in his seated body."[56] Just before the scene shifts, Ben realizes that "he is much drunker than he'd like to be and too drunk to realize it,"[57] an epiphany (of sorts) that serves as the abrupt ending to the scene. The next scene begins about one inch down the page, visually separated from the previous scene both by white space and by three club symbols, centered on the page. This visual break is instructive with respect to how readers are encouraged to experience the blackout and, more broadly, Ben's alcoholism. What this and other blackouts in the novel suggest is that, in *Leaving Las Vegas*, alcoholism constitutes a lived experience that, in many respects, cannot be contained. Here, specifically, Ben's experience resists the self-imposed logic of narrative coherence and closure, charting instead a somewhat discontinuous, at times even episodic, series of events, the sole throughline—if, indeed, this even can be considered a connecting motif—of which is excess. If Ben's experience is too unruly to be contained within narrative, then neither can it be

---

[56] Ibid., 90.
[57] Ibid.

appropriated and co-opted (again, in narrative) for alternative ends. Instead, that experience must be understood—as well as possible—on its own terms.

The next scene begins "ten miles and six hours away from [Ben's] last memory."[58] Ben discovers himself on the floor of his apartment, but unable to account for how he came to be there.

> As he sits at the kitchen table, tentatively gulping vodka and whatever-was-in-the-fridge, random memories of the night before flash in and out of his head. With no respect for chronology they are like a slide show at a stranger's house, the box of slides having been dropped and hastily reassembled just before presentation. He is always very uncomfortable with these absences of palpable participation in his own life, and the fact that they are increasing in both intensity and frequency makes him long to be anonymous.[59]

The many blackouts that pepper the narrative of *Leaving Las Vegas* are, for readers, experienced as incredibly disorienting. Without the coherence of temporal continuity, readers feel unmoored in the diegetic world and are forced to accept that the narrative might very well refuse to answer some of their most basic questions, such as "Where am I?" and "How did I get here?" (This sense of being unmoored within a narrative—of disorientation—is the topic of the final chapter of this volume, which focuses on Grace Krilanovich's *The Orange Eats Creeps*.) Furthermore, readers are challenged to confront the very real possibility that if the narrative cannot (or, perhaps, will not) answer basic questions of time, space and narrative action, then more complex questions regarding who addicts are and how it feels to stumble through the world as an alcoholic may also remain unanswered by the novel's end.

By abruptly and randomly interjecting these blackout moments into the narrative, O'Brien not only introduces a strong element of naturalism to the diegetic world, beautifully mimicking the unsettling experience of waking without a clear sense of time, space or continuous action, but also forcibly confronts readers with the blankness and absence that often characterizes the addict's lived experiences. It is a very clever tactic that suggests to readers that they may, through the act of reading *Leaving Las Vegas*, glimpse pieces of the addict's lived experiences, albeit pieces that sometimes are no more coherent or orderly than the "random memories of the night before [that] flash in and out of [Ben's] head," but readers will never completely see or understand who Ben is or how it feels to navigate the world as him. Stated differently,

---

[58] Ibid.
[59] Ibid.

the interjection of narrative gaps constitutes a powerful withholding gesture that challenges readers to acknowledge that labels like *addict* or *drunk* or *junkie* do very little to foster actual understanding and often, in fact, arm those who use such labels with little more than random misinformation—"a slide show" whose "box of slides [has] been dropped and hastily reassembled just before presentation." To withhold vital information about narrative action and character backstory is to refuse readers the privilege of understanding and, more importantly, the opportunity to co-opt the addict's experiences. It is a means of wresting control from readers and asserting in the addict's own voice, "It's not what the story's about."

This attitude is, at times, reinforced through the point of view that is adopted, which refuses to allow the narrator, the character or the readers to bear witness without resorting to easy judgment or simple moralism. In a later scene, for instance, Ben "awakens on a hard cold floor; it is wet. His eyes see only white. As consciousness returns, more or less fully, he realizes that he is on the floor of a public rest room, his head in a urinal."[60] Here, as in the earlier blackout scene, Ben (and, by extension, O'Brien's readers) experiences a profound sense of disorientation upon waking in "one of the public beach rest rooms."[61] However, unlike the previous blackout scene, here Ben cannot recall "random memories of the night before,"[62] and, in fact, he does not even attempt to do so. He simply "stands" and considers how "amazed [he is] at how well he is taking this." As Ben muses, "A year ago, if he had found himself sleeping in a urinal, he probably would have committed suicide on the spot—death by grossness. Instead he goes back to the rest room and cleans up as well as he can."[63]

Noteworthy here and elsewhere in Ben's blackout scenes is the disinterested, or objective, stance that Ben adopts toward the narrative action, even in those instances when the narrative action might, at other times and in other contexts, be deemed unpalatable, even foul. The voice in this scene invites readers to inhabit the addict's often chaotic world while "passing no comment on characters or events, and allowing the story to appear to tell itself."[64] The fade into oblivion, the loss of memory and the disorientation upon waking that accompany an en bloc blackout all are presented without the moralistic

---

[60] Ibid., 101.
[61] Ibid.
[62] Ibid., 90.
[63] Ibid., 101.
[64] "objective narration." *Oxford Dictionary of Media and Communication*, 2011, Oxford University Press. http://www.oxfordreference.com/view/10.1093/oi/authority.20110803100243605 (accessed February 2, 2019).

editorializing that is common fare in novels about addiction, particularly those written by US authors.[65] In fact, in this telling, the focal character is not even required to experience the residual shame and guilt that Western writers and their readers typically demand of their addict protagonists following a blackout-inducing binge. Ben simply awakens, discerns his location from context clues and then heads out for another day of binge drinking. No harm, no foul. To readers, this approach to narrative voice—so unfamiliar, and thus experimental in the context of Western addiction fiction—sends a clear and resolute message: Meet the addict where that person lives, even if that location is a public urinal, and understand her/him/them as best you can, without pity, without fear and without shame.

Bearing Witness

The ending of *Leaving Las Vegas* might at least initially appear to undermine my claim that the novel encourages readers to bear witness to Ben's lived experiences without resorting to pathos or easy moralism. After all, the final scene of the novel is, in a word, gruesome. Having withdrawn from everyday life and sequestered himself in a hotel room for 12 days with only his horde of alcohol bottles as company, Ben is "beyond drunk" and very near death when Sera visits him.[66] At the onset of the scene, the narrator (through the lens of Sera) observes that Ben's hotel room "is thick with the smell of liquor and the taste of atrophy,"[67] a remark that instantly equates alcoholism with degeneration and seems to underscore long- and widely held cultural attitudes that regard addicts as wastes of life. Furthermore, the focal character in this scene is Sera, not Ben, which might be read as a final gesture of silencing whereby

---

[65] Here, *The Lost Weekend* provides a telling contrast to the ways in which O'Brien departs from the traditional Western addiction novel, particularly with respect to how that category of fiction depicts the addict protagonist's relationship to her/his/their addiction. To be sure, *The Lost Weekend* and *Leaving Las Vegas* share many noteworthy similarities. Both novels, for instance, focus on a male alcoholic who aggressively embraces his addiction. Both novels, too, follow the addict protagonist's descent into alcoholism and imminent (Birnam) or eventual (Ben) death. And both addict protagonists insist that alcoholism is a choice that they willingly, if not happily, make; as Don Birnam reveals in interior monologue, "If he wanted to drink himself to death it was nobody's affair but his own; his life was *his* life to throw away, if that's what he wanted" (43). However, in *The Lost Weekend*, the addict protagonist repeatedly wakes up after a night of binge drinking feeling "sick with despair and regret" (41), and, in the end, the eponymous weekend constitutes little more than a seemingly endless cycle of "despair, depression, remorse" (41), an exercise in pathos and gratuitous tragedy.

[66] O'Brien, *Leaving Las Vegas*, 186.

[67] Ibid.

addiction forces the addict character to cede control of his life and his agency to the sober counterpart.

At the same time, more so than in any scene prior, here O'Brien permits readers to see, rather than merely glimpse, the extent of Ben's decline. Earlier in the novel, for example, Ben's physical decline is remarked upon, at best, in innuendo, as when a random bartender comments, "It's none of my business, but if you could see what I see you wouldn't do this to yourself."[68] By contrast, in this final scene, Ben's failing health is on open display—in his pallor (i.e., Sera observes, "You look so very sick. You're so pale."[69]), his speech (i.e., "Punctuated by frequent coughs and gasps, occasionally blocked by mucous, his broken speech is difficult to understand"[70]) and his obvious ataxia (i.e., "After several unsuccessful attempts, he manages to sit up in bed"[71]). In this final scene, readers are forced to bear witness to the ravages of addiction as they are physically manifested in the body of O'Brien's focal character, Ben. This novel is not, as O'Brien's sister, Erin, has long maintained, the "fantasy version" of the addict's otherwise pathetic exit;[72] it is, instead, an unrelentingly realistic, but never self-indulgent, portrait of the physical and the psychological pain that is addiction—the very same pain that is so frequently displaced by readers' disgust in more conventional examples of the addiction novel.

The final scene of *Leaving Las Vegas* also is significant for the ways in which it plays with the concept of mirroring, echoing key motifs and gestures from the first "meeting" between Sera and Ben as a means of directing the readers' response both to this scene and, more broadly, to the novel as a whole. Central to these two scenes is Sera's response to the spectacle of degradation that unfolds in her presence; and in both scenes, Sera reacts to what she witnesses by turning away. Read superficially this gesture might seem to connote avoidance, even self-willed ignorance, two important emotions that most certainly drive Sera's response to Ben in the opening scene of the novel. But her turning away in the last scene of *Leaving Las Vegas* is significantly more complicated in its emotional valences. In the final scene of the novel, this gesture is immediately preceded by another, more intimate gesture that hints at Sera's motivation in turning away. At this point in the narrative, Ben "has thrown the sheet off of himself and is masturbating furiously." Although "he doesn't seem to know that she is there," Sera "cover[s] his hand with hers"

---

[68] Ibid., 94.
[69] Ibid., 186.
[70] Ibid.
[71] Ibid.
[72] Lynn Cinnamon, "The Story Behind *Leaving Las Vegas*," *Lynn Cinnamon*, August 2014, http://lynncinnamon.com/2014/08/leaving-las-vegas/ (accessed August 12, 2018).

and helps Ben finish his task.[73] Far from either gratuitous or salacious, this act of sexual intimacy conveys the compassion and empathy that Sera has developed for Ben over the duration of their relationship. In this one gesture, Sera very simply illustrates that "to be [morally] responsible [...] is to care for the dying,"[74] in whatever manner the dying may need, without judgment and without prejudice. In the last moments of Ben's life, Sera finally understands the gravity of the commitment that she made when agreeing to never ask Ben to stop drinking and, in offering him this last gesture of kindness and comfort, she affirms that earlier commitment to allow Ben to live on, and to die by, his own terms.

At the same time, O'Brien avoids the kind of scopophilic impulse that drives the urge to look at (but not bear witness to) the suffering of addicts—including their sometimes graphically brutal deaths—by refusing to show readers Ben's final moments. Indeed, O'Brien withholds any details—visual, aural or otherwise—about Ben's death, allowing readers to realize (alongside Sera) that Ben is deceased only after the fact: "Suddenly feeling the vacuum in the room, petrified by relief and sorrow, exhausted by reality, she knows, even before she turns and sees his still body, that he is gone."[75] Representations of death, particularly those that involve individuals who belong to historically underrepresented or vulnerable groups, tend to be exercises in exploitation and co-optation. In representation, as in death, the character is stripped of agency and voice, becoming a puppet manipulated simultaneously by the puppeteer/author and the broader culture in which that representation was produced. The dead body, in this respect, is meaningful only insofar as it comes to stand in for something else. As Elisabeth Bronfen explains in *Over Her Dead Body: Death, Femininity, and the Aesthetic* (1992), "Narrative and visual representations of death, drawing their material from a common cultural image repertoire, can be read as symptoms of our culture."[76]

In addiction fiction, the addict's death/corpse often draws on a "common cultural image repertoire" that is designed to shame and blame the addict, while simultaneously affirming the shock and horror that readers experience in the presence of the addict character. Donald Goines's *Dopefiend* (1971), for instance, concludes with the suicide of a tangential addict character, Minnie, an event that precipitates the catatonia and institutionalization of one of Goines's focal addict characters, Terry. The scene that Goines describes is

---

[73] O'Brien, *Leaving Las Vegas*, 187.
[74] Sturken, *Tangled Memories*, 219.
[75] O'Brien, *Leaving Las Vegas*, 188.
[76] Elisabeth Bronfen, *Over Her Dead Body: Death, Femininity, and the Aesthetic* (New York: Routledge, 1992), xi.

brutally graphic, producing in Terry a repeated and increasingly intense "horror":[77]

> At first, the only thing she noticed was the dresser; then her eyes traveled upwards and the slowly swinging apparition came into view. She opened her mouth in horror. The sight in front of her froze her in her tracks. She stared in terror at the body swinging gently back and forth. The sight of Minnie hanging there was shocking enough, but when her eyes turned downward, away from the sight of her friend's contorted face, they fell on what looked to be a child's head protruding from between Minnie's naked legs.

Of particular note in this scene is the way in which Goines foregrounds the act of looking, both for Terry and for his readers. In the brief passage cited above, for instance, the narrative action follows the movement of Terry's gaze—her eyes determining what the readers see/know, and when. The slow reveal of the horrors that confront Terry unfolds simultaneously in diegetic and extra-diegetic time, inviting readers to see what Terry sees as she sees it, and, more importantly, to react as Terry reacts in "real time." Her horror at seeing the "afterbirth"[78] and the "feces"[79] is intended to provoke readers' horror, and, in fact, Goines almost ensures this melding of character and reader response by crafting an immersive and assaultive reading experience. The gruesome details accumulate rapidly over this one-page scene—suicide snowballs to still birth, for example—to the point that readers cannot step back from the narrative action to process what is being seen/experienced, but instead must simply follow Terry's gaze and mimic Terry's response.

The kind of exploitation witnessed in a work like *Dopefiend* is fairly common within the wider category of Western addiction fiction; indeed, such representations, similar to representations of female bodies in death, are "so excessively obvious that they escape observation. Because they are so familiar, so evident, we are culturally blind to the ubiquity of representations of" such topics.[80] In other words, representations of this sort facilitate a passive reading experience, actually discouraging readers from bearing witness. Further, because such representations tend to rely on a "common cultural image repertoire," which is fraught with overdetermined tropes and motifs, they strip the addict of identity, voice and experience. O'Brien rejects this tradition in

---

[77] Donald Goines, *Dopefiend* (New York: Kensington, 1999), 264, 265.
[78] Ibid., 264.
[79] Ibid., 265.
[80] Bronfen, *Over Her Dead Body*, 3.

one gesture; by allowing Sera to look away, thereby referencing but refusing to dwell on the gruesomeness of Ben's death, O'Brien does not permit readers to co-opt Ben's experience as just another tale of the generic addict's tragic devolution. In the end, as in the beginning, Ben is an alc, but that is neither what his life, nor what his death, are ultimately about, at least not in *Leaving Las Vegas*.

Finding Beauty in the Ruins

If alcoholism is not the central topical focus of the novel, then Ben's declaration begs the question, "What is the story about?" To address this question, it is necessary to return to the central dramatic conflict that fuels the action, as well as precipitates the climax and dénouement of *Leaving Las Vegas*—that is, Ben's struggle to maintain a sense of identity in the face of the pervasive sociocultural stigmas that persistently threaten to overwrite his self-image. While much addiction fiction regards this struggle as an either-or dilemma which the addict either overcomes through sobriety or succumbs to in death, *Leaving Las Vegas* creatively imagines another possibility for the addict. From its very first pages, this novel charts a story of a man who has committed to living and dying by the bottle, and throughout its pages, Ben remains undeterred in his mission, even when faced with the damning looks and comments of his fellow characters. Yet the end of the novel is affirmative, rather than condemnatory, of the addict's identity, experience and humanity, insisting that "the drunk, the prostitute, the will not, live not suicides" will *not* be "swept away [...] into the pit to burn." Ironically, it is a profoundly life-affirming novel that at once demands respect and dignity for the addict's journey, despite—or, perhaps, due to—its outcome simply by allowing the addict character to express without censure his authentic experiences. Ben is a human being, the novel insists, with all of the vulnerabilities, the traumas, the ugliness and the beauty that that distinction entails.

And, in the final analysis, there is, as Susan Sontag suggests of trauma photography in *Regarding the Pain of Others*, beauty in ruins,[81] much as there is beauty to be found amidst the garish postmodernity of Sin City. Of course, the beauty of O'Brien's novel is not that it has a happy ending in which Ben sobers up and he and Sera live happily ever after. Early on, readers know that Ben will die; his survival is not what the story is about, and it is certainly not the source of the novel's beauty. In part, what is beautiful about this novel is the way in which it so genuinely lays bare the pain, the degradation and even the pleasures of alcoholism—and, to be sure, there are pleasures that can be derived from an addiction, although those highs become increasingly less

---

[81] Sontag, *Regarding the Pain of Others*, 76.

frequent and shorter in duration as the addiction persists, and they are far too frequently eclipsed by the wealth of lows that addiction engenders. Also beautiful is the sharing of experience that takes place between writer, readers and character. Through his acts of narrative experimentation, O'Brien invites readers to actively bear witness to a set of lived experiences that has been rendered unbelievable, even unreal, by its world-destroying[82] sharpness—experiences that O'Brien shared with his character, and most certainly many of his readers, including this writer. In so doing, O'Brien underscores the very real materiality of the lived experiences of alcoholism, and reminds us that, as Zadie Smith has written in her short story "Now More Than Ever," "pain is the least symbolic thing there is."[83] By witnessing these experiences, readers corroborate them as unassailable, legitimate, absolute, which is a remarkable and potentially quite transformative feat given the systemic erasure of such experiences across the past two centuries of Western (literary) history. But what is perhaps most remarkable, and most remarkably beautiful, about O'Brien's novel is that, in the end, and in Ben's end, O'Brien enables his readers to creatively reimagine how we collectively understand who addicts are and how they navigate the world. In the ruins that are *Leaving Las Vegas*, O'Brien suggests, we ironically can imagine a better world: a world in which addicts are individuals, and not generic drunks; a world in which addicts can be loved, not in spite of their addictions, but simply because they are human; and, finally, a world in which readers hold themselves accountable for what they read, as well as for how they read, and, in so doing, those readers exercise greater compassion toward those about whom they read.

---

[82] I borrow this phrase from Elaine Scarry, who, in *The Body in Pain: The Making and Unmaking of the World* (1985), suggests that "intense pain is world-destroying" (29). Although Scarry writes specifically about the physical pain associated with bodily torture, her observations about the language- and world-destroying powers of torture are, in many significant ways, applicable to the lived experiences of addiction. For example, Scarry writes, "Torture inflicts bodily pain that is itself language-destroying, but torture also mimes (objectifies in the external environment) this language-destroying capacity in its interrogation, the purpose of which is not to elicit needed information but visibly to deconstruct the prisoner's voice" (19–20). In much the same way, addicts are by virtue of their addiction subjected to both physical and psychological pain, particularly from external sources who, in speaking for dominant (sober) culture, not only speak for (thereby objectifying) the addict, but also and simultaneously work to strip the addict of voice and agency.

[83] Zadie Smith, "Now More Than Ever," the *New Yorker*, July 16, 2018, https://www.newyorker.com/magazine/2018/07/23/now-more-than-ever (accessed July 29, 2019).

Chapter 2

BETRAYING: *DOPE* (2006)

Just as *Leaving Las Vegas* initially appears simply to recapitulate the topical, formal and ideological prescriptions of the Western addiction novel, so, too, does Sara Gran's *Dope* (2006) at once seem a virtual carbon copy of such classic roman noirs as James M. Cain's *The Postman Always Rings Twice* (1934), Patricia Highsmith's *Strangers on a Train* (1950) and Jim Thompson's *The Killer Inside Me* (1952). Like its literary forebears, *Dope* invites readers into "a negative utopia, a world stripped of all ethical values and inhabited by marginalized characters, who find it extremely difficult to apply the morals of the dominant class to their own action."[1] The marginalized character at the center of *Dope* is Josephine "Joe" Flannigan, a character that, given her former heroin addiction, as well as her questionable work history, which includes both grifting and prostitution, stands as one of the myriad noir "characters who live in a hostile or violent world where traditional moral codes do not always have the significance they are supposed to have."[2]

The hostility and violence that typify the mood of noir fiction are underscored in *Dope* by the ongoing antagonism between Joe and members of the New York City police force. Coerced into looking into the disappearance of a young, middle-class drug addict by the promise of a big payday, and then implicated in the murder of Jerry McFall, the young woman's dealer boyfriend, Joe spends much of the novel on the wrong side of a corrupt law enforcement that seeks to frame her for a crime that both she and readers know she did not commit. This conflict breeds within both the protagonist and Gran's readers the type of "isolation, fragmentation, alienation, and distrust in official institutions and values" that Jopi Nyman, in *Men Alone: Masculinity, Individualism, and Hard-boiled Fiction* (1997), regards as a defining characteristic of the roman noir.[3] At the same time, this conflict forces Joe to "[operate] outside and above the law [s]he professes to defend," another defining characteristic

---

[1] Jopi Nyman, *Men Alone: Masculinity, Individualism, and Hard-Boiled Fiction* (Amsterdam: Rodopi B.V., 1997), 331.
[2] Ibid., 30.
[3] Ibid.

of the noir form.⁴ By forcing characters (and readers) to exist outside of conventional ideological and social structures, noir fiction "projects a vision of a world filled with betrayal and deception"⁵ and encourages readers to consider "the price of law and order, the gap between the law and substantive justice and the impossibility of easy moral distinctions."⁶

Betrayal constitutes a key characteristic of the plot for much of noir fiction; indeed, in *The Roman Noir in Post-war French Culture* (2003), Claire Gorrara regards the "*noir* universe" as a site at which "betrayal and deceit seem to override friendship and loyalty."⁷ In *Murder Most Fair: The Appeal of Mystery Fiction* (2000), Michael Cohen similarly suggests that in noir fiction, "betrayal by the supposed innocent is often the spring for the plot: the attractive client, the lover or old friend of the detective, and the young girl seeking protection all turn out to be the culprits."⁸ Within the noir form, betrayal refers to a deliberate act that simultaneously violates a contract—one either assumed or tangible—between two or more individuals, and breaches the values of trust, loyalty and altruism on which such contracts typically are founded. In short, noir characters rarely are exactly what they initially might seem to be, and most are willing to double-cross their fellow human beings if doing so effects some sort of personal gain. Noir characters lie about their identities. They establish intimacy with other characters (often the protagonist) only as a means of fulfilling ulterior and self-serving ends. They cheat, steal and even murder without regard to how those actions will impact the other characters that occupy the diegetic world. They even defy the dictates of existing social and kinship formations, as when, in *The Maltese Falcon* (1930), Wilmer, having himself been betrayed by surrogate father figure Gutman, retaliates by shooting and killing Gutman. Of this action, Dashiell Hammett's protagonist Sam Spade remarks simply, "[Gutman] ought to have expected that."⁹

While betrayal recurs frequently as a plot point within the diegesis of the roman noir, it typically does not figure prominently, if at all, into the relationship between readers and text. As a category of popular fiction intended chiefly to appeal to a preexisting readership with a predilection for that style

---

⁴ Charles J. Rzepka, *Detective Fiction* (Cambridge, MA: Polity Press, 2005), 47.
⁵ Nyman, *Men Alone*, 331.
⁶ Alistair Rolls and Deborah Walker, *French and American Noir: Dark Crossings* (New York: Palgrave Macmillan, 2009), 167.
⁷ Claire Gorrara, *The Roman Noir in Post-War French Culture* (Oxford: Oxford University Press, 2003), 28.
⁸ Michael Cohen, *Murder Most Fair: The Appeal of Mystery Fiction* (Madison, WI: Fairleigh Dickinson University Press, 2000), 20.
⁹ Dashiell Hammett, *The Maltese Falcon, the Thin Man, Red Harvest* (New York: Alfred A. Knopf, 2000), 224.

of writing, noir fiction is as much defined by readerly expectations as it is by a set of formal features that typify works commonly placed within that category. Indeed, in "Objectivity and Immanence in Genre Theory," Paul Cobley goes even further, arguing that "genre is not a set of textual features that can be enumerated; rather, it is an expectation."[10] What appeals most to readers of popular fiction is the predictability of the form, or, the feeling as they are reading that they not only "ought to have expected" the events to unfold as they did, but also that they often did accurately predict the sequence and ideological course of narrative events.

This is not to suggest that popular fiction constitutes a "self-plagiarising form of literature" that "never changes or develops," that "seduces readers and empties their minds" and that "saturates" our culture with "'copy-cat' stories."[11] In fact, as a longtime reader of popular mystery fiction, I can attest to having encountered many formal innovations within that genre over my reading history, particularly in works written by feminist, hard-boiled mystery writers.[12] But it is to suggest that even when writers of popular fiction engage in formal innovation, they do so in a manner that ultimately affirms, rather than betrays, the literary tradition within which they are writing. At most, such writers typically only expose the problematic ideological prescriptions of the forms within which they work, raising questions like, *Who is permitted to inhabit this form? Who is excised from the form? And how do (or, Do?) these acts of excision help readers to understand better similar imbalances of power that exist in the extra-diegetic world?* While questions like these prove to be interesting thought exercises, they do not—and, indeed, cannot—undermine a deeply entrenched literary form precisely because the act of critique is predicated on the recapitulation of the ideologically questionable form as an illustration of said critique.

---

[10] Paul Cobley, "Objectivity and Immanence in Genre Theory," in *Genre Matters: Essays in Theory and Criticism*, ed. Garin Dowd, Lesley Stevenson and Jeremy Strong (Bristol: Intellect, 2006), 41.

[11] Ken Gelder, "The Fields of Popular Fiction," in *New Directions in Popular Fiction: Genre, Distribution, Reproduction*, ed. Ken Gelder (London: Palgrave Macmillan, 2016), 3.

[12] Three of my previous publications speak specifically of this topic, including: "'Listen to the Silence': Dismantling the Myth of a Classless Society in the Fiction of Marcia Muller and Sara Paretsky," in *Class and Culture in Crime Fiction: Essays on Works in English since the 1970s*, ed. Julie H. Kim (Jefferson, NC: McFarland, 2014), 49–68; "'There are times when an old rule should be abandoned, or a current rule should not be applied': Narration, Innovation, and the Hardboiled Mystery in Sue Grafton's *'T' Is for Trespass*," *TEXT: Journal of Writing and Writing Courses* 37(October 2016), http://www.textjournal.com.au/speciss/issue37/Diehl.pdf (accessed February 14, 2019); and "'W' Is for 'Woman': Deconstructing the Private Dick in Sue Grafton's Alphabet Series," in *Murdering Miss Marple: Essays on Gender and Sexuality in the New Golden Age of Women's Crime Fiction*, ed. Julie H. Kim (Jefferson, NC: McFarland, 2012), 120–41.

By contrast, Gran's *Dope* actively violates some of the foundational premises on which the noir genre has been built, and, in so doing, betrays the trust that exists between readers of popular fiction and the literary text. In Joe Flannigan, readers expect the same type of criminality that is witnessed in classic noir protagonists, like James M. Cain's Frank Chambers and Patricia Highsmith's Tom Ripley, especially given the widely held belief that addicts are compulsive liars and pathological narcissists. Of *Dope*, readers expect the kind of diegetic world in which "treachery and confusion blur the distinctions between detective, criminal, and victim,"[13] as foregrounded in a novel like *The Killer Inside Me*, which is narrated from the point of view of a sheriff's deputy-cum-sociopath. And from Gran, readers expect a work of fiction in which "characters' positions are unstable and subject to sudden change and role reversals that problematize notions of individual guilt and innocence."[14]

While Gran lures readers into *Dope* and creates a false sense of security by seeming to replicate many of the well-established formal features of noir fiction, what readers ultimately encounter in this novel proves to be quite the opposite of their initial expectations. In *Dope*, readers do encounter a diegetic world characterized by "treachery and confusion." However, while other "characters' positions are unstable and subject to sudden change and role reversals that problematize notions of individual guilt and innocence," in Joe Flannigan, readers discover a virtuous protagonist with a firm moral compass that unwaveringly guides her through the narrative action. As a noir protagonist, and especially as a noir protagonist who is both female[15] and a former addict, Joe is expected to be morally corrupt, and her firm commitment to the core values of truth, justice and altruism ultimately smacks of betrayal and serves to reframe the relationship between genre, text and readers. This betrayal is experienced as loss—loss of faith and trust in the very sociocultural institutions that once so authoritatively told us that addicts are narcissistic, morally bankrupt losers. But it also and simultaneously is experienced as renewal, for when we are forced to give up the narrative illusion that all

---

[13] Gorrara, *The Roman Noir in Post-war French Culture*, 6.
[14] Ibid.
[15] Here, I am alluding to the lengthy tradition of the femme fatale in the noir genre. In *Historical Dictionary of Film Noir* (2010), Andrew Spicer asserts that "the figure of the deadly female—the femme fatale or spider woman—is the most conspicuous representation of femininity in film noir" (329). Spicer goes on to suggest that this figure, who is distinguished by her duplicity, can be seen "as a symptom of male anxieties about women, a creature who threatens to castrate and devour her male victim" (329). In an interesting twist on the genre, Gran casts her addict protagonist as a kind of innocent who strives to maintain a relatively "virtuous and stable family life" (330), and Joe's seemingly "good girl" sister as the femme fatale and the malefactor.

addicts are mere carbon copies of Charles Jackson's Modernist antihero, Don Birnam, we allow ourselves to see addicts as complex individuals with rich interior lives, and we engage more meaningfully, more genuinely and more compassionately with both them and their lived experiences.

A "Woman Set between Contending Forces"

In order for readers to understand fully the ways in which Gran's *Dope* undermines dominant cultural scripts around the lived experiences of addiction, it is necessary first to locate the novel within the literary tradition with which it experiments: that is, the roman noir. This is so because the acts of betrayal that occur within this novel turn on and, indeed, presuppose at least a passing familiarity with the formal and ideological taken-for-granteds of the noir form. Stated differently, to feel the full force of the betrayal that Gran's novel enacts, readers must begin by examining what is being betrayed. In the initial three sections of the chapter, I will demonstrate the ways in which *Dope* initially appears to align with the formal expectations of the noir form. Then, in the final section of the chapter, titled "Poor, invisible Nadine," I will turn my attention to the acts of formal and ideological betrayal that work to "unsettle the limitations of genre and convention" and "subvert [readers'] familiarity"[16] with dominant cultural attitudes toward addicts and the lived experiences of addiction.

The most obvious parallel between *Dope* and the roman noir tradition is its focus on an outsider protagonist whose experience is characterized by loneliness, alienation and estrangement. In *Street with No Name: A History of the Classic American Film Noir* (2002), for instance, Andrew Dickos suggests that the noir protagonist "skirts the contours of an accepted social terrain";[17] Dickos goes on to explain that "the noir archetype is best understood as the character whose human weaknesses and passions receive no kind of reception in a social order structured to deny their existence."[18] The archetypal noir protagonist is typified by moral weaknesses that can, and often do, manifest themselves in tangible behavioral patterns (like addiction) that serve as both an illustration and a consequence of those weaknesses. Within the diegetic world, protagonists are ostracized from the dominant social order—their "weaknesses and passions,"

---

[16] Julie Armstrong, *Experimental Fiction: An Introduction for Readers and Writers* (London: Bloomsbury Academic, 2014), 9.
[17] Andrew Dickos, *Street with No Name: A History of the Classic American Film Noir* (Lexington: University of Kentucky Press, 2002), 66.
[18] Ibid., 65.

which are characterized as compulsive and excessive, at once marking them as pariahs and standing as a "justification" for the "den[ial of their] existence."

That Joe Flannigan is marked by the kinds of "weaknesses" that typify the noir protagonist is intimated from the first scene of the novel. Set in "a queer joint"[19] in New York City in the early 1950s, *Dope*'s opening chapter at once identifies Gran's protagonist with the geographic and moral margins of mid-century Manhattan. Throughout the novel, too, Joe repeatedly is associated with the marginal spaces that she frequents, both in present-tense narration and in past-tense flashback: the drug dens of the Bowery,[20] as well as the strip clubs,[21] the fleabag motels[22] and the houses of ill repute of Hell's Kitchen.[23] Like much noir fiction, *Dope* locates its primary action in red-light districts: that is, those areas of a gritty urban environ that are difficult to locate, given the ways in which they systematically are hidden from view by a dominant social order that is perpetually hostile to their existence, and sometimes dangerous to navigate, given the immoral characters who populate them.

Joe also is marked as an outsider given her sketchy backstory, which includes both heroin addiction and prostitution. This sense of outsiderhood is introduced explicitly in the second chapter of the novel, when Joe is hired by Mr. and Mrs. Nelson to locate their college-coed-turned-"dope fiend" daughter.[24] When asked by Joe why they want to hire her to locate the daughter, especially given that she lacks private investigation credentials, the couple quickly note that Joe possesses the "underworld connections"[25] that are needed to navigate the city and locate Nadine: as Mr. Nelson clarifies, "What we mean is, we need someone who knows about drug addicts, and girl addicts in particular."[26] Throughout the initial consultation, as Mr. Nelson describes his daughter's descent into heroin addiction, he consistently employs third-person pronouns and regularly refuses to make reference to his daughter's given name: "This man, Nick the Greek, he said that you would know where people like that go, how they make money and where they buy drugs and that sort of thing."[27]

Several aspects of this scene are noteworthy. First, Gran leads readers to believe that there is a significant class difference between Joe and the Nelsons, perhaps even choosing that particular surname as an overt homage to the

---

[19] Sara Gran, *Dope* (New York: Berkley Books, 2006), 1.
[20] Ibid., 36.
[21] Ibid., 52.
[22] Ibid., 64.
[23] Ibid., 223.
[24] Ibid., 9.
[25] Ibid., 14.
[26] Ibid.
[27] Ibid.

mid-century middle-class values embodied by *The Adventures of Ozzie and Harriet* (1952–66). This class difference marks Joe as marginal, as Other, especially in a nation where such class differences are systemically elided and citizens are fed the false belief that middle class is the default socioeconomic status.[28] Also significant is Mr. Nelson's rhetoric. The derisive phrase "people like that" gives lie to the myth of a classless society, alluding to the deep socioeconomic and moral chasms that typically separate sobriety from addiction and that cast the addict as a spectacle of degradation. Moreover, the repeated use of third-person pronouns in reference to addicts powerfully underscores the ways in which addicts are stigmatized in Western culture by recapitulating the binary logic that decisively, albeit problematically, divides "us" from "them." Despite the faulty logic undergirding this standpoint, it nonetheless gains added credence and authority with both Joe and Gran's readers because it is voiced from a position of racial, socioeconomic and gendered privilege. It is precisely the enduring power that such rhetoric has over Western culture that ultimately proves to be Joe's (and readers') undoing, a point that I will take up at greater length later in this chapter.

While a character like Mr. Nelson lends insight into how addicts as a class are regarded within the diegetic world of *Dope*, particularly outside of the red-light districts that they frequent, other characters, like Detective Springer, lend insight into how Gran's outsider protagonist specifically is viewed within this world. Midway through the novel, after Jerry McFall is murdered, Joe is visited by a homicide detective and his beat cop crony and questioned about her involvement in the crime. Joe repeatedly protests her innocence, explaining that she was only trying to track McFall down in connection with the disappearance of Nadine Nelson, whom she was engaged to locate. To these protestations, Springer responds, "You expect me to believe that out of everyone in New York City, [the Nelsons] hired a junkie whore like you to find their daughter? Don't treat me like a jerk, Josephine, that's all I ask of you. Don't treat me like a fool."[29] That Joe might possess some knowledge, skill or expertise that would render her a useful, contributing member of society is, at best, laughable to Springer. Operating under the kind of "Once an addict, always an addict" "logic" of Alcoholics Anonymous and like Twelve-Step programs, Springer refuses to acknowledge (let alone respect) Joe's sobriety, and instead simply dismisses her as a "junkie whore"—a more emphatic and colorful iteration of Mr. Nelson's "people like that." Moreover, Springer

---

[28] For more on the myth of a classless society that predominates in US culture, see Michael Zweig, *The Working Class Majority: America's Best Kept Secret* (Ithaca, NY: Cornell University Press, 2012).

[29] Gran, *Dope*, 133.

assumes Joe's guilt in the crime of murder based solely on what he perceives as the moral transgressions of addiction and prostitution. What these exchanges with the Nelsons and the New York City law enforcement drive home is that Joe functions within *Dope* as an outsider protagonist in the tradition of Sam Spade, Philip Marlowe and Mike Hammer: a "[wo]man set between contending forces"; "the stranger […] the unconnected [wo]man"[30] who exists outside of multiple systems of social organization, including morality, the law and even the family.

"I'd Been Places, and Far Too Many of Them"

Indeed, it is within traditional kinship structures that Joe's outsiderhood is particularly pronounced. Throughout *Dope*, Gran consistently characterizes Joe's relationship with her half-sister, Shelley, as one-sided and unbalanced. As the older sibling of a family in which the matriarch "was a good-for-nothing drunk […] and a whore," and the deadbeat patriarchs were multiple and absent,[31] Joe repeatedly made sacrifices so that the younger Shelley could enjoy a marginally "normal" childhood and adolescence; these sacrifices included, but were not limited to, Joe herself engaging in prostitution to make ends meet. In the opening scene of the novel, for instance, Joe relinquishes the bulk of the money she has earned from selling an engagement ring that she "boosted […] from Tiffany's the day before"[32] to pacify a fence whom Shelley had swindled out of $125.[33] Despite the many sacrifices that, over a lifetime, Joe has made on behalf of her sister, Shelley remains deeply ashamed of Joe—so much so that she ignores her sister's presence in public and refuses to invite Joe into her apartment building.

To Joe, Shelley's embarrassment and shame makes sense given the "long list of disappointments" that, as a "junkie," she made Shelley endure during their adolescence. As Joe justifies in interior monologue:

> [T]hat's what junkies do; they disappoint. They say they'll show up for dinner at eight, and they come at eight the next morning. They say they'll take care of the rent and then they shoot the money up their arm. They say they'll always be there for you and then they nod out on a park

---

[30] Lewis D. Moore, *Connecting Detectives: The Influence of the 19th Century Sleuth Fiction on the Early Hard-Boileds* (Jefferson, NC: McFarland, 2015), 76.
[31] Gran, *Dope*, 197.
[32] Ibid., 2.
[33] Ibid., 3–4.

bench when you need them the most [...] I was clean now, but there was no reason for her to forgive me. I wouldn't have.[34]

In light of Joe's sacrifices, Shelley's embarrassment and shame smack of ingratitude and point to the narcissism that is at the core of Shelley's characterization. That Joe has internalized Shelley's shame—evidenced by her concluding admission that she would not forgive (and, indeed, has not forgiven) herself for "becoming a junkie whore"—is not terribly surprising in a culture that demands that addicts, whether in the throes of an addiction, in recovery or even when dead, continuously engage in self-flagellation. In fact, in *Substance and Shadow: Women and Addiction in the United States* (1996), Stephen R. Kandall explains that the lived experiences of female addicts often are marked by a heightened degree (when compared to male addicts) of "self-loathing and despair [...] at being unable to control their own lives and a desire for self-anesthesia to dull unhappiness."[35] This perhaps is so because addiction seemingly runs counter to so many of the stereotypic "virtues" that historically have been attributed to the female sex—from temperance to sensitivity to gentleness and empathy.

While kinship structures traditionally are seen as a form of social organization "based on the reciprocal rights and obligations of the different family members,"[36] in *Dope*, the relationship between Joe and Shelley is unequal and incommensurate. Shelley is characterized as a narcissistic taker, while Joe is characterized as generous to a fault, a trait that Joe's ex-husband, Monte, challenges her to acknowledge when the pair run into each other midway through the novel:

> "Hey, how's Shelley doing? I saw her photograph in the paper this morning. An ad for soap or something like that."
> "She's good," I said. "She's good."
> "She helping you out?" Monte asked. "Throwing a little money your way?"
> "No," I said. "Why would she?"
> Monte shook his head. "If it wasn't for you that kid would be dead. Dead a hundred times over. If it wasn't for you—"

---

[34] Ibid., 119–20.
[35] Stephen R. Kandall, *Substance and Shadow: Women and Addiction in the United States* (Cambridge, MA: Harvard University Press, 1996), 137.
[36] Bryan Strong and Theodore F. Cohen, *The Marriage and Family Experience: Intimate Relationships in a Changing Society*, 13th ed. (Boston, MA: Cengage Learning, 2017), 18.

Typically, the addict does not function as a voice of moral authority in the Western novel; but here, in a twist on the genre that alludes to the act of betrayal that is central to the reading experience of *Dope*, Gran undermines the expectations that most Western readers bring to addiction novel. In this scene, it is the addict ex-husband, Monte, and not Gran's sober protagonist, Joe, who calls into question Shelley's self-serving nature. While Joe remains firmly trapped within the cycle of shame and blame that circumscribes many addicts' experiences, wondering aloud why Shelley, now a moderately famous model/actress on the verge of making it big, would possibly "[throw] a little money" her way, Monte insists that kinship is built on the core value of reciprocity, and that Shelley owes Joe for the many sacrifices that she made for her younger sister.

Moreover, the "if" statements that conclude this passage underscore the strength of Monte's conviction; unlike Joe, Monte refuses to shame her for resorting to grifting, prostitution or even illicit substances in an effort to support Shelley and ease her own pain. Instead, Monte challenges Joe to understand that her behaviors—while illegal—nonetheless are directly responsible for Shelley's success and that, if Shelley respected the kinship structure that not only saved her from imminent harm "a hundred times over," but also binds her—at least biologically—to Joe, then she would fulfill the reciprocal obligation of now providing for a sister that is less financially stable. But while Shelley accepts the rights, she consistently rejects the obligations that are an always and already to membership in existing kinship structures in the West; as Joe muses in interior monologue, "Without ever talking about it, Shelley and me had made a kind of deal. I wasn't her sister anymore. Not in public, at least. She was going places and me […] well, I'd been places, and far too many of them."[37] Shelley's public ostracization of Joe, which recurs multiple times within the narrative of *Dope*, reinforces Joe's outsiderhood and locates her squarely within the noir tradition—a tradition in which "family crises play [a significant] role,"[38] but the noir protagonist typically "has neither family nor friends [herself]."[39]

(Not) "in a Realm of Deferred Repentance"

Like her noir protagonist forebears, Joe not only lives in a world in which traditional forms of social organization fail to provide her comfort, stability or meaning, but she also operates according to a moral code that derives not

---

[37] Gran, *Dope*, 196.
[38] Moore, *Connecting Detectives*, 258.
[39] Ibid., 266.

from traditional legal systems, which, in *Dope*, are corrupt, nor from a kind of universal morality, which does not exist in this novel, but from her past experiences as a prostitute, as a grifter and, quite interestingly, as an addict. Writing about the moral code that Dashiell Hammett learned while working at the Pinkerton Agency, and that the writer used as a jumping off point for his Sam Spade novels, William Marling notes that the noir protagonist's morality is "strictly personal." In *The American Roman Noir: Hammett, Cain, and Chandler* (1995), Marling goes on to explain: "The bad guys did not live by a civil or religious morality, so to be bound by any rules in dealing with them was to put oneself at a disadvantage. In Wright's view, a detective might lie, cheat, steal evidence, and emotionally manipulate suspects. He lived in a realm of deferred repentance."[40] Within the diegetic world of the roman noir, virtue and integrity derive not from some external source that imposes its understanding of morality onto the individual, but from within. It is a contextual—although I would argue not relative—moral framework that empowers the noir protagonist to weigh her circumstances against her desired outcome to determine the most desirable and advantageous course of action in any given circumstance. As a result, the noir protagonist can (and often does) engage in all manner of questionable, if not illegal, behaviors and still be on the side of goodness, truth and justice.

Joe's investigation into the disappearance of Nadine Nelson initially appears to be driven largely by self-interest. In fact, in both the roman noir and hard-boiled detective fiction, the protagonist regularly is more invested in her/his/their own self-interest than "in seeking the truth,"[41] and more often than not, this self-interest is focused squarely on the protagonist's financial gain from undertaking a case. When Joe's investigation into the disappearance of Nadine Nelson hits a dead end, for example, Joe, unsure of how or even whether to proceed, muses in interior monologue:

> There wasn't really any reason for me to find her. The first thousand was already mine and the second—well, even if I did find Nadine, who knew if the Nelsons would pony up? I didn't have any reason to think they would, especially once they saw her [...] They probably wouldn't even want her in the house. And I couldn't exactly take them to court if they decided to renege.[42]

---

[40] William Marling, *The American Roman Noir: Hammett, Cain, and Chandler* (Athens, GA: University of Georgia Press, 1995), 97.
[41] Greg Martin, *Crime, Media and Culture* (New York: Routledge, 2019), 100.
[42] Gran, *Dope*, 85–86.

At this point in the narrative, Joe seems almost entirely motivated by the Almighty Dollar. She weighs aborting the investigation with the initial $1,000 in hand against the promise of a second payday. Joe worries about the financial and moral obligation that Nadine, once located, might become for her, given that "[Nadine's parents] were looking for a college girl whose biggest problem had been that she didn't fit in at the country club," but "if [Joe] brought them anything at all it would be an addict who'd been with more men than the rest of the country club combined."[43] Never once in this passage does Joe consider that Nadine is embroiled within a seedy and dangerous world that Nadine, as an affluent white woman, is entirely ill-equipped to navigate. Never once does altruism surface and Joe acknowledge that, given her own backstory, perhaps she is the best suited to guide Nadine out of the morass of her addiction.

What does surface is Joe's anger, even resentment, toward the young woman that she seeks to locate: "This girl was going to college, for Christ's sake. I'd never known anyone who'd been to college. I wasn't even sure what they did there […] [S]he'd thrown away what ninety percent of the world would kill for. I don't care if her parents did spank her or her mother did tip the bottle a little. She'd had no reason to do it. She'd had no right to do it."[44] At first, Joe's resentment of Nadine seems deeply rooted in the rigid class hierarchies that divide the "haves" and the "have-nots" in the United States, especially given the explicit contrast that she draws between her own meager origins and Nadine's markedly more privileged ones (i.e., "I never had much to lose to begin with. And I'd never been good at anything that was legal. But this girl […]").[45] The derisive references to college appear to reinforce Joe's class grievances given that, in the United States of the 1950s, only 50 percent of young adults—both male and female—completed high school and less than 10 percent of females earned an undergraduate degree.[46] The small percentage of US women who were attending college in the 1950s was almost exclusively drawn from the affluent classes; indeed, women like Joe were so divorced from the baccalaureate experience that most, like Joe, weren't "even sure what they did there."

But Joe's anger, if motivated at all by socioeconomic divisions, is equally if not more so prompted by the kinds of painful introspection in which this case forces her to engage. In the passage cited at length above, for instance, Joe

---

[43] Ibid., 86.
[44] Ibid., 87.
[45] Ibid.
[46] "120 Years of American Education: A Statistical Portrait," *National Center for Education Statistics*, U.S. Department of Education, January 1993, https://nces.ed.gov/pubs93/93442.pdf (accessed February 27, 2019).

repeatedly contrasts her lived experiences with Nadine's, arriving at the conclusion that while she (Joe) was environmentally—if not genetically—predisposed to becoming a "junkie whore," Nadine, with her many advantages, should have had "no reason" to travel down that same path. Of course, this line of thinking is flawed, both logically and ideologically, in that it both presupposes and perpetuates a faulty causal relationship between class status, broken family structures and addiction. Joe's realization that anyone can become an addict—even someone like Nadine who enjoys many of the advantages that an affluent, Western life has to offer—angers Joe, causing her to direct her frustrations seemingly at Nadine as she proclaims, "She'd had no reason to do it. She'd had no right to do it." But to read this line as an indictment of Nadine would, I think, be inaccurate. It is telling that Joe's thoughts proceed from "reason," a term that alludes to an internal motivation within the individual, to "right," a term that suggests an external force, or entitlement, that prompts an individual to behave in a certain manner. To conclude this passage with "She'd had no right to do it," with the pronoun "it" referring to illicit drug use, is to rail not against Nadine but against the drugs and, more broadly, the addiction that has stripped Nadine of her "reason" and compelled her to use.

This epiphany serves as a motivating force for Joe, propelling her to pursue the case even when all signs suggest that she simply should take the money and run. The shared experiences of addiction and prostitution fuel an empathic bond between Joe and Nadine—a bond that repeatedly is reinforced by how other characters speak about and treat the two women. For instance, once Joe learns that the "Mr. and Mrs. Nelson" that initially hired her are con artists and not Nadine's biological parents, she visits the real Mrs. Nelson, who resides with her hyper-controlling husband in the suburb of New Village. The quintessential 1950s housewife, Mrs. Nelson clearly suffers from what Betty Friedan would, in *The Feminine Mystique* (1963), go on to term "the problem that has no name"—"liv[ing her] life putting on makeup to watch cereal commercials all day."[47] Mrs. Nelson admits to having last seen Nadine in the city about a month earlier, at, she reveals, "[a] cafeteria, coffee shop—someplace like that. I mean I can't take her someplace nice. Not looking like she does."[48] To this statement, Joe inquires, "And what does she look like?" to which Mrs. Nelson, in a passage that echoes Detective Springer's verbal assault on Joe, says, "Skinny, dirty—well, like a whore. Like a drug addict and a street whore."[49] Long saddled with similarly demeaning epithets, and long treated like a pariah by both strangers and intimates, Joe identifies with

---

[47] Gran, *Dope*, 155.
[48] Ibid., 156.
[49] Ibid.

Nadine, despite their dissimilar origin stories and the markedly disparate opportunities that those origin stories afforded them. This connection that Joe feels with Nadine is at least partially responsible for her initially taking the case, and it is almost exclusively the reason why she persists in her efforts to locate Nadine.

"Poor, Invisible Nadine"

While Joe initially appears to be driven largely by self-interest, over the novel Gran makes clear that Joe is more motivated by an internal need to do right by a woman who has been abused, discarded and rendered invisible many times over. Early in her investigation into Nadine's disappearance, Joe visits Rose's Hi Class Lounge—a dive bar featuring exotic dancers where "the girls look good, the guys were cheap, and the price of liquor was up."[50] When she shows Tony, the manager, a photograph of Nadine and asks him if he can identify the woman, he hedges: "She looks like a girl who might have worked here a couple of months ago [...] Raquel? [...] Roxanne? [...] After a while, they all look alike."[51] Although Joe already has identified Tony as a relatively virtuous man who protects the dancers from unwanted advances by the patrons,[52] here readers see that even to kind-hearted characters like Tony, the addicts who pass through Rose's are little more than nameless, faceless junkies akin to the "staggering drunk" who stumbles through the opening pages of *Leaving Las Vegas*. Tony's inability to correctly identify Nadine—accentuated by the dramatic linguistic and phonetic differences between "Nadine," "Raquel" and "Roxanne"—reinforces the ways in which even white, privileged women like Nadine are rendered socially invisible by their addictions.

Nadine's invisibility also is reinforced by the fact that, within the primary narrative of *Dope*, she is set up as a MacGuffin. In *Dictionary of Film Terms: The Aesthetic Companion to Film Art* (2007), Frank Eugene Beaver describes the MacGuffin as "a plotting device for setting a story into motion." Beaver goes on to explain, "The term is frequently applied to that object or person in a mystery film that at the beginning of the plot provides an element of dramatic curiosity [...] The MacGuffin can [...] be someone or something that is lost and is being sought [...] Once the dramatic plot is under way [...] the MacGuffin often ceases to be of major importance."[53] Introduced in the

---

[50] Ibid., 54.
[51] Ibid., 54–55.
[52] Ibid., 52.
[53] Frank Eugene Beaver, *Dictionary of Film Terms: The Aesthetic Companion to Film Art* (New York: Peter Lang, 2007), 153.

second chapter of the novel, Nadine's disappearance, indeed, does appear to be the inciting incident of *Dope*, setting the dramatic action in motion and seemingly providing for readers the central conflict that propels the narrative action toward some as yet unidentified, but looming climax. After all, it is the investigation into Nadine's disappearance that implicates Joe in the major events of the narrative, including the murder of Jerry McFall, the death of Joe's friend Jim and the eventual unmasking of Shelley and the revelation of the key role that she, from the onset, has played in the entire sequence of events.

However, once "the Nelsons" are unmasked as con artists paid to impersonate Nadine's parents in order to frame Joe for the murder of Jerry McFall, Nadine "ceases to be of major importance" to anyone except Joe. In fact, in the final, climactic scene in which Shelley admits that she murdered McFall and then set Joe up to take the blame, Shelley justifies the impending murder of Joe by saying, "You should have taken the jail time [...] That's what you were supposed to do. You should have taken the murder rap for McFall and let the girl disappear. You should have let her go [...] She probably would've killed herself sooner or later anyway."[54] For Shelley, who is finally on the verge of stardom with the possible offer of a lead role in a television sitcom,[55] McFall represented a liability given that he had in his possession some nude pictures of her taken years earlier when she "needed the money."[56] But this passage also suggests that Shelley views both Nadine and Joe as equally disposable— mere "plot devices" in the narrative web that she spins around her criminal actions, insignificant in their own right, and important only insofar as they enable Shelley to achieve her self-serving ends.

Key to understanding the act of narrative betrayal at the heart of *Dope* is Joe's relentless search for Nadine, despite the many entreaties by other characters for her to abandon the quest. It is during a conversation with Shelley that Joe's desire to find Nadine is made clear to Gran's readers:

> "Anyway," Shelley said. "I guess it's all over now. I mean, Jim's dead. And the girl, Nadine—she turned out not to have anything to do with it all, right?"
>
> I thought about it for a minute. I had enough money left to live on for a few months. I didn't have any reason to work. I didn't have any reason to do anything, really. "I guess I'll find her anyway."

---

[54] Ibid., 237.
[55] Ibid., 117.
[56] Ibid., 236.

> Shelley took off her sunglasses and looked at me. "Why? [...] She might not even be alive [...] I mean, you know what happens—"
>
> "Either way," I said. "I guess I'll find her."[57]

Shelley's "you know what happens [to girls like that]" echoes Springer's "I guess [Nadine] ended up wherever girls like that go," which concludes the previous chapter. Both statements strike at the core of Joe's identity, linking her to Nadine, as well as to a sea of other nameless, faceless "junkie whores," by way of a shared personal history. Joe asks Springer, "Whatever happened to the girl? Nadine?"[58] even after she has been cleared of McFall's murder in part because she understands that but for the miracle of sobriety (which even she does not quite believe after two years), she might easily have suffered the same fate as "poor, invisible Nadine,"[59] except she may not have had a sober champion and savior in the world who relentlessly pursued her whereabouts. Joe also understands, even before Shelley cruelly speaks these words in the climactic scene of the novel, that to the larger diegetic world she and Nadine are just "two junkie whores" whose murders won't even "mak[e] the papers."[60] In short, part of what propels Joe to the final, climactic showdown with her half-sister is a psychological desire—perhaps need—to save herself (via Nadine as proxy) from the emotional pain and physical abuses of addiction and prostitution.

However, Joe's motives are not exclusively self-serving and, in fact, her character is equally (if not more so) defined by a strong commitment to altruism. At several points in the novel, Joe encounters a seemingly insurmountable obstacle and muses "there was no reason at all for me to keep looking for Nadine Nelson. But I did."[61] While Joe fails (or, refuses) to acknowledge her motivation for continuing to search for Nadine, readers are very carefully guided to the conclusion that Joe's actions are motivated by an unwillingness to allow Nadine to "slowly fade away" like the scores of other young women who become victims of addiction, prostitution and misogynistic exploitation. In the Introduction to *Substance and Shadow: Women and Addiction in the United States*, Kandall notes that while "women have always made up a significant portion, and at times a majority, of America's drug users and addicts," "guilt and shame, both self-imposed and societal, have pushed them to the margins of society."[62] The guilt and shame to which Kandall makes reference drives

---

[57] Ibid., 217.
[58] Ibid., 214.
[59] Ibid., 219.
[60] Ibid., 240.
[61] Ibid., 91.
[62] Kandall, *Substance and Shadow*, 8.

Joe to accept her murder at the hands of Shelley as preordained and rightfully earned: "It seemed now like it couldn't have happened any other way. Like this was the way it was supposed to be. This was how it had to end. All the disappointments added up to this."[63] The self-hatred that Western cultures breed in addicts blinds Joe to the sociopathic narcissism and unchecked ambition that drives Shelley to commit multiple murders in an effort to advance her career.

But before Joe becomes a willing participant in her own murder, she sets out to locate "poor invisible Nadine"[64] because, in the words of her former stepfather Yonah, she "always [has been] a stand-up girl" who acts in the interests of what is good, virtuous, right.[65] By the end of the novel, neither Nadine's parents nor law enforcement have any investment in locating the missing girl. As Joe muses, "To the rest of the world they're already dead. It's only them that can't see it. It's only the girls themselves who think that somehow, in some way, they still matter. That they're still alive."[66] At the core of Joe's ruminations is an intimate understanding of the ways in which Western cultures lay waste to addicts in myriad ways. At least since the 1970s, for instance, our drug-related legislation has become increasingly draconian, designed to punish rather than to heal and driven by the fallacious equation that uncritically is drawn between addiction and criminality, even when the object of an addiction is a controlled, rather than an illicit, substance. Within the "treatment" industry, our efforts to heal have been equally cruel and misguided, offering addicts a program for addiction recovery that consistently has been proven ineffectual, yet shames and blames the addict for failing to work the steps when relapses occur. Such recovery programs forcibly instill within addicts a sense of shame at their lack of willpower and fuel a sense of self-hatred that ultimately tells addicts that they deserve whatever violence or/and misfortune that comes their way. And within the popular imaginary, from the Temperance movement to *The Lost Weekend* to the most recent iteration of *A Star Is Born* (2018), we have for over two centuries been regularly reminded that addicts are a class of persons that forfeits all dignity and value as human beings the moment that they seek a fix.

A Powerful Reimagining of the Noir Form

The act of betrayal that is central to the reading experience of *Dope* centers precisely on Joe's unwillingness to regard "poor, invisible Nadine" as "already

---

[63] Gran, *Dope*, 241.
[64] Ibid., 219.
[65] Ibid., 220.
[66] Ibid., 224.

dead"—a gesture that undermines not only generic prescriptions of the roman noir, but also dominant cultural attitudes regarding addicts. As I mention earlier in the chapter, the roman noir typically is inhabited by "marginalized characters, who find it extremely difficult to apply the morals of the dominant class to their own action";[67] within this kind of diegetic world, "treachery and confusion blur the distinctions between detective, criminal, and victim."[68] To be sure, Joe is a marginalized character who refuses to adhere to "morals of the dominant class" and apply those morals to her own actions; but she does so not because those values (which in the prototypical roman noir are honesty, loyalty, compassion and the like) stand as an obstacle between her and some self-serving ends, but rather because the values of the dominant class, in *Dope*, are themselves perverted and self-serving: dishonesty, disloyalty, animosity and the like. In characters like Detective Springer and Shelley, both of whom represent different subgroups of the "dominant class," readers bear witness to the kinds of solipsism and ruthlessness by which the noir protagonist historically has operated—an ironic commentary on the ways in which both systems of jurisprudence and kinship structures are compromised within this diegetic world.

By contrast, Joe remains steadfast in her quest to save Nadine, which is also and simultaneously a quest to salvage the values of honesty, loyalty and compassion in a (diegetic) world circumscribed by narcissism and cruelty. This commitment that readers witness in Joe undermines the expectations that readers of noir fiction bring to the genre and, in so doing, encourages—perhaps even facilitates—a critical distance between readers, subject matter and text. The distance that is created in the act of fundamentally altering the character of the archetypal noir protagonist enables readers to engage in critical acts of introspection that begin to unsettle noir's "tendency to vilify women or relegate them to" the status of "minor characters, with little power and agency."[69] In Joe, readers bear witness to a protagonist marked not by moral weakness but by moral fortitude; further, readers experience within the context of a traditionally masculinist and misogynistic genre a female protagonist who refuses the positions of angel, whore or femme fatale. In this respect, *Dope* constitutes a powerful reimagining of the noir form that neither ignores the ideological pull of, nor accepts as an a priori, an exclusionary social order that is designed to deny the existence of historically underrepresented or/and vulnerable groups like women, people of color, the poor and addicts. In

---

[67] Nyman, *Men Alone*, 331.
[68] Gorrara, *The Roman Noir in Post-war French Culture*, 6.
[69] Deborah Walker-Morrison, *Classic French Noir: Gender and the Cinema of Fatal Desire* (London: I. B. Tauris, 2019), 201.

the diegetic world that Gran creates, the female addict may still "[skirt] the contours of an accepted social terrain,"⁷⁰ but in so doing, she challenges the reader to grapple with the implications of that generic prescription as well as their own acquiescence to it.

At the same time, Gran constructs the addict as a voice of truth, virtue and altruism, which ultimately undermines at least two centuries' worth of cultural narratives that doggedly regard the addict as the antithesis of these values. Unlike the protagonists of Charles Jackson's *The Lost Weekend* and Jay McInerney's *Bright Lights, Big City*, for instance, Joe is not a chronic liar whose tall tales are designed to cover over "some dreadful deed committed"⁷¹ during one of a perpetual string of binges. Unlike the unnamed narrator in Luke Davies's *Candy: A Novel of Love and Addiction* or Bobbie in Eddie Little's *Another Day in Paradise* (1997), she does not engage in an endless cycle of "pathetic misadventures,"⁷² going about the single-minded pursuit of her next fix indifferent to how her actions impact anyone—intimates or strangers—in her path. Unlike Darlene in James Hannaham's *Delicious Foods* and Doc in Steve Earle's *I'll Never Get Out of This World Alive* (2011), Joe refuses to use controlled or illicit substances to self-medicate against the physical and emotional traumas that litter her backstory. As a consequence, Joe escapes the kind of self-loathing that leads heroin addict Jules, in Heather O'Neill's *lullabies for little criminals* (2006), to the epiphany, "I'm always going to be a misfit [...] There's always going to be something wrong with me,"⁷³ or that leads the alcoholic male protagonist to die by suicide in every iteration of *A Star Is Born* since its debut in 1937.

While *Dope* most certainly concerns itself with the ways in which Gran undermines the roman noir tradition, and Joe undermines readerly expectations of "the addict," what ultimately is experimental here is how these twin acts of betrayal potentially can spur readers to acknowledge and grapple with a more fundamental act of betrayal: the reader's betrayal of self. For many Western readers, the act of reading *Dope* most certainly is an exercise in disappointment, not in the novel, which is an imaginative and compelling riff on the noir tradition, but in the self and the kinds of presuppositions about addicts that self brings to the reading experience. Reading about Joe's unflagging virtue serves as a powerful reminder of how deeply entrenched the equation between addiction and immorality is, especially when that virtue is experienced as a violation of readers' trust, confidence and expectation.

---

⁷⁰ Dickos, *Street with No Name*, 66.
⁷¹ Jackson, *The Lost Weekend* (New York: Vintage Books, 2013), 181.
⁷² Jay McInerney, *Bright Lights, Big City* (New York: Vintage, 1984), 89.
⁷³ Heather O'Neill, *Lullabies for Little Criminals* (New York: Harper Perennial, 2006), 319.

With every act of Joe's kindness and altruism, Gran insists on confronting her readers with the addict's humanity, on saying unequivocally to those readers that addiction is a condition that does not rob addicts of their dignity or their integrity. In fact, Gran suggests that it is precisely Joe's own struggles with addiction, both in the past and in the present, that fuel her decency and compassion. Over and again, readers may expect Joe to relapse, or to take the money and run, relinquishing poor, invisible Nadine to the parasitic world of drugs, sex and violence that is Gran's Hell's Kitchen; but time and again, Joe resists the most damning stereotypes with which Western culture has saddled addicts, challenging readers to consider why they repeatedly and uncritically have accepted these stereotypes as Truth—itself another act of betrayal, this time of the addict—and how such problematic "understandings" of addicts and the lived experiences of addiction might, in the extra-diegetic world, have as deadly of consequences as they do in the diegetic world of *Dope*.

In this way, reading *Dope* is nothing short of a journey to becoming woke. The myriad violations and betrayals of readerly expectations serve as a powerful object lesson in the struggles associated with becoming—and remaining—alert to social discrimination and injustice. The figure of Joe Flannigan stands as a compelling testament to the responsibility concomitant with becoming woke. She reminds readers of the need to remain vigilant against oppression, to remain alert, even in the face of imminent danger and violence, even death. The murders of Joe and Nadine allude to the many perils of being woke: the inability to look away from, or unsee, injustice and the traumatic, often violent, consequences that result from looking. And, finally, the novel at large is at once a haunting and a sobering, even liberating, reminder that being woke means that you can never be unwoke again.

Chapter 3

GASLIGHTING: *THE GIRL ON THE TRAIN* (2015)

Paula Hawkins's *The Girl on the Train* (2015) shares with Gran's *Dope* a firm commitment to entering well-established genres from alternative angles to wrest new meanings about addiction from those forms. Hawkins's debut novel locates itself squarely within the murder mystery tradition, specifically the classic whodunit, casting its alcoholic protagonist, Rachel, as an unwitting amateur sleuth in the disappearance and, as readers eventually learn, murder of Rachel's former neighbor, Megan Hipwell. In most ways, the novel adheres to long- and widely held formal expectations for the Western mystery novel. At its center, for example, is a complex, plot-driven narrative that presents a crime to be solved, or, in the words of Roland Barthes in *S/Z: An Essay* (1974), "a truth to be deciphered":[1] namely, who murdered Megan Hipwell and why? Like other works within the whodunit tradition, *The Girl on the Train* is predicated on the commission of a criminal act, often but not exclusively murder, and its plot advances by degrees through the uncovering and interpretation of a series of clues that helps identify suspects, motives and, in the end, a single, guilty perpetrator.

At the same time, *The Girl on the Train*, like all good mysteries, charts a second narrative that runs parallel to "the story of the crime," and that is, as Tzvetan Todorov discusses in *The Poetics of Prose* (1977), "the story of the investigation."[2] Drawing on the work of Todorov, Rita Felski, in *The Limits of Critique* (2015), explains this double narrative more thoughtfully:

> The detective novel is organized around [...] an original act of violence that sets the text in motion [...] Nothing significant happens in the classic detective novel that is not tied to this first act of transgression [...]

---

[1] Roland Barthes, *S/Z: An Essay*, trans. Richard Miller (New York: Hill and Wang, 1974), 75.
[2] Tzvetan Todorov, *The Poetics of Prose*, trans. Richard Howard (New York: Cornell University Press, 1977), 44.

> [The genre] proceeds from an effect (the corpse) to the deduction of a cause (the killer). The job of the detective is thus to reason backward in order to bring a constellation of past events to light.[3]

Indeed, the process by which Rachel parses out the events leading up to and including Megan's murder, bringing the "constellation of past events to light," consumes the narrative of *The Girl on the Train*, in some ways eclipsing in significance the "first act of transgression" itself. Rachel, for instance, admits that she "cant let go of [Megan's murder],"[4] and her obsession with investigating and solving the crime leads Megan's husband, Scott, eventually to label Rachel "insane"[5] and the police detectives to regard her as "a fantasist."[6]

In addition to its by now signature double narrative, the classic whodunit also is distinguished by the close relationship that it forges among readers, text and character. In *Murder Most Fair: The Appeal of Mystery Fiction* (2000), Michael Cohen suggests that the mystery novel is typified by "the identification of the detective, and sometimes the reader, with the murderer,"[7] a dynamic that facilitates the readers' investment in the narrative and, in particular, in searching for the solution to the crime that serves as its "first act of transgression." Within this dynamic, readers and the detective are posited as healthy rivals. As Janice Marion Shaw has written about the work of P. D. James, "Detective fiction exploits the [reader's] interest […] to enter a world in which seemingly unreadable clues can be interpreted by the detective," while at the same time, the form encourages "the reader [to compete] with the detective to find both the solution and the motive for the crime."[8] This rivalry between protagonist-sleuth and readers is a precondition of the whodunit— the "game" that is "afoot" in every Sherlock Holmes story ever penned. It demands the author's commitment to "fair play among the competitors"[9] in order to advance the narrative and bring about narrative closure; in other words, all clues related to the crime, while not necessarily presented in context or in a logical order, nonetheless, must be presented accurately to readers in order to ensure that those readers have equal (to the protagonist) access to

---

[3] Rita Felski, *The Limits of Critique* (Chicago, IL: University of Chicago Press, 2015), 92.
[4] Paula Hawkins, *The Girl on the Train* (New York: Riverhead Books, 2015), 187.
[5] Ibid., 244.
[6] Ibid., 250.
[7] Michael Cohen, *Murder Most Fair: The Appeal of Mystery Fiction* (Madison, WI: Fairleigh Dickinson University Press, 2000), 20.
[8] Janice Marion Shaw. "P.D. James's Discontinuous Narrative: A Suitable Job for a Reader," in *New Perspectives on Detective Fiction: Mystery Magnified*, ed. Casey Cothran and Mercy Cannon (New York: Routledge, 2016), 100.
[9] Charles J. Rzepka, *Detective Fiction* (Cambridge: Polity, 2005), 14.

the information needed to solve the crime and are able (albeit perhaps not capable) of doing so.

In *The Girl on the Train,* Hawkins refuses to play fairly with her readers, a choice that not only marks this "murder mystery" as experimental in form but also that highlights the reading experience as an exercise in power, one that reveals much about the many false or simply misguided preconceptions regarding addicts and the lived experiences of addiction that readers often bring to the Western novel. From the onset of *The Girl on the Train,* Rachel appears to be a garden variety homodiegetic unreliable narrator whose failed marriage and chronic alcoholism render the narrative incomplete, jumbled and ultimately untrustworthy. The many fragmentary and en bloc blackouts that punctuate the narrative suggest that Rachel's every memory is suspect and raise serious doubt regarding whether Rachel, as a first-person narrator, can ever "[speak] for or [act] in accordance with the norms of the work" which, in *The Rhetoric of Fiction* (1961), constitutes Wayne C. Booth's benchmark for narrative reliability.[10] Rachel's alcoholism, though, does not merely render her narrative suspect; rather, it also renders her an object of pity, scorn and even derision within the narrative, which further erodes the trustworthiness of her account. As a result, readers are set adrift within a confounding diegetic world in which the narrative voice is itself repeatedly called into question, posed as a red herring designed deliberately to divert the readers' attention from significant clues related to the identity of Megan Hipwell's murderer.

"I Am Not the Girl I Used to Be"

With a garden variety homodiegetic unreliable narrator, that character becomes, as Vera Nünning explains in *Unreliable Narration and Trustworthiness: Intermedial and Interdisciplinary Perspectives* (2015), "the object of dramatic irony while a story is told 'behind his back' in a communication between implied author and reader."[11] On the surface of such a narrative, the narrator shares a version of the diegetic events that is compromised and rendered untrustworthy by a lack of experience, lack of access to resources, diminished mental capacity and so forth. The narrator's limited access to information or/and compromised ability to communicate information may be unintentional (e.g., Emma Donoghue's *Room,* 2010) or intentional (e.g., Mohsin Hamid's *The Reluctant*

---

[10] Wayne C. Booth, *The Rhetoric of Fiction,* 2nd ed. (Chicago, IL: University of Chicago Press, 1983), 158.
[11] Vera Nünning, "Conceptualising (Un)reliable Narration and (Un)trustworthiness," in *Unreliable Narration and Trustworthiness: Intermedial and Interdisciplinary Perspectives,* ed. Nünning (Berlin: Walter de Gruyter, 2015), 2.

Fundamentalist, 2007); further, readers may be made aware of the narrator's unreliability from the onset of the narrative (e.g., S. J. Watson's *Before I Go to Sleep*, 2011), it may be revealed gradually as the narrative unfolds (e.g., Ian McEwan's *Atonement*, 2001), or it may function as a surprising plot twist (e.g., Gillian Flynn's *Gone Girl*, 2012). But beneath this surface-level narrative, the narrator's untrustworthiness is shared as an open secret between author and readers, a precondition of the reading experience that heightens the readers' awareness of the many discontinuities between what the narrator says/does and how those events should actually be interpreted.

To understand how Rachel proves incapable of "speak[ing] for or [acting] in accordance with the norms of" Hawkins's diegetic world, we must first establish what those "norms" are. Within the genre of mystery fiction, the amateur sleuth, like her/his/their more professionally oriented peers (e.g., the hard-boiled P.I., the law enforcement officer, the criminal prosecutor), exists first and foremost to solve the crime at the center of the narrative. To successfully fulfill this role, the sleuth-protagonist must possess heightened curiosity, cunning and reasoning abilities, and must be driven by an unwavering commitment to justice. At the same time, the mystery places particular (and particularly telling) demands on the amateur *female* sleuth, who has comprised the majority of this type of protagonist since the earliest origins of this subgenre. As Kimberly J. Dilley writes in *Busybodies, Meddlers, and Snoops: The Female Hero in Contemporary Women's Mysteries* (1998):

> The woman amateur sleuth represents the women who, like most women in Western society, live their lives according to the rules. She is "inside" the ideology. The woman amateur sleuth works to find a place for the "feminine" within masculine-dominated society. She illustrates how it is possible to protest against gender stereotypes and constraints while remaining a part of the community.[12]

The female amateur sleuth exists at the intersection—and experiences the coercive force of—a number of competing interests. She is expected to be the standard bearer for the traditional "virtues" of femininity, like sensibility and temperance, while at the same time she must of necessity venture into the stereotypically male domains of logic and intellect in order to fulfill her raison d'être: namely, identifying the motive for and perpetrator of the "original act of violence that sets the text in motion."

---

[12] Kimberly J. Dilley, *Busybodies, Meddlers, and Snoops: The Female Hero in Contemporary Women's Mysteries* (Westport, CT: Greenwood, 1998), 96.

Rachel's alcoholism immediately sets her up as a woman who does not live her life according to the rules of responsibility, self-discipline and vigilance—rules with which females in Western society have been perpetually saddled. A substance use disorder marks the female body as unruly, a particular burden that women must bear in a culture that chronically shames them for never quite "measuring up" in any sense of the phrase. Stated differently, while all addicts in Western society are subject to public humiliation and ignominy, female addicts experience especially pronounced issues of guilt, shame and stigma around their substance use disorders precisely because addiction is widely perceived as antithetical to, and simultaneously as violation of, the deeply entrenched gender norms that so often dictate actions, behaviors and perceptions. As Dr. Valery Yandow has written, "There is no other illness a woman can have that carries such a sense of shame and guilt as addiction. Even breast cancer does not bring the same feelings of failure, of being bad, or of being an outcast."[13] In this respect, Rachel might at once be regarded as "unfit" to be a first-person narrator since she proves incapable of conforming to traditional (albeit problematic) conceptions of femininity and womanhood. To be sure, reviews of the novel, which frequently dismissed Rachel as "unlikeable"—a moniker that often is revealed to be synonymous with "unfeminine"—bear out the validity of this claim.[14]

Rachel's alcoholism, though, does not simply mark her as a failed woman, but also identifies her as incapable of "speak[ing] for or [acting] in accordance with the norms of" Hawkins's diegetic world; this point is intimated and explicitly reinforced in a number of ways throughout the novel, beginning with her own self-presentation and self-perception, both of which are intimately interconnected with her alcoholism. In the first chapter of the novel, Rachel alludes to her substance use disorder when she openly sips from a pre-mixed can of gin and tonic while riding the train home from London and observes, "It's Friday, so I don't have to feel guilty about drinking on the

---

[13] Valery Yandow, "Alcoholism in Women," *Psychiatric Annals* 19, no. 5 (1989): 243. For more contextual information on this topic, see Edith S. Lisansky Gomberg, "Shame and Guilt Issues among Women Alcoholics," *Alcoholism Treatment Quarterly* 4, no. 2 (1988): 139–55; Ann Dowsett Johnston, *Drink: The Intimate Relationship between Women and Alcohol* (New York: Harper Wave, 2013); and Michelle L. McClellan, *Lady Lushes: Gender, Alcoholism, and Medicine in Modern America* (New Brunswick, NJ: Rutgers University Press, 2017).

[14] One exemplar of this trend is David Shaffer, who, in his *Star Tribune* review describes Rachel as "so pathetically unlikable that there's a danger you'll slap the book down in distaste." Koa Beck responds to this trend of assessing female characters' literary value in relation to a vague "standard" of likability in "Female Characters Don't Have to Be Likable."

train."[15] The following Monday, Rachel can once again be found on the train, this time drinking a can of Chenin Blanc and musing, "It's less acceptable to drink on the train on a Monday, unless you're drinking with company, which I am not."[16] Still later in the same chapter, Rachel observes the 30-something male professional seated opposite her gazing at her and "the little bottle of wine on the table in front of [her]" with obvious "distaste."[17] After realizing that the young, male professional seated opposite her on the train finds her "distasteful," Rachel considers, "I am not the girl I used to be. I am no longer desirable, I'm off-putting in some way. It's not just that I've put on weight, or that my face is puffy from the drinking and the lack of sleep; it's as if people can see the damage written all over me, they can see it in my face, the way I hold myself, the way I move."[18] To Rachel, she is damage incarnate—someone whose value, usefulness or/and "normal" function has been so compromised by alcoholism as to render her virtually worthless.

Like many addicts, Rachel is rendered hyper aware of her alcohol consumption patterns and how those behaviors might be perceived by onlookers, particularly in public spaces where such behaviors are indirectly regulated by contextual factors like day, time and company (or, lack thereof, as in Rachel's case). While these early references to alcohol consumption might, in another context, be viewed as entirely innocuous, Rachel's obsessive preoccupation with what she is doing and how it is being perceived by those who share her train car clearly point to, at minimum, problem drinking and, in the extreme, chronic alcoholism.

Rachel's self-consciousness regarding her drinking contributes directly to both a lowered self-image and, by association, an abiding sense of unreliability with respect to her role as a first-person narrator. Regardless of how exaggeratedly negative Rachel's self-assessments sometimes may be, Hawkins's narrator clearly has internalized the widespread cultural attitudes that addicts are damaged, worthless and, in so doing, has seemingly compromised her own abilities to narrate the events that unfold around her in an accurate and reliable manner. After all, those who suffer from low self-image typically hold a distorted view both of themselves and of the world. Strengths can be minimized or ignored completely. Weaknesses can be amplified, sometimes so dramatically that the person's self-image becomes virtually unrecognizable to onlookers. And always the individual with low self-esteem views the surrounding world through the distorted lens of confirmation bias, "actively

---

[15] Hawkins, *The Girl on the Train* 12.
[16] Ibid., 15.
[17] Ibid., 20.
[18] Ibid.

seek[ing] out and assign[ing] more weight to evidence that confirms their [beliefs], and ignor[ing] or underweigh[ing] evidence that could disconfirm their [beliefs]."[19] In the absence of sound logic and reasoning skills, Rachel at once seems entirely ill-suited for the role of sleuth, even amateur sleuth, given that the primary charge of that role is to unravel and reorder a series of events surrounding a criminal infraction to determine who did what, when and why.

Rachel explicitly admits to her inability to "[speak] for or [act] in accordance with the norms of the work" immediately after she sends a deceptive e-mail to Scott Hipwell:

> I can feel the heat come to my face, my stomach a pit of acid. Yesterday—sensible, clear-headed, right-thinking—I decided I must accept that my part in this story was over. But my better angels lost again, defeated by the drink, by the person I am when I drink. Drunk Rachel sees no consequences, she is either excessively expansive and optimistic or wrapped up in hate. She has no past, no future. She exists purely in the moment. Drunk Rachel—wanting to be part of the story, needing a way to persuade Scott to talk to her—she lied. *I* lied.[20]

The contrast that Rachel draws between Drunk Rachel and Sober Rachel is telling with respect to the question of reliability. When sober, Rachel regards herself as "sensible, clear-headed, and right-thinking," all attributes that would mark her as ideally suited for the role of amateur sleuth in a murder mystery novel. By contrast, Drunk Rachel is prone to emotional excess and hyperbole, unable to understand the concepts of accountability and consequence, both of which exist at the center of the mystery genre, broadly defined. Since Rachel spends the majority of *The Girl on the Train* in a state of inebriation, readers are led to conclude that she is ill-suited for the role of detective, amateur or otherwise. The near-constant conflict that exists between Rachel and actual law enforcement officers only underscores the validity of this conclusion.

"Do You Know How Idiotic [...] Damien Felt?"

The self-loathing that repeatedly is witnessed in Rachel is, at least within the diegetic world, normalized by other characters like Cathy's boyfriend, Damien, Rachel's ex-husband, Tom, and the law enforcement officers tasked with solving Megan Hipwell's murder, all of whom echo, and, in so doing, lend

---

[19] *Confirmation bias*, Science Daily, https://www.sciencedaily.com/terms/confirmation_bias.htm (accessed March 30, 2019).
[20] Hawkins, *The Girl on the Train*, 109.

authority to, her self-assessments. Of the characters whose opinions attain this kind of gravity and credibility, one of the more unusual is Cathy's boyfriend, Damien. At the opening of the novel, Rachel has lived as a tenant in "Cathy's bland and inoffensive duplex" for two years.[21] Although much of the novel takes place within the flat that Cathy owns, Damien is mentioned only a handful of times, and most of those references are intended simply to identify Cathy's whereabouts during any given scene. For instance, one evening, Rachel receives a message from Cathy informing her roommate that "she's going to Damien's for the night, she'll see me tomorrow."[22] In another scene, later in the novel, Rachel lies to Cathy, telling her that she "ha[s] not had a drink for three days." Cathy condescendingly responds, "I'm so pleased for you, Rach […] Getting yourself sorted. You've had me worried," before telling Rachel that "she was going to spend the weekend at Damien's."[23] What I find especially interesting about these particular references is the way in which Damien consistently functions as an absent-presence both in the flat and in Rachel's narrative. Not an active participant in the diegetic action, and rarely occupying the same fictional setting as Hawkins's narrator, Damien nonetheless ghosts the narrative action, his distaste for Rachel lingering within (and, at times, extending beyond the walls of) Cathy's flat and reminding Rachel every time she takes a drink that she is a "filthy, stinking drunk."[24]

What Damien signifies is a culture of sobriety that maintains itself through the systemic shaming and blaming of addicts for what is perceived to be at best a lack of willpower, and at worst a moral failing, but what is in actuality a serious medical condition. That Damien's presence is most frequently felt in the absence of his physical self indicates that this culture of sobriety functions not simply as an attitude of disdain expressed toward alcoholics like Rachel, but as an ideology—that is, as a set of shared normative (and normalizing) beliefs that are so deeply entrenched within a given culture that they do not merely frame, but instead determine political and social realities.

Even in the one instance when Damien plays a pivotal role in the rising action and the escalation of narrative tension, his participation in the unfolding of the drama is relegated to a past-tense recounting by Cathy, and Damien himself remains decidedly ensconced in the wings of the narrative action:

> Cathy is waiting for me when I get home. She's standing in the kitchen aggressively drinking a glass of water.

---

[21] Ibid., 17.
[22] Ibid., 48.
[23] Ibid., 103.
[24] Ibid., 255.

"Good day at the office?" she asks, pursing her lips. She knows.

"Cathy [...]"

"Damien had a meeting near Euston today. On his way out, he bumped into Martin Miles [...] You haven't worked there in *months!* Do you know how idiotic I feel? What an idiot Damien felt? Please, *please* tell me that you have another job that you just haven't told me about. Please tell me that you haven't been pretending to go to work. That you haven't been lying to me—day in, day out—all this time."[25]

One of the key conflicts of the novel is posed between Rachel and Cathy; indeed, it is precisely this conflict, born out of Rachel's having been fired from her job, that forces Rachel onto the eponymous train every day—a ruse to suggest continued employment—in order to avoid Cathy's passive aggressive judgment. Readers are clued in early that Rachel is deceiving Cathy, a narrative choice that only helps to build suspense as Rachel's secret by degrees comes increasingly closer to being revealed, and over the first half of the novel, the narrative of *The Girl on the Train* builds to and anticipates the eventual clash that occurs in the passage cited above.

But when the clash inevitably comes, it seems almost anti-climactic that the conflict is instigated by a third party (i.e., Damien). What Hawkins seems to be alluding to is the often invisible circulation, but always incredibly coercive machinations of dominant ideology: in this case, the dominant ideology of Puritanical sobriety. In *Ideology: A Very Short Introduction* (2003), Michael Freeden suggests that ideology manifests itself as the imposition of a pattern—"some form of structure or organization—on how we read (and misread) political facts, events, occurrences, actions, on how we see images and hear voices."[26] Freeden goes on to describe dominant ideology as an "artificially constructed [set] of ideas, somewhat removed from everyday life, [that is] manipulated by the powers that be—and the powers that want to be. They attempt to control the world of politics and to force us into a rut of doctrinaire thinking and conduct."[27]

Within Hawkins's diegetic world, Damien stands as a compelling illustration of dominant Western ideology around addiction. Outside of the narrative action for the bulk of the novel, and thereby "somewhat removed from everyday life," Damien nonetheless retains a heightened degree of control over other characters' "thinking and conduct," most particularly Cathy's

---

[25] Ibid., 158.

[26] Michael Freeden, *Ideology: A Very Short Introduction* (Oxford: Oxford University Press, 2003), 3.

[27] Ibid., 1.

as in the scene cited above where she becomes a glorified mouthpiece for him. However, Hawkins does not present Damien (or, his ideas regarding Rachel's drinking) as either self-evident or innocuous, instead casting doubt on their accuracy and credibility through the way that she crafts Damien as unlikeable: censorious and sanctimonious to the point of blatant ignorance where the nature of substance use disorders is concerned. In so doing, Hawkins challenges her readers—many, perhaps most, of whom might share Damien's views of Rachel's alcoholism—to see the shame and blame that Westerners typically foist onto addicts not as an always and already that reflects "an objective, external reality,"[28] but as a particular type of "doctrinaire thinking and conduct" reflecting an invested standpoint that finds its origins in, among other sociohistorical currents, the Temperance movement, Puritanism and even Judeo-Christian notions of self-discipline and self-sacrifice.

"Please, Rachel. You've Got to Sort Yourself Out."

While Damien serves as a reminder of the kinds of external ideologies that shape dominant perceptions of addicts, Tom perhaps is the most influential on Rachel's own self-image, and therefore on readers' perception of and reactions to Hawkins's first-person narrator. The backstory regarding the demise of Tom and Rachel's marriage unfolds gradually over the novel, as readers piecemeal learn of miscarriages, failed in virto fertilization (IVF) treatments, increasingly heated arguments, chronic alcoholism and repeated instances of public humiliation. For Rachel, Tom is the personification of "the anguish of shame"[29] that her alcoholism produces within her. When Rachel thinks about or, on rare occasions, sees Tom in person, he calls to mind a seemingly endless series of half-remembered indignities brought about by Rachel's excessive drinking. At times, Tom pities Rachel for these behaviors, although not for her drinking which he (like Damien and Cathy) consistently intimates is a choice that reflects poorly on Rachel's character and morality;[30] more often, he reminds Rachel, with equal parts anger and resentment, that she is the sole reason for the disintegration of their marriage: "I remember his coldness the next day, his refusal to speak about [our fight]. I remember him telling me, in flat disappointed tones, what I'd done and said, how I'd smashed our framed wedding photograph, how I'd screamed at him for being so selfish,

---

[28] Ibid., 3.
[29] Hawkins, *The Girl on the Train*, 22.
[30] Ibid., 50.

how I'd called him a useless husband, a failure. I remember how much I hated myself that day."[31]

Here, as elsewhere in the novel, Tom describes Rachel as an emasculating shrew, and a "filthy, stinking drunk,"[32] suggesting that her inability to adhere to social norms regarding femininity, matrimony (read patriarchy) and sobriety—that is, her unwillingness to "live [her life] according to the rules"—is wholly responsible for their failed marriage and her current misery. It is, I think, significant that in Tom's recounting of this marital row one of the key milestones in the devolution of their marriage is the destruction of the framed wedding photograph at Rachel's unruly, drunk hands. Here, the wedding photograph functions as a symbol of the matrimonial bond that it sentimentally captures, and Rachel's smashing of that frame is both a symbolic and a literal desecration of her relationship with Tom. That Rachel's alcoholism is identified by Tom as wholly responsible for the transgression marks addiction and Rachel, its presumably witting conduit, as antitheses to the social order and ideological stability that institutions like marriage and family, patriarchy and heterosexism traditionally connote. By advancing as Truth this narrative regarding the smashed wedding frame, Rachel simultaneously locates Tom in the position of Author(ity) vis-à-vis the narrative action of *The Girl on the Train*.

That Rachel has internalized Tom's view of her, thereby normalizing the loathing and resentment with which he regards her alcoholism, is evidenced in many of Rachel's actions and thoughts. Most particularly, Rachel regularly drunk dials Tom, leaving him rambling, often incoherent, messages that cause conflict between Tom and his current wife, Anna. Indeed, Rachel's calls are so frequent that time and again Tom must ask her to desist: "His voice sounds leaden, he sounds worn out. 'Listen, you have to stop this, OK? [...] Please, Rachel, you can't call me like this all the time. You've got to sort yourself out.'"[33] These phone calls, which occur frequently enough to leave Tom sounding "worn out," can be understood as both a validation of Tom's perceptions of Rachel and simultaneously a plea for Tom's forgiveness. By repeatedly reinserting herself back into her ex-husband's life, Rachel is confirming as accurate Tom's account of their past and present relationship; in effect, Rachel looks to Tom for validation of who she is and, more often than not, the reflection that Tom provides is of a stereotypical, "filthy, stinking drunk" prone to excess and ignominy; at the same time, by subjecting herself to Tom's loathing and resentment, Rachel is attempting to atone for her transgressions against Tom and their marriage—a somewhat manic iteration

---

[31] Ibid., 193.
[32] Ibid., 255.
[33] Ibid., 24.

of Steps 8 (i.e., "Ma[k]e a list of all persons we ha[ve] harmed, and bec[o]me willing to make amends to them all") and 9 (i.e., "Ma[k]e direct amends to such people wherever possible, except when to do so would injure them or others") of Alcoholics Anonymous.[34] In so doing, Rachel reveals to readers that she has blindly accepted Tom's version of herself and their marriage as Truth, a revelation that is underscored by Rachel's willingness to justify Tom's cruelty and adultery (i.e., "I was extremely difficult to live with and Tom sought solace elsewhere"[35]).

Normalizing Tom's version of events serves as one of the key means through which Rachel is marked as unreliable. However, narrative unreliability in *The Girl on the Train* functions rather differently than in most other works of fiction. Typically, narrative unreliability manifests itself in one of two forms: either the first-person narrator is unaware (often blissfully so) of her/his/their unreliability (e.g., Ottessa Moshfegh's *Eileen*, 2015) or the narrator actively tries to conceal the lapses in accuracy and credibility that pepper her/his/their narrative (e.g., Lionel Shriver's *We Need to Talk about Kevin*, 2003). In both cases, readers are clued in—either from the onset or gradually over the rising action—to the questionable authority of the narrator and the question of reliability comes to shape profoundly every aspect of the diegetic world and the reading experience. In Hawkins's novel, by contrast, Rachel's unreliability is a taken-for-granted. Throughout the novel, Rachel regularly acquiesces to other characters' perceptions of her, buying wholeheartedly and uncritically into the cultural script that equates alcoholism, untruth and lack of integrity. In so doing, Rachel shifts narrative authority from herself to the other characters who populate Hawkins's diegetic world, but especially to Tom, whose version of events attains particularly heightened authority given the internalized shame that Rachel feels as a result of her infertility and substance use disorder.

"Something Happened. Something Bad."

Rachel's internalization of Tom's (and other characters') view of her as damaged contributes significantly to readers' perceptions of her as an unreliable narrator; however, Rachel's authority and credibility are further called into question by her penchant for lying and the alcoholism-induced blackouts that mar her memory. A key narrative event that immediately appears to

---

[34] *The Twelve Steps of Alcoholics Anonymous*, Hazelden Betty Ford Foundation, https://www.hazeldenbettyford.org/articles/twelve-steps-of-alcoholics-anonymous (accessed May 23, 2019).

[35] Hawkins, *The Girl on the Train*, 158.

confirm Rachel's unreliability is the elaborate architecture of deception and untruth that she has carefully crafted around both her professional life, or lack thereof, and her "friendship" with Megan Hipwell. Several months prior to the start of Hawkins's narrative, Rachel "was sacked [...] for turning up blind drunk after a three-hour lunch with a client during which [she] managed to be so rude and unprofessional that [she] cost the firm his business."[36] Yet, for most of the novel, she lies to Cathy, taking the train to London every weekday as if she is still employed as a means of avoiding conflict between her roommate/landlord and herself.

From Rachel, readers learn that this cohabitation situation began when her husband, Tom, threw her out of the house and filed for divorce. As Rachel reveals, "Cathy and I were friends at university. Half-friends, really, we were never that close [...] But in my hour of need she happened to have a spare room going and it made sense."[37] Here and elsewhere in the novel, Cathy is depicted as a savior of sorts—a kindhearted, if a bit "forceful,"[38] peer who repeatedly displays compassion toward Rachel and attempts, time and again, to help Rachel conquer her alcoholism. That Rachel compulsively deceives such a "nice"[39] character as Cathy works to undermine her own likability factor and further erodes her credibility. Readers might conclude that if Rachel is willing to betray someone, like Cathy, who has extended both generosity and hospitality in spite of the many times that Rachel has disrespected her host, then she most likely would be only too willing to deceive readers—virtual strangers—and betray their trust should doing so prove favorable to her.[40]

---

[36] Ibid., 148.
[37] Ibid., 17.
[38] Ibid., 18.
[39] Ibid.
[40] At least since the nineteenth century, alcoholism (and, more broadly, substance use disorders) has marked those afflicted with the condition as individuals who persistently distort or conceal the truth, often but not exclusively out of pure self-interest or/and self-preservation. In *Becoming Whole after Addiction* (2017), Clayton R. Hall Jr. articulates this widespread, albeit highly problematic, "understanding" of addicts:

> When addicts are focused on their own needs, when they are feeding the monster of their addiction, it is easy to forget everyone else around them so that they can concentrate on their own desire. The only thing that matters to the addict is their own desires. Addicts lie, cheat, steal, and even kill in extreme cases, nothing can be allowed to interfere with the desire to feed their addiction, nothing. (90)

While Hall's book peddles in misinformation and stereotype, the view of addicts that he outlines in the passage cited above enjoys support among Western audiences. Indeed, even Rachel buys into the idea that addicts will do anything to "feed their addiction" when she

Rachel also creates an elaborate ruse in order to weasel her way into Scott Hipwell's life, posing as "a friend from the [art] gallery"[41] at which Megan worked to establish both contact and credibility with Scott; and this act of deception is perhaps even more damning than her transgressions against Cathy given Scott's fragile emotional state. Scott is, first and foremost, emotionally raw from the very public revelations of his wife's adultery, murder and pregnancy. At the same time, he is plagued by the not-knowing-ness surrounding Megan's disappearance and murder, and he is overwhelmed by the intense public scrutiny that both Megan and he are receiving at the hands of the 24-hour news cycle. As he admits to Rachel, "I find it hard to sleep [...] It's her. She's everywhere. I can't stop seeing her."[42] Scott is under further scrutiny by law enforcement who, for most of the novel, believe him to be responsible for Megan's disappearance and murder; as Detective Riley cautions Rachel after a physical altercation with Scott, "You were warned to stay out of this [...] [T]his is a person who, at best, is under a great deal of strain and is extremely distressed. At best. At worst, he might be dangerous."[43] Although readers gradually come to realize that Scott was not the best husband to Megan, subjecting her to both psychological and physical abuse, the novel nonetheless still encourages readers to sympathize with Scott where Rachel's many deceptions are concerned, to see her "total fucking disaster" of a life as a "picnic" compared to Scott's existence.[44]

Another narrative event that seems to underscore Rachel's unreliability is the frequent memory loss that she experiences as a consequence of her chronic binge drinking. That Rachel experiences blackouts is intimated relatively early in the novel, but not addressed directly until about a quarter of the way into *The Girl on the Train*: "Blackouts happen, and it isn't just a matter of being a bit hazy about getting home from the club or forgetting what it was that was so funny when you were chatting in the pub. It's different. Total black; hours lost, never to be retrieved."[45] What Rachel describes here is an en bloc blackout, or complete memory loss. In "What Happened?: Alcohol, Memory Blackouts, and the Brain," Aaron M. White explains, "People experiencing en bloc blackouts are unable to recall any details whatsoever from events that occurred

---

remarks quite uncritically, "I once read a book by a former alcoholic where she described giving oral sex to two different men, men she'd just met in a restaurant on a busy London high street. I read it and I thought, I'm not *that* bad. This is where the bar is set" (23).

[41] Hawkins, *The Girl on the Train*, 109.
[42] Ibid., 205.
[43] Ibid., 249–50.
[44] Ibid., 183.
[45] Ibid., 74.

while they were intoxicated, despite all efforts by the drinkers or others to cue recall [...] [I]t is as if the process of transferring information from short-term to long-term storage has been completely blocked."[46] To be sure, any degree of compromised ability to recall events in an accurate and complete manner would of necessity mark a narrator—whose central charge is to recount a series of events in an accurate and truthful manner—as unreliable; but here, Rachel's matter-of-fact attitude toward these lapses in memory (i.e., "Blackouts happen") suggests that such en bloc blackouts occur with enough frequency as to render them commonplace and to mark her as patently untrustworthy.

Of course, Rachel understands herself to be untrustworthy, admitting to other characters (and, by association, readers) on multiple occasions that she is "an unreliable witness,"[47] and reminding readers many times over that her account of events is not to be believed. When she struggles to recall the events that she witnessed on the night of Megan's disappearance, Rachel muses in interior monologue, "I can't stop thinking about the argument I saw, or imagined, or dreamed about on Saturday night."[48] At a later point in the novel, Rachel, still consumed by her inability to decipher her fragmented "memories" of the events that took place on that fateful Saturday night, considers, "I was in an argument. Or perhaps I witnessed an argument [...] I heard someone call Megan's name. No, that was a dream. That wasn't real."[49] The slippage that occurs in these passages with regard to whether an event recalled is a legitimate memory, a product of the imagination or a mere dream points to the massive self-doubt that addicts experience with respect to the timeline of their lives. But it also highlights the significant ways in which substance use disorders—especially, but not exclusively, alcoholism—can compromise a person's mental agility, unmooring that person from everyday reality by withholding the kinds of categorical distinctions that otherwise would ground her/him/them in time, space and identity.

Not only do these blackouts contribute to Rachel's characterization as a seemingly unreliable narrator, but also they fuel the suspense that is characteristic of both the mystery genre, and the newly emergent genre of domestic noir, of which *The Girl on the Train* is an exemplar.[50] An early example of this

---

[46] Aaron M. White, "What Happened?: Alcohol, Memory Blackouts, and the Brain," *Alcohol Research & Health* 27, no. 2 (2003): 186–96. *National Institute on Alcohol Abuse and Alcoholism*, https://pubs.niaaa.nih.gov/publications/arh27-2/186-196.htm (accessed April 1, 2019).

[47] Hawkins, *The Girl on the Train*, 185.

[48] Ibid., 71.

[49] Ibid., 186.

[50] For a thoughtful discussion of how domestic noir fiction is built upon the foundation of a compromised female witness/narrator, see Joyce Carol Oates, "The Domestic Thriller Is Having a Moment," *The New Yorker*, February 19, 2018, https://www.newyorker.com/magazine/2018/02/26/the-domestic-thriller-is-having-a-moment

occurs on the morning following Megan Hipwell's disappearance, when Rachel, in a panic, articulates in interior monologue:

> Something is wrong. For a second, I feel as though I'm falling, as though the bed has disappeared from beneath my body. Last night. Something happened. The breath comes sharply into my lungs and I sit up too quickly, heart racing, head throbbing. I wait for the memory to come. Sometimes it takes a while. Sometimes it's there in front of my eyes in seconds. Sometimes it doesn't come at all. Something happened. Something bad.[51]

The repeated use of the indeterminate pronoun "something" to characterize an experience that is unspecified or/and unknown points to the type of memory impairment that often accompanies heavy alcohol consumption. In this passage, Rachel admits to both fragmentary (i.e., "Sometimes [memory recovery] takes a while.") and en bloc blackouts (i.e., "Sometimes [memory recovery] doesn't come at all.")—an admission that marks her as "a narrator who may be in error in his or her understanding or report of things."[52] These blackouts situate readers in a confusing position vis-à-vis the narrative action, unsure of what events have transpired in the interim between Saturday evening when Rachel disembarks from the train at Witney and Sunday morning when Rachel awakens in her own flat.[53]

In some ways, these blackouts initially might be understood as simply a clever means to retard the narrative action, a central defining feature of the mystery genre. In *S/Z*, Barthes discusses the concept of narrative "delay," which, while not exclusively drawn from the mystery nonetheless has direct relevance to that genre. Barthes writes, "Narratively, an enigma leads from a question to an answer, *through a certain number of delays*. Of these delays, the main one is unquestionably the feint, the misleading answer, the lie, what we will call the *snare*."[54] In mystery fiction, announcing the solution to the crime, or, what Barthes terms "an enigma," is forestalled time and again as a means of cultivating in readers a sense of excitement and simultaneously anxiety regarding what might happen within the diegetic world. Some actions/events

---

(accessed May 31, 2019). For further examples of this trend, see Louise Doughty, *Apple Tree Yard* (New York: Faber & Faber, 2013); A. S. A. Harrison, *The Silent Wife* (New York: Penguin, 2013); and Ruth Ware, *The Lying Game* (New York: Scout Press, 2017).

[51] Hawkins, *The Girl on the Train*, 46.

[52] C. Hugh Holman and William Harmon, *A Handbook to Literature*, 6th ed. (New York: Macmillan, 1992), 490.

[53] Hawkins, *The Girl on the Train*, 45–46.

[54] Barthes, 32.

are misinterpreted by the detective, thereby ensnaring readers in the trap of a red herring and derailing for a brief time the detective's and the readers' quest for resolution. Certainly, blackouts work to forestall the unravelling of the narrative enigma; however, they are not merely delays, but rather stand as dead ends, especially when the I-narrator—readers' sole foothold in the diegetic world—experiences complete memory loss. In a genre in which the narrative turns on readers' anticipation of eventually learning answers to the twin questions of *What happened?* and *What happens next?*, the narrator's inability to recall key narrative events, or to determine whether the forgotten narrative events even are key to the solving of the crime, works to build not suspense but frustration and, in so doing, does not merely delay but prevents the protagonist and readers from solving the crime thereby undermining the very operations of the genre within which both character and readers find themselves.

At the same time, readers are uncertain whether to trust Rachel's intuition that the events that have transpired are "anything to be frightened of,"[55] although the "painful and tender" lump on the right side of Rachel's head, paired with her "filthy" fingernails,[56] suggests that "something" is, indeed, amiss. But what kind of "something" actually happened to Rachel? Was that "something" really as "bad" as Rachel fears? Or is this indeterminate fear merely another product of Rachel's rich and active imagination—the same imagination that enabled Rachel to create entirely fanciful alternative lives for Scott and Megan Hipewell[57] from the voyeuristic safety of her seat on the train? In an interesting twist on first-person narration, Rachel does not merely provide readers with a possibly untrustworthy, albeit complete, account of the narrative events, as is typical with an unreliable narrator; rather, Rachel leaves readers completely adrift within the narrative, not simply unsure if she is telling the truth, but confused as to what exactly Rachel experienced, if, indeed, she experienced anything at all, since she also has a proclivity for confusing the real and the imagined. It is as if readers are, to some degree, experiencing the very same blackouts that Rachel experiences.

"Everything Is a Lie"

While Hawkins represents Rachel as untrustworthy and, for many readers, unsympathetic, from early in the novel, Rachel's ex-husband Tom is, by contrast, cast as a long-suffering victim of Rachel's substance use disorder. During one of Rachel's first benders that readers are permitted to witness,

---

[55] Hawkins, *The Girl on the Train*, 47.
[56] Ibid., 46.
[57] Ibid., 13–15.

for example, Rachel recalls an instance when she "humiliated [her] husband at a summer barbecue by shouting abuse at the wife of one of his friends" and another when they "got into a fight one night at home and [she] went for him with a golf club, taking a chunk out of the plaster in the hallway outside the bedroom."[58] The barbecue debacle concerns the vicarious embarrassment and shame that Tom, as the husband of an alcoholic, feels when his inebriated wife unwarrantedly lobs verbal abuse at an innocent bystander during a social engagement. Through the chapters that are narrated by Tom's second wife, Anna, and less so through Rachel's own voice, readers are reminded that such behaviors constitute one of the key reasons why Tom eventually began an extramarital affair and the once-happy relationship between Tom and Rachel disintegrated. By contrast, the golf club incident is about the unpredictability of substance use disorders and the fear that unpredictability provokes in those who must bear witness to them. Within his own home—a space that should engender feelings of safety, security—Tom cowers in the shadow of his golf-club-wielding wife, who swings at him with wild and violent abandon for no discernible reason other than that she has been consuming alcohol to excess.

Tom also is, as I have alluded above, readers' window into Rachel's backstory—the one character entrusted (by both Rachel and Hawkins's readers) with supplying the necessary narrative exposition for the present action and conflict to be meaningfully understood. In this way, Tom functions as readers' surrogate within the world of the novel—at least until the narrative climax occurs. He is not our entry point, and neither is he our anchor in the diegetic world nor our guide through it. Those roles are filled by Rachel, whose sometimes disjointed first-person narrative serves as the focal point of *The Girl on the Train*. But Tom does function as a substitute for readers within the diegetic world—his treatment at the hands of Rachel metaphorically mirroring our own. To be sure, readers are not physically abused by Rachel, and neither do her actions serve as a public embarrassment that reflects poorly on us. But her alcoholism—and, more specifically, the blackouts that accompany it—repeatedly disrupt the reading process, sometimes violently so. As readers, we are denied access to key scenes and significant pieces of information that would enable us to better understand the events that transpired on the night that Megan Hipwell disappeared and was murdered. We also sometimes receive conflicting information from our focal narrator, or we are presented with a piece of information without context or further explanation—a technique that perhaps is intended to mimic the disorientation that alcoholics feel in the throes of a blackout. And the result is that our sympathies are, for most of the reading experience, decidedly aligned with Tom. As readers, we might

---

[58] Ibid., 22.

wonder why, after everything he endured during their brief marriage, Tom remains emotionally supportive of Rachel and even weathers—most of the time quite good-naturedly—Rachel's incessant postdivorce drunk dials. We might even marvel at how protective Tom is of Rachel, especially with respect to the wrath of his current wife, Anna. Tom may seem at times like an enabler, but through it all, he remains an admirable and virtuous man.

Or so readers are led to believe [...] at least until the climax of the novel.

Typically, in a novel about substance use disorders, the narrative climax occurs when the addict protagonist hits "rock bottom" and realizes that she/he/they needs/need to stop using and must willingly enter into a treatment program—preferably one patterned on the Twelve Steps. Some novels—like Charles Jackson's *The Lost Weekend* and Tony O'Neill's *Down and Out on Murder Mile*—conclude precisely at this climactic moment, fueling in readers both a hope for recovery and doubt that such an ending is actually possible. Other novels like Marian Keyes's *Rachel's Holiday* (1998), Anna David's *Party Girl* (2007), and Martha Southgate's *The Taste of Salt* (2011) follow a more conventional narrative trajectory, identifying the addict character's rock bottom as a mere turning point on their journey toward recovery, which is posited as the narrative resolution.

Interestingly, the climax of *The Girl on the Train* does not involve an epiphany that requires Rachel to acquiesce to the many problematic cultural narratives with which addicts are saddled. She does not have to concede to being a "filthy, stinking drunk," nor does the narrative demand that she enter rehab or insist that she will always and only be an addict. Instead, the climax occurs when Rachel realizes that Tom has systematically overwritten her memories of their marriage and of the night that Megan Hipwell was murdered in the interests of his own self-preservation. "Everything is a lie," she concludes,[59] finally understanding that while her alcoholism has produced some fragmented memories, she nonetheless "remember[s], it's just that [she] had confused [some] memories."[60] In short, Rachel's epiphany is that the man she has trusted for much of her adult life has been systematically gaslighting her.

A Figure for Readers' Own Identity

Although the term "gaslight" finds its origins in Patrick Hamilton's 1938 stage play of the same name, the concept of psychologically manipulating an individual as a means of convincing that person to question her/his/their sanity did not enter the vernacular until several years later when George Cukor

---

[59] Ibid., 266.
[60] Ibid., 267.

adapted Hamilton's play for film.[61] Gaslighting typically occurs within intimate, albeit not necessarily romantic or sexual, relationships and refers to the act of overwriting someone's reality "to manipulate [that person] into believing [they are] imagining things" and to cause that person "to mistrust the evidence of [their] senses."[62] In *The Gaslight Effect: How to Spot and Survive the Hidden Manipulation Others Use to Control Your Life* (2007), Robin Stern explains the operations of gaslighting in greater detail: "Gaslighting is always the creation of two people—a gaslighter, who sows confusion and doubt, and a gaslightee, who is willing to doubt his or her own perceptions in order to keep the relationship going [...] [T]hat shared responsibility was the essence of gaslighting. It wasn't only emotional abuse. It was a mutually created relationship."[63]

What is particularly insidious about gaslighting is that it speaks to deep-seated, "malevolent intentions" against the person being gaslit; as James B. Meigs explains in *Commentary Magazine*, "Those engaged in gaslighting aren't just wrong, or even simply lying [...] they're conducting an insidious campaign to undermine the judgment and mental stability of their interlocutors. In other words, gaslighters aren't trying to convince us, they're trying to confuse us, even unhinge us."[64] The principal intent of gaslighting is to erode

---

[61] Around 2016, gaslighting gained a foothold in conversations around twenty-first-century politics with the nomination and eventual "election" of Donald Trump to the US presidency; while a wealth of articles and books that examine Trump's masochistic rhetoric exist, some representative ones include: Bobby Azarian, "Trump Is Gaslighting America Again—Here's How to Fight It," *Psychology Today*, August 31, 2018, https://www.psychologytoday.com/us/blog/mind-in-the-machine/201808/trump-is-gaslighting-america-again-here-s-how-fight-it (accessed May 29, 2019); Amanda Carpenter, *Gaslighting America: Why We Love It When Trump Lies to Us* (New York: Broadside Books, 2018); Lauren Duca, "Donald Trump Is Gaslighting America," *Teen Vogue*, December 10, 2016, https://www.teenvogue.com/story/donald-trump-is-gaslighting-america (accessed May 29, 2019); Paul Rosenberg, "Lies, Bulls**t and Gaslighting: A Field Guide to Trump's Reality-Warping Mendacity," *Salon*, February 24, 2019, https://www.salon.com/2019/02/24/lies-bullst-and-gaslighting-a-field-guide-to-trumps-reality-warping-mendacity/ (accessed May 29, 2019); and Stephanie Sarkis, "Donald Trump Is a Classic Gaslighter in an Abusive Relationship with America," *USA Today*, October 3, 2018, https://www.usatoday.com/story/opinion/2018/10/03/trump-classic-gaslighter-abusive-relationship-america-column/1445050002/ (accessed May 29, 2019).

[62] Katy Waldman, "From Theater to Therapy to Twitter, the Eerie History of Gaslighting," *Slate*, April 18, 2016, https://slate.com/human-interest/2016/04/the-history-of-gaslighting-from-films-to-psychoanalysis-to-politics.html (accessed May 29, 2019).

[63] Robin Stern, *The Gaslight Effect: How to Spot and Survive the Hidden Manipulation Others Use to Control Your Life* (New York: Harmony Books, 2007), xix.

[64] James B. Meigs, "A Gaslight unto the Nations: How a Word Became the Cliché of the Trump Years," *Commentary Magazine*, December 2018, https://www.commentarymagazine.com/articles/gaslight-unto-nations/ (accessed May 29, 2019).

the credibility of an individual's memory, perception and voice, both for that person and for those with whom that person shares her/his/their memories and perceptions. The result is to cast the individual being gaslit as mentally unbalanced, even deranged, while the person performing the gaslighting is elevated to the status of long-suffering, compassionate and trusted intimate. Gaslighting takes on a particularly Machiavellian dimension when targeted at addicts, whose credibility and sanity are always and already in question, both within and outside of themselves, and whose self-image is at once undermined by confusion and doubt.

As I discuss in detail above, within the narrative of *The Girl on the Train*, Rachel functions as the gaslightee who, as a result of infertility and alcoholism, willingly cedes control over her narrative voice and her memories to Tom, who functions as the gaslighter. But within the reading experience of *The Girl on the Train*, there exists another relationship that is founded on the concept of gaslighting and that is central to the narrative experimentation evinced within the novel: that is, the relationship between the author and her readers. Like the relationship between a gaslighter and a gaslightee, the reading experience is predicated on a pact of mutual agreements between author and readers; this is especially true within genre fiction, like the mystery novel, where readerly expectation regarding generic conventions determine and are determined by the reading experience.

At the heart of the mystery reading experience is the expectation that readers will be able to successfully gain access to the diegetic world through the trustworthy intermediary of the sleuth-protagonist, with whom readers are persistently encouraged to identify. In *A Theory of Narrative*, Rick Altman explains this dynamic as follows: "The reader's decision to continue reading always constitutes an investment of desire. Once that desire has been fixed on the protagonist, the protagonist becomes an extension of the reader's own self, an indirect method of self-expression, a figure for the reader's own identity."[65] Whether narrated in first- or third-person, mystery novels turn on the creation of an intimate, if competitive, relationship between readers and sleuth—that is, the sleuth becomes the lens through which readers view the diegetic world, as well as the sieve used to filter information and differentiate clues from extraneous information. While this relationship is marked by healthy competition to see who can solve the crime before the other, ultimately for the mystery to "work" as a genre, readers must strongly identify with the sleuth-protagonist—not necessarily "like" that character, and not always even "approve" of that character's actions (which, as I discussed in the previous chapter, is especially true within the subgenre of the roman noir), but definitely readers must share

---

[65] Rick Altman, *A Theory of Narrative* (New York: Columbia University Press, 2008), 181.

the sleuth's core values and must invest in the sleuth-protagonist's destiny, which is, of course, also and simultaneously readers' shared destiny.

The identification that typically is fostered between mystery readers and protagonist-sleuth—the self-same relational dynamic of identification that, for the initial three-quarters of *The Girl on the Train*, is fostered between Hawkins's readers and Rachel—demands that readers look with the protagonist, "measuring the world against the protagonist's desires instead of just measuring the protagonist against the world."[66] Stated differently, while characters like Tom, Damien, Anna, Cathy and Detective Riley may judge Rachel's actions and character, particularly when she is inebriated, against the measuring stick of manic sobriety, the readers, as an extension of Rachel, navigate much of the novel saddled with a shame and self-deprecation similar to Rachel's.

When Rachel experiences her epiphany regarding Tom, readers are forcibly extracted from their identificatory relationship with Hawkins's protagonist through a kind of *lectio interruptus* and thrust into what Altman terms "a participatory present, sharing the protagonist's position, [while also adopting a] retrospective stance permitting recognition of the central character's foibles."[67] This participatory present disallows identification with Rachel, prohibits immersion within the narrative and demands a heightened self-awareness on the part of readers. In *Self-Reflexivity in Literature* (2005), the editors of the volume suggest that self-reflexivity occurs when writers "violate poetological norms [...] in order to comment on their writing [...] or to [...] openly question how literary assumptions and conventions transform and filter reality, thus trying to ultimately prove that no singular truths or meanings exist."[68] At once inside and outside of the text, readers must come to grips—both emotionally and ideologically—not only with their having been duped into trusting Tom's version of the narrative events, but also with their having willingly entered into a toxic, emotionally abusive relationship with the text's author, Paula Hawkins. In effect, I am arguing here that there are two acts of gaslighting in which readers become enmeshed: one at the diegetic level, the other at the extra-diegetic level. The gaslighting that occurs within the diegesis—that is, identifying with Rachel, who cedes narrative authority to Tom—is, in most ways, just a riff (albeit an inventive and interesting one) on the traditional unreliable narrator. But the extra-diegetic gaslighting that involves Hawkins's willful (and skillful) violation both of generic conventions

---

[66] Ibid.
[67] Ibid., 183.
[68] Werner Huber, Martin Middeke and Hubert Zapf, "Introduction," in *Self-Reflexivity in Literature*, ed. Huber, Middeke and Zapf (Würzburg, Germany: Königshausen & Neumann, 2005), 7–12 (9).

and of readerly trust is what marks *The Girl on the Train* as remarkably experimental and what challenges readers to adopt a more compassionate view of addicts and substance use disorders.

To begin with, it is important to acknowledge that while the gaslighting that occurs between Hawkins and her readers is not entirely "mutually created," the reader nonetheless is complicit in that toxic and abusive relationship. This is so because the novel at once presents itself as a kind of classic whodunit and, as such, invites readers to participate in a particular type of reading experience whereby they invest their trust in the sleuth-protagonist. In such a reading experience, if the sleuth-protagonist insists that she is untrustworthy, and her ex-husband should be believed, then readers most likely will adopt that viewpoint as well, and will do so uncritically, trusting not only in Rachel but also in the long-standing generic prescriptions of the mystery genre that demand they *look with* the protagonist. But Hawkins creates a narrator who is only unreliable with respect to the question of her own unreliability and then refuses to share this secret behind Rachel's back, thereby rendering her protagonist an object of dramatic irony trafficked between implied author and readers. Readers take for granted that the taken-for-granteds of the mystery genre are operative within Hawkins's diegetic world, and, when, at the climax of the novel, that assumption proves erroneous and readers realize that it is Hawkins (and not her characters) who has not been playing fairly with them, those readers are rendered self-conscious about and implicitly shamed for their gullibility.

To cast readers as gullible is to directly confront those readers with their willingness to buy wholeheartedly into cultural scripts that equate addicts with liars and cheats, and that always and only characterize addiction as a state of compromised morality. In this respect, the novel engenders among its readers an examination of why they believe what they believe about addiction. *Why*, the reader is forced to consider, *was I so quick to accept Rachel's untrustworthiness? Do I really believe that addicts are, by nature, liars, and, if so, then where did I learn that bit of "wisdom" and what are the implications of my investing faith and trust in that belief?* Such questions not only illustrate the epistemological struggles at the heart of the reading experience in *The Girl on the Train*, but also point up the pervasive pull of ignorance where substance use disorders are concerned. Readers' gullibility hinges on their inability, or more likely unwillingness, to acquire trustworthy and valid knowledge about the lived experiences of addicts and, instead, to lean into long-standing and widely held belief systems that simply are taken for granted. *The Girl on the Train*, then, serves up a powerful reminder that simply because a belief system is widely taken for granted does not by default mean that that belief system is true.

In raising questions regarding the taken-for-granted nature of certain belief systems, Hawkins is also and simultaneously challenging readers to exercise greater mindfulness with respect to those "areas on which ideology is silent." Indeed, *The Girl on the Train* reminds its readers that ideology is most reticent—and most powerful—when it becomes so deeply ingrained within a culture, so pervasive, as to be rendered invisible and taken for granted. The very invisibility and silence within which many ideologies are cloaked is what lends to those belief systems the force of legitimacy, Truth and privilege, and renders them nearly impossible to be dislodged and undone. Within the Western novel and, more broadly, Western culture at large, unruly, narcissistic and self-destructive behaviors commonly are seen as symptomatic of substance use disorders, and these beliefs are reinforced by a medical community, a system of jurisprudence and a treatment industry that regularly refuse to recognize the nuances and complexities of substance use disorders.[69] At the moment that Rachel steps decisively out of the role of gaslightee, unmasking both Tom and Hawkins as gaslighters, *The Girl on the Train* gives lie to some of the most frequently taken-for-granted truisms about substance use disorders. It is a powerful and empowering gesture that affirms the humanity and the self-efficacy of the addict, and in those respects *The Girl on the Train* marks itself as a rarity in the trajectory of Western literary history.

Even more empowering is the resolution of the novel when Rachel, in an act of self-defense, kills Tom by stabbing him in the neck with a corkscrew: "Tom's lips are moving, he's saying something to me, but I can't hear him. I watch him come, I watch him, and I don't move until he's almost upon me, and then I swing. I jam the vicious twist of the corkscrew into his neck. His eyes widen and he falls without a sound."[70] In a novel that is so deeply concerned with acts of silencing, particularly those that result from instances of gaslighting, it is, I think, significant that the key event in the narrative resolution involves a particularly brutal and vivid form of silencing. Although readers are not necessarily immersed in this series of events, as they are by now looking at rather than with Rachel, readers nonetheless are invested in the sleuth-protagonist's fate and, for me, this moment reads like a much-deserved contemporary illustration of Hammurabian justice. Having been silenced and shamed for her alcoholism by a rabidly misogynistic ex-husband who gaslit or killed women when they "just wouldn't fucking shut up,"[71] Rachel here enacts the ultimate silencing by stabbing Tom in the neck, thereby rendering him physically incapable of producing any sounds during the final moments of his pathetic life.

---

[69] Peter R. Martin, Bennett Alan Weinberg and Bonnie K. Bealer, *Healing Addiction: An Integrated Pharmacopsychosocial Approach to Treatment* (Hoboken, NJ: John Wiley, 2007), 8–9.
[70] Hawkins, *The Girl on the Train*, 311.
[71] Ibid., 303.

Here, at the close of *The Girl on the Train*, the gaslighter is not merely being gaslit, but instead is being unequivocally silenced.

Ironically, the weapon used to murder Tom serves as a very powerful commentary on the ways in which Rachel's alcoholism was used to render her, if not mute, then unreliable, especially since that weapon is used to enact justice against Tom for, at least in part, the acts of gaslighting perpetrated against Rachel; further, Rachel's killing of Tom with a corkscrew very powerfully wrests ideological control from dominant (sober) culture. To survive, Rachel must kill off her ex-husband, the man responsible for the suffocating shame and self-hatred that defines Rachel for the majority of the novel, and, in so doing, she also symbolically murders those demeaning and fatally flawed cultural scripts about substance use disorders that were weaponized and used against her for Tom's self-serving ends. In the end, Rachel does not just kill Tom and, in so doing, bring about narrative and ideological closure to *The Girl on the Train*; rather, she also and simultaneously exposes and systematically disembowels the literary forms and cultural scripts that, to borrow Jill Dolan's assessment of lesbian subjectivity in dramatic realism, are "so determined to validate dominant culture" that the addict "can only be moralized against or marginalized."[72] At the close of Hawkins's novel, Rachel is a self-assured woman who acts both decisively and courageously to save herself, Anna and Anna's child from Tom. At the close of the novel, too, readers feel as if Tom got exactly what he deserved, although this feeling is accompanied by more than a modicum of unease given readers' complicity in Tom's gaslighting. In this way, the end of *The Girl on the Train* also is an object lesson in the value and importance of what Eve Kosofsky Sedgwick termed "unknowing *as* unknowing, not as a vacuum or as the blank it can pretend to be but as a weighty and occupied and consequential epistemological space."[73] And, finally, at the close of the novel, readers ultimately feel compassion for Rachel neither because she is an addict, nor because she has sobered up, but because she is an addict who exists within a culture in which her identity as a woman and her medical condition as an alcoholic can be weaponized and used against her to near-fatal ends. On this point, Hawkins's novel is decidedly not silent.

---

[72] Jill Dolan, *Presence & Desire: Essays on Gender, Sexuality, Performance* (Ann Arbor: University of Michigan Press, 1993), 162–63.

[73] Eve Kosofsky Sedgwick, *Epistemology of the Closet* (Berkeley: University of California Press, 1990), 77.

Chapter 4

TRANSGRESSING: *LESS THAN ZERO* (1985)

To transgress is, by nature, to play, to test, to experiment. But, in the novel, acts of formal transgression can extend beyond trial to violation, which is what differentiates the acts of experimentation discussed in the current and the following chapters from those discussed in earlier chapters of this volume. In the preceding chapters, all three of the texts under consideration were read and analyzed in the context of existing categorical, generic or/and topical expectations; while each of these texts undertakes, by varying degrees, an exploration of the unknown by pushing at the boundaries of these expectations, ultimately *Leaving Las Vegas*, *Dope* and *The Girl on the Train* are recognizable as iterations of particular literary traditions—such as the addiction novel, literary realism, the roman noir and the classic whodunit—even as they pose challenges to how twenty-first-century readers understand and interpret both those traditions and the subject matter at hand (i.e., addiction). At the center of this and the following chapter, by contrast, are two novels that "go beyond the bounds or limits prescribed"[1] by genre, history and sometimes even the existing literary marketplace at the time of their original publication. Bret Easton Ellis's *Less Than Zero* (1985) and Grace Krilanovich's *The Orange Eats Creeps* (2010) break quite decisively, even violently, with a number of the formal, ideological or/and topical traditions that have, for over two centuries, defined the addiction novel in the West, trespassing against readerly expectations for the reading experience, offending readers' beliefs and sensibilities and ultimately forcing readers to confront addiction in new and often quite confounding ways.

---

[1] "transgress, v." *OED Online*, June 2019, Oxford University Press http://www.oed.com.ezproxy.bgsu.edu/view/Entry/204775?rskey=BFADjt&result=2 (accessed June 9, 2019).

Black Neon: **Exploitative Self-Flagellation**

To articulate the textual and ideological trespasses in which Ellis's novel engages, I need first to locate the novel within and against both the conservative history of the addiction novel and the more progressive tradition of transgressive fiction. The addiction novel traditionally has been an extremely punitive genre with regard to addict characters and addict-readers, offering, as I note in the Introduction to the current volume, two equally unappealing resolutions to the lived experiences of addiction: either addicts suffer cruel and painful deaths, or addicts magically (and too rapidly) "recover" from addiction[2] only to be saddled with the specter of relapse and the albatross of shame for the remainder of their lives, which predictably are steeped in pathos. In either case, the addiction novel—or, more specifically, the narrative trajectory of literary realism that inevitably leads the addiction novel to one of these two, common dénouements—often reads like a cautionary tale in which, whether alive or dead at the close of the book, addicts suffer severe consequences for their substance use disorders, consequences that clearly are designed to shame and blame the addict while simultaneously warning readers away from such deplorable behaviors. Throughout its history, then, the addiction novel has been typified by a firm, and firmly conservative, moral logic that punishes excess while championing self-restraint and personal accountability, despite mounds of scientific research that clearly document the ways in which illicit and controlled substances neurochemically undermine the addict's agency.

The cautionary tale thread that runs prominently through the addiction novel takes on a particularly violent form in the writing of some addicts; works like Charles Bukowski's *Women* (1978), Dan Fante's *86'ed* (2009), Mark SaFranko's *Hating Olivia* (2010) and Ryan Leone's *Wasting Talent* (2014) manifest

---

[2] In *Dopesick: Dealers, Doctors, and the Drug Company That Addicted America* (2018), Beth Macy reports that "the latest research on substance use disorder from Harvard Medical School shows it takes the typical opioid-addicted user eight years—and four to five treatment attempts—to achieve remission for just a single year. And yet only about 10 percent of the addicted population manages to get access to care and treatment for a disease that has roughly the same incidence rate as diabetes" (243). To be sure, Macy here is writing about a very specific set of circumstances that contribute to the dire remission rates facing opioid addicts, including the chemical composition of the drug, as well as the lack of financial and geographical access to extended, comprehensive treatment programs in the rural areas of the United States where the opioid epidemic is most deeply felt. However, research on the effectivity of various forms of treatment (and on various substance use disorders) confirms that the "30 days and done" narrative common to novels like Jo Piazza's *Love Rehab* (2013) and Farrah Penn's *Twelve Steps to Normal* (2018) offers false hope to addicts who desperately struggle to achieve sobriety. For more on this research, see Bankole A. Johnson, ed., *Addiction Medicine* (New York: Springer, 2010).

the consequences of addiction as gratuitous self-loathing and self-flagellation, often delving into the underbelly of drug culture and urban violence in an act of exploitative self-shaming. Tony O'Neill's *Black Neon* (2012) is highly representative of this trend, particularly the storyline that focuses on filmmaker Jacques Seltzer, whose one-hit-wonder debut, *Dead Flowers*, catapulted him to cult stardom, much like O'Neill's debut novel, *Digging the Vein*, almost instantaneously became a cult classic when published in 2006.

Since the release of *Dead Flowers*, O'Neill's narrator reveals, Seltzer has spent his time taking and exhibiting degrading photographs of historically under- and misrepresented populations:

> His first book was a collection of portraits of Dutch amputee prostitutes entitled *Wide Eyed and Legless* [...] His images of Palestinian refugees—published in France as *An Auschwitz of Their Own*—won several awards and cemented his reputation as an *enfant terrible*, a provocateur and a lightning rod for controversy [...] [His] latest masterpiece [was] a dark collection of images showing the squalid lives of working class youths in stagnant Northern English mill towns.[3]

Seltzer's willful exploitation of vulnerable individuals for his own professional gain casts him as an unprincipled miscreant with little to no regard for basic human dignity. And the types of populations he exploits should heighten readers' disdain for Seltzer. For refugees who are displaced—often violently—from their homes/homeland to be treated so disrespectfully registers contempt not only for the individuals being photographed, but also for the decades of political and religious strife on which their displacement is predicated. But to posit a patently inaccurate and politically problematic analogy between the Palestinian refugee crisis and the Holocaust is, at best, to peddle revisionist history and, at worst, to engage in what has been termed "soft Holocaust denial," which Zach Ben-Amots describes as "the exploitation of the Holocaust to attack Israel and its supporters, as well as the trivialization of the Holocaust in order to serve political ends."[4] Granted, in the case of Seltzer's book title, the reference to the Holocaust is intended more for shock, than political effect, but it nonetheless undermines the historical gravity of and the reverence that should be expressed toward the genocide of six million human beings.

---

[3] Tony O'Neill, *Black Neon* (West Yorkshire: Bluemoose Books, 2014), chapter 2, Kindle.
[4] Zach Ben-Amots, "The Rise of 'Soft' Holocaust Denial," *The Tower*, October 2016, http://www.thetower.org/article/the-rise-of-soft-holocaust-denial/ (accessed June 21, 2019).

Seltzer's photography work, though, is not the only aspect of his character that marks him as morally grotesque; his drug-fueled behaviors also are increasingly illegal and reprehensible. At the opening of the novel, Seltzer accepts an offer to complete his much-anticipated second film, the eponymous *Black Neon*.[5] Over the course of the novel, as Seltzer sinks ever-deeper into his polysubstance use disorder, he steps out from behind the camera, "like some junkie Alfred Hitchcock,"[6] to become a participant-observer in his work. One character describes some video footage shot for *Black Neon* as follows: "I don't even know who *shot* half of this stuff. It sure as hell wasn't Jacques. I mean, there he is, all flushed and tweaked out, sucking on the tit of some bugged-out, toothless transsexual meth freak, or fixing a shot while some underage hooker turns a trick in the bed next to him [...] it's really sick shit, man!"[7]

The scenes described above are riddled with grotesque imagery that serves as a not-so-subtle condemnation of the filmmaker's character and actions, particularly as that character and those actions are refracted through his polysubstance use disorders. Seltzer's flushed countenance alludes to the hypertension that has resulted from his compulsive consumption of massive amounts of food, alcohol and illicit substances, and that ultimately contributes to his death at the novel's close. High blood pressure is a medical condition signified by excess—an escalation of heart rate, a narrowing of arteries and a concomitant increase in resistance to blood flow through those arteries. That Seltzer's hypertension is the result of myriad "risky" behaviors—behaviors that widely are regarded as "choices"—marks the condition as deserved, a warranted punishment for his transgressions against the sanctity of body and health.

Furthermore, that the meth freak transsexual whose tit Jacques suckles is toothless offers an interesting commentary on the filmmaker's morality and character when read against the backdrop of a culture that is obsessed with teeth whitening, teeth straightening and, more broadly, dental hygiene. Extreme tooth decay and loss are common side effects of repeated methamphetamine use, but they also speak to an absence of personal hygiene, and a general sense of "dirtiness" that often intimates not simply poor self-care, but a lack of moral fortitude on the part of the addict. Methamphetamine also is associated with poverty, stereotyped as a white trash drug,[8] and thus, as a

---

[5] O'Neill, *Black Neon*, chapter 2.
[6] Ibid., chapter 33.
[7] Ibid.
[8] For thoughtful discussions on the intersections of meth culture, socioeconomic status and whiteness, see Jeffery Chaichana Peterson, Aline Gubrium and Alice Fiddian-Green, "Meth Mouth, White Trash, and the Pseudo-Racialization of Methamphetamine Use in the U.S.," *Health Communication* 34, no. 10 (2018): 1–10; and Travis Linnemann and

meth freak, the transsexual (and, by association, Seltzer) stands as an affront to notions of self-reliance, personal accountability and upward mobility that are deeply imbricated in and, indeed, constitutive of the Western cultural imaginary, particularly in the United States. Equally telling is the fact that Seltzer engages in these acts of depravity with a transsexual which, I suspect, is intended to serve as a further taint on his character, an additional marker of debasement. This type of transphobia is not unsurprising in a body of literature that frequently trafficks in misogyny, homophobia and heterosexism. Finally, the reference to the underage hooker reinforces the problematic, but widely held, belief that addiction inevitably leads to criminal behavior, even when the addiction involves controlled, rather than illicit, substances.

Black Neon ends, quite predictably, with Seltzer's gruesome death in a seedy Budget Inn on Sunset Boulevard that the narrator describes as "a faceless sleaze-pit sandwiched between an outpatient drug rehab and an auto shop."[9] His body is sweaty and bloated as a result of his insatiable appetites, and his corpse becomes a symbol of the destructive excess that is assumed to characterize the lived experiences of addiction. After Seltzer's death, the "sleazy, disjointed mess" of footage that he shot during his time in Los Angeles is cobbled together and released under the title *Black Neon*. While the film experiences "a successful theatrical run and huge sales on DVD and Blu-Ray," the narrator of O'Neill's novel regards it as "profoundly unprofound, about as deep and meaningful as a puddle of skid row piss," and, in the end, this narrator concludes that Jacques Seltzer is "just another dead junkie, and not even a particularly talented one."[10] To be fair, O'Neill's narrator is regularly unlikeable, and often unreliable, given his own struggles with substance use disorders; yet his assessment of the filmmaker rings true with readers' own, and, in the end, *Black Neon* leaves readers with a simplistic and predictable moral truism that has been echoed ad nauseum across the expansive history of the addiction novel: namely, addicts deserve to die gruesome and degrading deaths because they are addicts.[11]

Tyler Wall, "'This Is Your Face on Meth': The Punitive Spectacle of 'White Trash' in the Rural War on Drugs," *Theoretical Criminology* 17, no. 3 (2013): 315–34.

[9] O'Neill, *Black Neon*, chapter 33.

[10] Ibid., Epilogue.

[11] One particularly startling extra-diegetic example of this trend can be seen in the "Chris Farley death photos" that have circulated some of the seedier corners of the internet for decades. Allegedly taken by a prostitute whose services were (again, allegedly) engaged by Farley on the final day of his life, the photographs picture an aubergine-faced Farley sprawled face up on the floor of his Chicago apartment, brown froth oozing from his mouth. The images are graphic and brutal, rendering Farley an obvious spectacle of degradation to be trafficked among spectators who take pleasure in the visual display and consumption of traumatic injury. As such, these images serve as a sanction against

Transgressive Fiction: The New as Shocking

Less Than Zero is no less graphic (content-wise) than *Black Neon*, which is not especially surprising, or perhaps even noteworthy, given that Ellis's novel belongs to the loosely defined category of literature known as "transgressive fiction." Transgressive fiction constitutes a category of fairly diverse contemporary literary production that primarily hails from the United States and the United Kingdom and includes such representative authors as Kathy Acker, J. G. Ballard, Angela Carter, Dennis Cooper, A. M. Homes and Chuck Palahniuk. Coined by *Los Angeles Times* contributor Michael Silverblatt in 1993,[12] the phrase *transgressive fiction* refers to texts that, in subject matter and in form, challenge, violate or/and dismantle preexisting sociocultural, ideological, behavioral or/and generic expectations that a reading public might share in a given historical moment. James Gardner of the *New York Times*, for instance, notes that transgressive fiction typically includes "books pitched to young adults, written by authors descended from William Burroughs and the Marquis de Sade, that explore aberrant sexual practices, urban violence, drug use and dysfunctional families in graphic detail."[13] At the heart of transgressive fiction is the notion of assault—specifically, the author wages an assault on readers' expectations, sensibilities, values or/and morals through a graphic exploration of monstrous characters, grotesque behaviors or/and abject experiences. Kathy Acker's *Blood and Guts in High School* (1978),[14] for instance, presents readers with a young woman's uncensored journey through adolescence against the backdrop of incest, sexual violence and human sex trafficking. Similarly, Chuck Palahniuk's *Haunted* (2005) focuses on a motley cast of social and sexual deviants who are trapped in an abandoned theater and who pass the time telling one another graphic stories that concern everything from a chronic masturbator whose proclivities lead to his own disembowelment ("Guts") to a social worker who places razor blades in the orifices of anatomically correct dolls to prohibit law enforcement officers from "molesting" them ("Exodus").[15]

---

his immoral "choices" and a mark of his transgressions. They also and simultaneously deny Farley even a modicum of humanity or integrity in death.

[12] Michael Silverblatt, "Shock Appeal/ Who Are These Writers, and Why Do They Want to Hurt Us: The New Fiction of Transgression," *Los Angeles Times*, August 1, 1993, https://www.latimes.com/archives/la-xpm-1993-08-01-bk-21466-story.html (accessed June 9, 2019).

[13] James Gardner, "Naked Breakfast, Lunch and Dinner," *New York Times*, April 23, 1995, 49.

[14] Kathy Acker, *Blood and Guts in High School* (New York: Grove, 1978).

[15] Chuck Palahniuk, *Haunted* (New York: Anchor, 2005).

Transgressive fiction, though, is not simply identified by its controversial subject matter; also central to the genre is the treatment of that subject matter. In "Abjection/Abjectivism," Allan Lloyd-Smith explains that transgressive fiction enacts "a refusal to engage with the recuperated articulations of the dominant culture."[16] Robin Mookerjee, author of *Transgressive Fiction: The New Satiric Tradition* (2013), offers a more detailed explanation of this characteristic of the genre, suggesting that authors of transgressive fiction "treat flashpoint subjects without taking any kind of moral stand and treat bizarre behavior as if it were absolutely normal."[17] Dennis Cooper's *Frisk* (1991), for instance, confronts the reader with violently explicit depictions of physical torture, sexual sadism and bodily mutilation, narrated through the disinterested perspective of a drug-addled serial murderer.[18] Similarly, A. M. Homes's *The End of Alice* (1996), which was dubbed "the most vile and perverted novel I've ever read" by the spokesperson for the National Society for the Prevention of Cruelty to Children,[19] is principally narrated from the point of view of a middle-aged pedophile and treats the subject of child sexual molestation as unremarkable, even banal.[20]

Finally, the label of *transgressive* is determined as much by audience reception as it is by the subject matter of a given text and its treatment by a given author. As Mookerjee writes, "'Transgressive' as a label applied to literature or other media is a comment on the content's reception which is very much a function of the atmosphere of the time."[21] Many factors—social, cultural, political—play into the "atmosphere of the time" and, by association, the reception of a given cultural text. Due to shifts in social mores around taboo sexual practices or/and recreational drug use, for instance, what once was deemed "transgressive" might in a later historical moment seem passé, unremarkable, even boring. In "After the Shock Is Gone," for example, Eric Felten of the *Wall Street Journal* illustrates this point quite vividly: "When Bob Fosse first put his dancers on stage in fishnets and bowlers, eyebrows were duly raised. How many decades will Madonna continue to wear that same costume

---

[16] Allan Lloyd-Smith, "Abjection/Abjectivism," *European Journal of American Culture* 24, no. 3 (December 2005): 195.

[17] Robin Mookerjee, *Transgressive Fiction: The New Satiric Tradition* (New York: Palgrave Macmillan, 2013), 2.

[18] Dennis Cooper, *Frisk* (New York: Grove, 1991).

[19] "The End of Alice—A. M. Homes," *Books, Time, and Silence*, April 10, 2009, http://bookstimeandsilence.blogspot.com/2009/04/end-of-alice-am-homes.html (accessed June 9, 2019).

[20] A. M. Homes, *The End of Alice* (New York: Scribner, 1996).

[21] Mookerjee, *Transgressive Fiction*, 15.

100   ADDICTION, REPRESENTATION & THE EXPERIMENTAL NOVEL

as if it were a racy innovation?"[22] At the same time, desensitization can occur when cultural artists are so bent on pushing boundaries that transgression becomes the norm, rather than the exception, or anomaly; when this situation occurs, cultural artists (and even consumers) are left to wonder, "Once all the boundaries have been blurred, what's left?"[23] Salman Rushdie has suggested that "what's left" often is the presentation of "transgressive" subject matter merely for shock value: "Once the new was shocking, not because it set out to shock, but because it set out to be new. Now, all too often, the shock is the new. And shock, in our jaded culture, wears off easily."[24]

Less Than Zero as Transgressive

When *Less Than Zero* originally was published in the summer of 1985, the novel was widely dubbed as "*Bright Lights, Big City West*"[25] given its similarities in subject matter, tone and literary stylings to Jay McInerney's novel, which was published the previous year. Written in one month (so the lore goes) by Ellis, who at the time was a junior at Bennington College, the novel chronicles the narrator's four-week holiday break following the completion of his first semester as a college student. At its core, the novel reads like a commentary on 1980s materialism with its emphasis on all manner of excessive consumption—from engaging in promiscuous sexual activities with both men and women (sometimes simultaneously) to watching seemingly endless hours of MTV and ingesting massive amounts of illicit and controlled substances (again, sometimes simultaneously). The events of the novel unfold episodically as the narrator, Clay, drifts almost aimlessly from this party to that club, from this sexual partner to that drug, without any sense of chronological time to anchor him or the narrative. At multiple points, for example, Clay loses track of "how many days [he's] been home,"[26] even though his winter break is only four weeks in length. The characters of the novel (including the narrator) are so vaguely drawn as to be virtually indistinguishable from one another—perhaps an allusion to the "Disappear Here" billboard that both symbolically and thematically looms large in the novel. In the end, it is difficult to identify what this novel is "about" (at least in a conventional sense) and, in some ways,

---

[22] Eric Felten, "After the Shock Is Gone: Postmodern Times," *Wall Street Journal*, December 3, 2010, https://www.wsj.com/articles/SB10001424052748703377504575650882413327998 (accessed June 9, 2019).
[23] Ibid.
[24] Ibid.
[25] Larry McCarthy, "Less Than Zero," *Saturday Review* July/August 1985: 80.
[26] Bret Easton Ellis, *Less Than Zero* (New York: Vintage Contemporaries, 1998), 115.

I would concur with *Film Comment* reviewer John Powers, who wrote of the novel, "[*Less Than Zero*] has no real plot, no likeable characters, few evident emotions, and scarcely any growth by its hero."[27]

In 1985, the content of *Less Than Zero* was regarded as transgressive in part given the graphic and unapologetic manner in which polysubstance use disorder was represented. Indeed, against the backdrop of a literary tradition in which addiction historically had served as the central preoccupation of the narrative, as well as the protagonist's scarlet letter, a novel in which characters blithely admit to dosing with animal tranquilizers in the same breath that they recount attending a music concert[28] most certainly pushes at readers' preconceived notions of what constitutes appropriate social behavior and discourse. But also included in Ellis's novel are scenes in which characters voraciously consume snuff films to the point of sexual arousal[29] and regard a dead addict who has overdosed in an alleyway as a tourist attraction.[30]

Perhaps the most representative example of the transgressive content that is threaded through Ellis's novel occurs in the scene when Rip invites Clay to his apartment on Wilshire to see "something that will blow [Clay's] mind" and the scene is described as follows:

> There's a naked girl, really young and pretty, lying on the mattress. Her legs are spread and tied to the bedposts and her arms are tied above her head. Her cunt is all rashed and looks dry and I can see that it's been shaved. She keeps moaning and murmuring words and moving her head from side to side, her eyes half-closed. Someone's put a lot of makeup on her, clumsily, and she keeps licking her lips, her tongue drags slowly, repeatedly, across them. Spin kneels by the bed and picks up a syringe and whispers something into her ear. The girl doesn't open her eyes. Spin digs the syringe into her arm. I just stare.[31]

The 12-year-old girl in this scene suffers multiple violations at the hands of her male captors. Most obviously, she is drugged up against her will, at least in this scene, and then violently gang raped. But more subtle violations also pepper this scene, including the forced shaving of her vagina, indicated by dryness and rash, and the application of make-up by her rapists, a gesture that

---

[27] John Powers, "The MTV Novel Arrives," *Film Comment* 21, no. 6 (November–December 1985): 46.
[28] Ellis, *Less Than Zero*, 126.
[29] Ibid., 152–54.
[30] Ibid., 185–87.
[31] Ibid., 188.

underscores her sexual objectification. All of these actions suggest that the girl is viewed as a plaything to be drugged and fucked and discarded; this attitude would be disturbing enough if expressed toward an adult—as, in *Leaving Las Vegas*, when the college-aged men anally gang rape Sera because they view her as a possession, rather than as a person—but when targeted at a "really young" minor in a culture that actively—at times maniacally—legislates age of consent, these actions read as salacious. Even more offensive is Rip's justification for holding the girl hostage—"If you want something, you have the right to take it. If you want to do something, you have the right to do it"[32]—which could be seen as the overarching philosophy of both *Less Than Zero* and, more broadly, transgressive fiction. In the end, this scene, and, indeed, many of the scenes of *Less Than Zero*, does not simply refuse "to engage with the recuperated articulations of the dominant culture," but actively and violently decimates the status quo with respect to consent, personal autonomy and sexual expression.

The subject matter of *Less Than Zero* can be regarded as transgressive simply because it is so often beyond the pale with respect to dominant social mores around personhood, sexuality, sobriety and youth culture; however, in the remainder of this chapter, I want to explore a different manifestation of transgressiveness in the novel—one that not only reveals the experimental nature of Ellis's prose vis-à-vis literary realism but also illustrates the ways in which Ellis undermines the dictates of the addiction novel with respect to the addict's "inevitable" fate. Specifically, I want to address the author's creation of a diegetic world in which conventional, extra-diegetic notions of morality and legality are suspended and the addict ultimately is not punished (or, perished) simply for being an addict.

As I note briefly above, the absence of a firm moral compass is a staple of transgressive fiction. In her postgraduate thesis, titled "Outrageous Insights: The Ethical Value of Transgressive Literature," Ekin Ulas explains specifically how "literature which depicts morally condemnable characters and their behavior while adopting a perspective that does not condemn [those characters]" impacts readers: "When readers engage imaginatively with this kind of literature, responding emotionally as solicited by the text, they may end up caring for these morally condemnable characters, and thus be forced to go beyond their habitual moral attitudes."[33] Ulas is especially interested in the ways in which reading such fiction "will affect how we consider the real world counterparts of such characters," and how the reading experience can

---

[32] Ibid., 189.
[33] Ekin Ulas, "Outrageous Insights: The Ethical Value of Transgressive Literature" (Master's Thesis, University of Hong Kong, 2014), 1.

provide "emotional and intellectual insight into [...] people to whom we do not easily relate, but who we easily ignore."[34] Like Ulas, I believe that transgressive fiction can facilitate a compassionate reading experience, encouraging readers to listen and relate to those who are easily and frequently ignored, here specifically addicts, by removing the lens of condemnation through which readers have been socioculturally indoctrinated to view that population, thereby forcing readers to see addicts with fresh eyes.

Only Stubble: The Mirror as Site of Self-Examination

Less Than Zero is rife with references to drug use, promiscuous sexual practice, prostitution and even domestic violence that vary only in terms of degree of explicitness and severity; yet the narrator's attitude toward these subjects—regardless of how graphically they are represented—can most accurately be described as *apathetic*. With respect to illicit drug use, in which the narrator routinely engages, the behavior is viewed as an unremarkable part of Clay's everyday existence, neither more significant nor more noteworthy than any other event or behavior that he experiences and certainly not cause for self-criticism or self-censure. On Christmas, for instance, Clay notes without emotion or judgment, "It's Christmas morning and I'm high on coke, and one of my sisters has given me this pretty expensive leather-bound datebook, the pages are big and white and the dates elegantly printed on top of them, in gold and silver lettering."[35] The terse, minimalist prose in this passage, coupled with the absence of a censorious tone, highlights the ways in which transgressive fiction often turns on the inversion of conventional binary relationships—that is, the "abnormal" becomes "normal(ized)," the "immoral" becomes if not "moral" then banal, and so on. Moreover, that Clay's intoxication is joined by a simple "and" to a fairly elaborate description of the Christmas present that he receives reinforces the banality of his heavy drug use—the practice being compared, at least implicitly, to something as commonplace and generic as a datebook, albeit an "expensive" one. The datebook seems, in this instance, also ironic given that Clay's abuse of illicit substances disallows him—and, I would argue, Ellis's readers—from differentiating between and among the days of Clay's holiday break, creating an incoherent and at times confusing temporality for the novel. In this respect, it is telling that one of the songs from the soundtrack of the filmic adaptation was a cover of "Hazy Shade of Winter" by The Bangles. The confusing temporality of the narrative thus echoes the confused thematic morality operative within the novel.

---

[34] Ibid., 4.
[35] Ellis, *Less Than Zero*, 71–72.

At other points in *Less Than Zero*, illicit drug use and addiction are treated as merely a backdrop for the narrative that unfolds—little more remarkable than the designer sunglasses that the characters don or the colorful nightclubs that they frequent. Addiction, for instance, can manifest itself in specific "stage properties" (such as a cocaine vial, a mirror adorned with lines of white powder or a drug spoon) that lend a feeling of verisimilitude to the fictional milieu inhabited by Clay and his insular coterie of privileged friends. When, for instance, Clay visits his friend Rip early in the novel, he offers the following clinical description of the setting: "I walk into Rip's bedroom and he's still in bed, nude, and there's a mirror on the nightstand, next to the bed, and he's cutting a line of coke. And he tells me to come in."[36] In a similar manner, substance use disorders figure into the novel as a means of implicit characterization—that is, as a way to allude to the characteristics that are shared by members of the affluent lost generation of 1980s youth culture, and to indicate what differentiates that generation from others. However, such aspects of characterization are depicted in as banal a manner as watching MTV,[37] listening to New Wave music[38] and playing video games.[39] For instance, late in the novel, Clay remarks about an evening out with a friend: "We do some of the coke and then go to an arcade in Westwood and play video games for close to two hours and end up spending something like twenty bucks apiece and we stop playing only because we run out of quarters."[40] Here, the act of snorting cocaine is implicitly (and uncritically) likened to spending a couple of hours hanging out at the arcade (a popular activity among youth in the 1980s); in making this comparison, Ellis underscores the idea that the Los Angeles of *Less Than Zero* is a world turned upside down—a world devoid of conventional morality in which cocaine addiction is characterized as commonplace, as ordinary and even, at times, as boring.

On two specific occasions, Clay directly is confronted with the consequences of substance abuse and addiction (e.g., overdose and death), yet those consequences barely register in Clay's stream-of-consciousness-inspired narration, a marked deviation from the traditions of both literary realism and the addiction novel. In the first instance, Clay's friend, Trent, mentions that a mutual friend, Scott, has overdosed, to which Clay emotionlessly responds, "I don't know who Scott is. It keeps raining. And that night, after I get three of the weird silent phone calls, I break a glass by throwing it against the wall.

---

[36] Ibid., 48.
[37] See, for instance, Ellis, *Less Than Zero*, 12, 40, 58, 71, 86, 103, 115, and 152.
[38] See, for instance, Ellis, *Less Than Zero*, 57, 74, 96, 104, 151, and 200.
[39] See, for instance, Ellis, *Less Than Zero*, 23, 128, 152, and 199.
[40] Ellis, *Less Than Zero*, 127–28.

No one comes in to see what the sound was. Then I lie on the bed, awake, take twenty milligrams of Valium to come off the coke, but it doesn't get me to sleep. I turn MTV off and the radio on."[41] Several pages later, Rip suggests that Julian is responsible for selling drugs to the "thirteen-year-old kid who O.D.'d at Beverly"; Clay registers neither shock nor disgust at this suggestion, and instead turns the conversation to Rip's recent activities—which include taking "some animal tranquilizers" and going "to see The Grimsoles."[42] For Clay and his ilk, addiction and death by overdose constitute mere staples of the landscape of affluent US youth culture in the 1980s, neither more nor less remarkable than Clay's chronic insomnia, middle-of-the-night prank telephone calls and typical southern California weather patterns. While much of the rest of US culture (at least outside of the diegesis of the novel) was staging Drug Awareness Weeks and joining chapters of Students against Drunk Driving (SADD), Clay pops "twenty milligrams of valium to come off the coke" and listens apathetically as a friend blandly admits to taking "some animal tranquilizers."

To the close of *Less Than Zero*, Clay remains unselfconscious regarding his substance use disorder. In one especially telling scene, for example, Ellis highlights Clay's lack of introspection by simultaneously referencing and subverting a common literary symbol (i.e., the mirror). Ellis writes, "The bathroom door opens and a man and a woman come out together, laughing, and they pass me and I go in and shut the door and open a small vial and notice that I don't have too much coke left, but I do what's left of it and I take a drink from the faucet and look at myself in the mirror, run my hand over my hair, and then across my cheek, decide I need to shave."[43] The import of this scene turns on the inversion of the symbolic meanings of the mirror. In addition to a wide range of symbolic connotations, many of which are explored thoughtfully in *The Symbolism of Mirrors in Art from Ancient Times to the Present* (1999) by Hope B. Werness, the mirror often serves as an impetus and a locus for self-examination by characters in Western literary and artistic production.[44]

---

[41] Ibid., 114–15.

[42] Ibid., 125–26.

[43] Ibid., 180–81.

[44] Interestingly, a number of cultural studies scholars have devoted significant attention to the history, evolution and symbolic import of the mirror. For more on this topic, see Miranda Anderson, ed. *The Book of the Mirror: An Interdisciplinary Collection Exploring the Cultural Story of the Mirror* (Newcastle upon Tyne: Cambridge Scholars, 2007); Benjamin Goldberg, *The Mirror and Man* (Charlottesville: University of Virginia Press, 1985); Arnaud Maillet, *The Claude Glass: Use and Meaning of the Black Mirror in Western Art*, trans. Jeff Fort (New York: Zone Books, 2004); Sabine Melchoir-Bonnet, *The Mirror: A History* (New York: Routledge, 2000); and Mark Pendergrast, *Mirror, Mirror: A History of the Human Love Affair with Reflection* (New York: Basic Books, 2004).

In his Introduction to *The Book of the Mirror: An Interdisciplinary Collection Exploring the Cultural Story of the Mirror* (2007), Mark Pendergrast explains, "Mirrors are meaningless until someone looks into them. Thus a history of the mirror is really the history of looking, and what we perceive in these magical surfaces can tell us a great deal about ourselves—whence we have come, what we imagine, how we think, and what we yearn for. The mirror appears throughout the human drama as a means of self-knowledge or self-delusion."[45] Within Western literary and artistic production, a mirror often functions as a means through which a character undergoes self-examination. The act of looking into the mirror foregrounds the self as a site for inquiry and investigation, which is perhaps why Jacques Lacan identified the mirror as the metaphoric and literal site at which the ego is formed. Within the looking glass, the looker sees a reflection of the self—that is, a visual simulacrum of the looker's physical appearance that is at once familiar and strange. The reflection is familiar in its seeming exact replication of the physical features that distinguish the self from others. At the same time, the strangeness of the reflection arises due to the perceived distance between the self and its reflection, between the real and the representational, between the "I" and the "not I." In the act of looking, the individual stages a confrontation between these two selves, a confrontation that ultimately engenders a greater degree of self-awareness and self-knowledge precisely through attempts to reconcile the two. A mirror in this respect simultaneously signals and triggers an existential crisis. For the character who gazes into the looking glass, then, the literal image reflected in the mirror often prompts and facilitates a process of introspection whereby the looker considers "whence [he has] come, what [he] imagine[s], how [he] think[s], and what [he] yearn[s] for."

Clay, by contrast, undergoes no such introspection. When Clay peers into the bathroom mirror, what he sees is what I refer to above as the "visual simulacrum" of his physical being. His narration—as is true throughout the novel—is terse, is clinical and focuses only on the literal details that he observes in the reflection. He sees himself "run [his] hand over [his] hair, and then across [his] cheek." In the stubble that has formed across his lower jaw, Clay perceives a need to shave. What he fails to perceive—or even acknowledge—is the addiction that quickly empties his "small vial." Clay never once experiences the kind of internal shame that often plagues long-term drug addicts and that, in the end, leads them either to a final, fatal overdose or to a successful

---

[45] Mark Pendergrast, "Introduction: Mirror Mirror: A Historical and Psychological Overview," *The Book of the Mirror: An Interdisciplinary Collection Exploring the Cultural Story of the Mirror*, ed. Miranda Anderson (Newcastle upon Tyne: Cambridge Scholars, 2007), 1–14.

intervention. Clay also never once examines the causal link between his various addictions and his dysfunctional life. In other words, Clay never achieves the classic epiphany moment that leads flawed protagonists to literary climax and dénouement. In fact, instead of devoting serious critical reflection to his substance use disorder (which is alluded to here in the nearly empty cocaine vial), Clay, in a classic act of self-deception,[46] gazes into the mirror and sees only stubble.

The significance of this lack of insight is underscored when seen in the context of Ellis's larger body of work. One scene in *Imperial Bedrooms* (2010), the sequel to *Less Than Zero*, illustrates my point. *Imperial Bedrooms* returns readers to the familiar characters and settings of *Less Than Zero* 25 years after the earlier novel ends. Like *Less Than Zero*, *Imperial Bedrooms* focuses its attention principally on the character of Clay who, in the sequel, is a 45-year-old screenwriter based in New York City. Early in the novel, Clay confides in interior monologue, "I can suddenly see my reflection in a mirror in the corner of the bedroom […] an old-looking teenager."[47] In *Imperial Bedrooms*, Clay's character arc is circumscribed by the experience of a traumatic midlife crisis—one that prompts a consideration of the poor judgment and the missed opportunities that mark the period between Clay's early adulthood (as represented in *Less Than Zero*) and his middle adulthood (as represented in *Imperial Bedrooms*). When the Clay of *Imperial Bedrooms* gazes into the mirror, he acknowledges (albeit in an implicit and still unexamined manner) one of the key faults that has defined his character since *Less Than Zero*: namely, his immaturity. The juxtapositioning of an allusion to Clay's chronological age (i.e., he self-identifies as "old-looking") with an allusion to his self-image (i.e., "teenager") points up the marked disparity between who Clay *is* and who Clay *perceives himself to be*. Author Donna Tartt makes a similar observation

---

[46] To be clear, I am not trying to perpetuate the widely held falsehood that all addicts are liars—a falsehood that Anne M. Fletcher tackles (14–16) in *Inside Rehab: The Surprising Truth about Addiction Treatment—and How to Get Help That Works* (2013). Nor am I suggesting, as put forth in the Big Book, that "Denial is the most cunning, baffling and powerful part of my disease, the disease of alcoholism"—another falsehood that Lance and Zachary Dodes tackle in *The Sober Truth: Debunking the Bad Science behind 12-Step Programs and the Rehab Industry* (2014). Instead, here I merely acknowledge that any human being, when faced with circumstances that challenge her/his/their self-image, might engage in denial, self-deception and other behaviors that enable that person to maintain a consistent and favorable (or, at least, not unfavorable) sense of "self." See Anne M. Fletcher, *Inside Rehab: The Surprising Truth about Addiction Treatment—and How to Get Help That Works* (New York: Viking, 2013), and Lance Dodes and Zachary Dodes, *The Sober Truth: Debunking the Bad Science behind 12-Step Programs and the Rehab Industry* (Boston, MA: Beacon Press, 2014).

[47] Bret Easton Ellis, *Imperial Bedrooms* (New York: Vintage, 2010), 60.

of the novel in her Amazon.com review, noting that *Imperial Bedrooms* "marks a return to the characters of *Less Than Zero*, twenty-five years on, where it's still the same old scene, camera flashes and sun-blinded gloss—only this time, there's a persistent echo of unease, *the sadness of moving in a young world while no longer young in it*."[48] The juxtapositioning also suggests that middle-aged Clay is capable of seeing more than just his surface-level reflection (or, his stubble)—that is, that he is capable of greater (albeit still limited) introspection than his younger counterpart. The absence of even this modicum of self-reflection in *Less Than Zero* illustrates quite powerfully the ways in which the earlier novel (and perhaps the genre of transgressive fiction more broadly) refuses to moralize against the characters and their addictions.

Compassionate Listening

To be sure, just because the novel refuses to shame and blame the addict does not mean that it excuses or sanctions addiction, although some reviewers misunderstood the novel in precisely this manner. Mary Jo Salter of the *New York Times*, for instance, regarded the characters of *Less Than Zero* as "incapable of moral or critical thought," as "too burnt out to change."[49] Views like Salter's are born out of deeply entrenched, extra-diegetic cultural narratives that identify substance use disorders as morally reprehensible behaviors and addicts as expendable, collateral damage of their willfully chosen transgression; this is what, in an earlier book, I refer to as "the metaphor of waste" that, for over two centuries, has dictated how Western audiences view and understand addiction both within and beyond representation.[50] *Less Than Zero* poses a challenge to the metaphor of waste (and to readings like Salter's). In particular, the novel refuses to condemn its characters or their behaviors, relating the experiences of addiction in clinical, disinterested prose and failing to kill off or redeem (usually by way of a Twelve-Step Program) the addicts at the close of the narrative in order to reinforce the ideological status quo.

What *Less Than Zero* does is challenge readers to engage both imaginatively and critically with a set of unfamiliar ideas about addiction, and to do so within the safe space of the reading experience. Most particularly, this novel posits the

---

[48] Donna Tartt, Review of *Less Than Zero*, by Bret Easton Ellis, *Amazon.com*, n.d., https://www.amazon.com/Imperial-Bedrooms-Vintage-Contemporaries-Easton-ebook/dp/B0036S49VY (accessed June 27, 2019) (emphasis added).

[49] Mary Jo Salter, "In Short: Fiction," Review of *Less Than Zero*, by Bret Easton Ellis, *New York Times*, June 16, 1985, https://www.nytimes.com/1985/06/16/books/in-short-fiction-050756.html (accessed June 24, 2019).

[50] See Heath A. Diehl, *Wasted: Performing Addiction in America* (London: Routledge, 2016).

question: What if the resolution of a text does not hinge on the addict's death or ability to achieve sobriety? In the mid-1980s, this was a revolutionary idea with respect to addiction, as evinced through the film adaptation of *Less Than Zero* (1987) which radically (read conservatively) reimagines Ellis's transgressive narrative through these twin frames, ultimately sacrificing cocaine addict Julian at the altar of Clay's sobriety. Even at the time of this writing, during the summer of 2020, the idea that addiction does not have to be the central narrative enigma to be solved and expunged by the turn of the last page of the novel is fairly uncommon, as my research for the current volume revealed. To unhinge addiction from questions of morality, as Ellis does by treating the subject in such banal terms, and to allow addict characters simply to exist *as addicts* without being censured or fixed by novel's end, is to advance the idea that addiction is a chronic medical condition, and not the ultimate mark of moral failure. While this idea has been acknowledged as medical fact by both the American Medical Association and the American Psychiatric Association since the mid-twentieth century, sadly the disease model of addiction often still is rejected in favor of the morality model and the mere suggestion that addiction is a medical condition remains a transgressive idea.

The novel also forces readers to consider whether they are able to listen to an addict's experience without trying to fix or solve the addiction and without offering (typically unsolicited) advice. Ellis's characters persistently stretch readers' ability to listen, let alone react, compassionately. It's not just that those characters indiscriminately consume all manner of controlled and illicit substances. They also engage in myriad illegal activities that contribute to the exploitation of self and others. Indeed, *Less Than Zero* is not an easy novel to traverse, even in 2020 when, in contrast to 1985, the assaults of transgressive fiction have become, at least for readers with a certain degree of literary competence, rather predictable and even, at times, passé. The content is graphic and assaultive. And it is presented without judgment or commentary, so readers cannot look to the novel for ideological guidance or affirmation.[51] Instead, held in a kind of (self-en)forced captivity, readers must confront addiction head-on without the safety net of the moral always and already that Western culture bequeaths to its citizenship.

---

[51] This point was driven home to me when, in the fall of 2019, I taught a senior-level, undergraduate seminar on the topic of experimental addiction fiction and my students almost unanimously expressed equal parts disgust and outrage at the way in which Ellis so blithely represents violence, trauma and exploitation in his novel. What was so unsettling to students was the lack of ideological guidance that they experienced when reading the novel—a not unsurprising response given how deeply entrenched these students' reading histories are in the tradition of literary realism.

It is important to clarify that *Less Than Zero* stages a very different type of confrontation between subject matter, text and readers than *Leaving Las Vegas*, even though both novels ultimately force readers to look directly at addiction in ways that they may previously have been reluctant, even unable, to do. In the latter novel, the narrative unfolds in the presence of an overarching moralism regarding addiction, but it simultaneously calls that attitude into question with an addict protagonist who insists, "It's not what the story is about." The reading experience of *Leaving Las Vegas*, then, is characterized as a process of unlearning whereby readers' preexisting attitudes toward addiction, particularly those that condemn the addict as weak-willed, are simultaneously acknowledged and undermined. In this way, Ben's journey stands as a powerful counterargument against the moral model of addiction, forcing readers to grapple with the painful and traumatic lived experiences of addiction without easy sentiment or simplistic morality. O'Brien, though, does not abandon his readers within an unfamiliar (and unwelcoming) diegetic world, but instead inserts Sera between readers and the text as a kind of guide to navigating the fictional landscape of *Leaving Las Vegas*.

By contrast, *Less Than Zero* refuses even to acknowledge the kinds of easy sentiment and simplistic morality that historically and traditionally have determined Westerners' responses to addiction. In the spirit of literary minimalism, a movement which includes much transgressive fiction, *Less Than Zero* is characterized by a "consistent abstention from social criticism"[52] and a general unwillingness to "place [its] characters in the midst of ethical crises."[53] Stated differently, Ellis not only confronts readers with an unfamiliar and unwelcoming diegetic world, but also abandons readers within that world without any clear sense of how to navigate and respond to it. A staunch moralism is rendered inappropriate by a text that refuses to condemn the illicit and illegal behaviors represented within its pages. And shame and blame prove ineffective when lobbed at characters who, in sheer boredom, aimlessly wander through their lives without any sense of self-consciousness or self-censure.

What remains is the option to just listen without the compulsion, or the expectation, to fix, solve, judge. *Less Than Zero* demands that readers free fall into the reading experience and the diegetic world, accepting early on that they are going to be faced with behaviors and characters that they may not understand or believe to be acceptable, morally or otherwise. These readers must come to terms with the fact that, if they persist in reading this novel, then they will of necessity have to find their own ways of making sense of the

---

[52] Robert C. Clark, *American Literary Minimalism* (Tuscaloosa: University of Alabama Press, 2014), 149.

[53] Ibid., 138.

characters, their behaviors and even the often-confounding world that Ellis has built.

There is great compassion involved in the act of "just" listening; indeed, as Dr. Hyder Zahed reports, "Listening is an accepting and nonjudgmental invitation for others to be themselves, without any worry about disapproval."[54] To listen is to take heed—to say to someone, "You and your experiences are worthy of my time and attention," which is a statement rarely offered to addicts, at least not unconditionally. Often when an addiction becomes too complicated, or/and when an addict's behavior becomes too unruly, Western culture, with the backing of Twelve Step philosophy, encourages us to stop listening as a gesture of "tough love." *Less Than Zero* suggests that perhaps it is more loving, and most certainly tougher, to exercise the "emotional strength, patience, openness and [...] desire to understand" the addicts' experiences, especially but not exclusively when those experiences are graphic, violent, offensive and morally transgressive.

Compassionate listening originally was conceived by international peacemaker Gene Knudsen Hoffman as a personal practice, a skill set, a process and a healing gift that requires listeners to "seek the truth of the person speaking, seeing through 'masks of hostility and fear to the sacredness of the individual.'"[55] The compassionate listener "seek[s] to humanize the 'other'" by "accept[ing] what others say as their perceptions, and validat[ing] the right to their own perceptions."[56] Within the pages of Ellis's novel, Clay is not to be regarded as an addict, and, in fact, that moniker is used only a single time in *Less Than Zero*, and then only in reference to a tertiary character named Larry who was refused admission to film school "because he's a heroin addict."[57] In fact, from the very opening of Ellis's novel, the narrator insists that "All it comes down to is that I'm a boy coming home for a month and meeting someone whom I haven't seen for four months and people are afraid to merge."[58] There is a kind of self-effacing humility underlying Clay's admission that he is just another "boy coming home" from college. There is also a vulnerability to the observation that "people are afraid to merge," although Clay remains throughout this novel unable to own his inability to connect with and relate to others. And there is trepidation about "meeting someone whom

---

[54] Hyder Zahed, "Compassionate Listening," *HuffPost*, July 11, 2017, https://www.huffpost.com/entry/compassionate-listening_b_10921036 (accessed June 25, 2019).
[55] "About Us," *Compassionate Listening Project*, n.d., https://www.compassionatelistening.org/about-us (accessed June 25, 2019).
[56] Ibid.
[57] Ellis, *Less Than Zero*, 111–12.
[58] Ibid., 9–10.

[he hasn't seen] for four months," although this feeling, too, Clay refuses to directly own. These are the masks that readers are challenged to see through and understand, not as triggers for his addictions, not as symptoms of a problematic childhood and not as harbingers of a horrible fate, but merely as the lenses through which Clay sees and navigates his world.

Some readers, of course, might suggest that the disaffected style of narration employed throughout *Less Than Zero* might pose a significant obstacle to readers' efforts to view Clay as a genuine "human" subject worthy of their compassion. To such readers, Clay, at best, likely stands as a stereotype of white, privileged, narcissistic masculinity, although I would remind such readers that, in the novel, and even more so in the film adaptation, Rip more frequently exhibits the twin behaviors of "sexual conquest and violence" that, as *HuffPost* Contributor Ryan Douglass notes, are constitutive of toxic masculinity.[59] Moreover, Ellis goes to great lengths to establish Rip as an obvious foil for Clay throughout *Less Than Zero*, most noticeably in their vastly different reactions to the tied-up girl. This is, of course, not to suggest that Clay is, or should be regarded as, a benchmark of virtue. His apathy toward morally problematic behaviors most definitely discourages the degree of psychological and emotional intimacy that typically is fostered between first-person narrators and their readers. But placing the reader at a remove from the protagonist does not de facto produce apathy—or, worse, antipathy—and to suggest that such distance always and only precludes compassionate listening advances an incredibly simplistic model of the reading experience generally and the operations of transgressive fiction more specifically.

In fact, I would suggest that Clay elicits compassion from readers precisely because Ellis employs a disaffected narrative voice to forge distance between this character and his readers. Writing about *The Sopranos*, philosopher Murray Smith, in his essay "Just What Is It That Makes Tony Soprano Such an Appealing, Attractive Murderer?," argues that one of the more remarkable aspects of the series' reception is that "though most committed viewers of the show will be repelled by Soprano's dishonesty and violence and the gang's quiescence, they'll continue to find Soprano a fascinating, and even

---

[59] Ryan Douglass, "More Men Should Learn the Difference between Masculinity and Toxic Masculinity," *HuffPost*, August 4, 2017, https://www.huffpost.com/entry/the-difference-between-masculinity-and-toxic-masculinity_b_59842e3ce4b0f2c7d93f54ce (accessed June 6, 2020). For a thought-provoking critique of the phrase "toxic masculinity," see Ronald F. Levant and Shana Pryor, *The Tough Standard: The Hard Truths about Masculinity and Violence* (New York: Oxford University Press, 2020), especially pages 26–28.

appealing, character."[60] Smith goes on to suggest that characters like Tony Soprano, Patty Hewes (*Damages*, 2007–12), Don Draper (*Mad Men*, 2007–15), and Walter White (*Breaking Bad*, 2008–13)[61] simultaneously attract and repulse television viewers because the villainy of such characters is intimately conjoined with their vulnerability.[62] Clay, for example, is both young and sheltered—observations that are intended to contextualize, but not excuse his jejune behaviors, and to provide some further explanation for why readers not only stick with him as a narrator, even when the narrative takes fairly gruesome turns, but also listen to that narrative with compassion. Clay also is the least immoral or Ellis's cast of characters, and, as Smith remarks, readers have an almost "evolutionary" "propensity to detect and ally ourselves with the most moral—and thus the most trustworthy—agents in a given community or situation."[63] To this end, Clay may not verbally object to or halt any of the morally or legally problematic situations that he encounters in *Less Than Zero*, but unlike his peers, Clay at least removes himself from the situations.

Left alone in the diegesis with only this character as our companion, though not guide, readers are forced to accept what Clay says as his perception and to validate Clay's right to that perception, even if Clay's perceptions are not always necessarily accurate and certainly not always palatable. Further, I would venture that the question of reliability does not (or, should not) even arise for readers of *Less Than Zero* if those readers are attentive to the ways in which the text encourages compassionate listening. Instead, readers hopefully will move beyond their habitual moral attitudes about addiction, pushing beyond (or, transgressing) what has long been regarded as "natural" or "instinctual," and removing the fears that so often prohibit meaningful human connections, to discover the humanity and the integrity that lurks within all of us, even those characters/individuals who are cast as most deserving of their suffering and are deemed most morally condemnable.

---

[60] Murray Smith, "Just What Is It That Makes Tony Soprano Such an Appealing, Attractive Murderer?," *Ethics at the Cinema*, ed. Ward E. Jones and Samantha Vice (Oxford: Oxford University Press, 2011), 67–88 (68).

[61] While I do understand that the antihero figure and the protagonist of transgressive fiction are not always synonymous, the two often share important commonalities that impact significantly the politics and poetics of reception. Like the antihero, for instance, Clay often is depicted as unsympathetic and "more or less bad by dominant social and legal norms" (Vaage "Preface"). See Margrethe Bruun Vaage, *The Antihero in American Television* (New York: Routledge, 2016), Kindle.

[62] Smith, "Just What Is It That Makes Tony Soprano Such an Appealing, Attractive Murderer?" 85.

[63] Ibid., 77.

Chapter 5

DISORIENTING: *THE ORANGE EATS CREEPS* (2010)

In her introduction to *Compassion: The Culture and Politics of an Emotion* (2004), titled "Compassion (and Withholding)," Lauren Berlant acknowledges the deep and uncomfortable links among suffering, compassion and aversion, explaining:

> Scenes of vulnerability produce a desire to withhold compassionate attachment, to be irritated by the scene of suffering in some way. Repeatedly, we witness someone's desire to not connect, sympathize, or recognize an obligation to the sufferer; to refuse engagement with the scene or to minimize its effects; to misread it conveniently; to snuff or drown it out with pedantically shaped phrases or carefully designed apartheids; not to rescue or help; to go on blithely without conscience; to feel bad for the sufferers, but only so that they will go away quickly. In this book's archive, the aesthetic and political spectacle of suffering vulnerability seems to bring out something terrible, a drive not to feel compassion or sympathy, an aversion to a moral claim on the spectator to engage, when all the spectator wants to do is to turn away quickly and harshly.[1]

Berlant's words call to mind the many overt and subtle acts of aversion targeted at addicts on a daily basis as a consequence of their perceived suffering and vulnerability. That addiction continues to be regarded as a foul invective within the vernacular, as well as the popular imaginary, despite volumes of scientific research confirming that it is, in fact, a real and documented medical condition speaks to the powerful "desire to not connect, sympathize, or recognize an obligation to the sufferer." Indeed, the systemic manufacturing of

---

[1] Lauren Berlant, "Compassion (and Withholding)," in *Compassion: The Culture and Politics of an Emotion*, ed. Berlant (New York: Routledge, 2004), 1–14 (9–10).

"mythological stereotypes that feature in public stigmatization of addiction"[2] points decidedly to a deeply entrenched desire to "withhold compassionate attachment, to be irritated by the scene of suffering in some way."

Further, the ubiquitous nature of the metaphor of waste, which regards the addict as disposable in myriad ways, provides a potent illustration of the ways in which Western culture systematically minimizes the intrapersonal, interpersonal and social effects of addiction. This same metaphor, which I write about at length in *Wasted: Performing Addiction in America* (2015), operates as both a "pedantically shaped" discourse designed to condescend to and shame addicts, as well as a "carefully designed [apartheid]" that discursively and tangibly segregates the addict from normal (read sober, moral) culture. In a similar way, Twelve-Step philosophy implicitly preaches a rhetoric of aversion, even as it actively promotes itself as a highly effective means of helping addicts "achieve and maintain abstinence from substances of abuse";[3] in effect, when Twelve-Step programs insist that addicts take responsibility for their actions, even as scientific researchers repeatedly have confirmed that addiction impairs, if not erodes, an individual's power of choice, those programs and their most vocal proponents affirm their own willingness "to go on blithely without conscience" in their refusal to offer actual help to someone who is deeply enmeshed in, and enslaved by, the spectacle of suffering vulnerability. And the practice of "tough love," which often manifests among "long-suffering" family members and experience-hardened rehab counselors at precisely the moment when an addict relapses and is most vulnerable, offers a sobering example of what Berlant describes as "[the] drive not to feel compassion or sympathy, an aversion to a moral claim on the spectator to engage, when all the spectator wants to do is to turn away quickly and harshly." More subtly, this drive manifests itself in the sidelong, "knowing" glances shared between bartenders, friends, acquaintances or even strangers when a suspected addict simply walks into a pub and orders a cocktail.

Storytelling, broadly defined, and the realist novel more specifically have long charted a history that runs counter to the methodical aversion to suffering witnessed in Western culture more widely. Writing about nineteenth-century realist fiction, Rae Greiner notes that at the heart of realism is a sustained effort to "pull [readers] more closely into characters so that we can see

---

[2] Steve Matthews, "Self-Stigma and Addiction," in *The Stigma of Addiction: An Essential Guide*, ed. Jonathan D. Avery and Joseph J. Avery (Basingstoke, UK: Springer, 2019), 5–32 (13).

[3] Scot Thomas, MD, "12 Step Drug Rehab and Alcohol Treatment Programs," *American Addiction Centers*, June 11, 2019, https://americanaddictioncenters.org/rehab-guide/12-step (July 24, 2019).

ourselves reflected in them and thus better understand what makes them tick." Greiner goes on to explain, "Often this intimacy is presented loosely as a matter of sympathetic identification, the assumption being that we are predisposed to sympathize with those we perceive as most like ourselves."[4] Even realistic fiction about addiction, which, as I explain in the Introduction to this volume, tends to lean narratively toward rehabilitation or death, attempts to build connections between readers and characters through the addict's graphic suffering and the pathos that that character labors under post-addiction, either in rehab or in the grave.

Experimental fiction, by contrast, typically is characterized by a highly clinical portrayal of characters who are suffering and vulnerable, encouraging readers "to look, to judge, to assume—in a manner that is anything but sympathetic."[5] At times, as Ellen E. Berry notes in *Women's Experimental Writing: Negative Aesthetics and Feminist Critique* (2016), experimental fiction manufactures an "extreme intimacy" between readers and characters due to the use of "first-person point of view combined with the intimate confessional nature of the narrator's descriptions"; Berry goes on to suggest that this type of writing "invite[s], even demand[s], our sympathy—if not always our identification or approval."[6] More generally, and regardless of what point of view is employed, experimental fiction, as R. M. Berry explains in *The Routledge Companion to Experimental Literature* (2012), tends not to "[progress] toward the identification of represented and representing selves," but toward "displacement of both self and representation."[7] What Entin, Berry and Berry collectively describe is the lack of identification between readers and characters that typifies experimental fiction. Readers may be encouraged to sympathize with the character—that is, simply to understand and care about the character's trials and travails—but typically readers are actively discouraged from seeing themselves in the fictional character and, to rework a statement by Janice A. Radway, they are not permitted to live the protagonist's relationship to the other characters, to her/his/their situation or to the diegetic world without distraction.[8]

---

[4] Rae Greiner, *Sympathetic Realism in Nineteenth-Century British Fiction* (Baltimore, MD: Johns Hopkins University Press, 2012), 40.
[5] Joseph B. Entin, *Sensational Modernism: Experimental Fiction and Photography in Thirties America* (Chapel Hill: University of North Carolina Press, 2007), 95.
[6] Ellen E. Berry, *Women's Experimental Writing: Negative Aesthetics and Feminist Critique* (London: Bloomsbury Academic, 2016), 107.
[7] R. M. Berry, "Metafiction," in *The Routledge Companion to Experimental Literature*, ed. Joe Bray, Alison Gibbons and Brian McHale (London: Routledge, 2012), 128–40 (136).
[8] Janice A. Radway, *Reading the Romance: Women, Patriarchy, and Popular Literature* (Chapel Hill: University of North Carolina Press, 1984).

At first blush, Grace Krilanovich's *The Orange Eats Creeps* appears to be precisely the type of novel that discourages identification between readers and characters, or, for that matter, readers and diegetic world. The action takes place in the Pacific Northwest of the early 1990s and follows a nomadic band of "Slutty Teenage Hobo Vampire Junkies"[9] who spend much of the novel strung out on methamphetamine. The unnamed I-narrator is a runaway who spent her adolescence in the foster care system, enduring myriad indignities and acts of violence as a result, and now she searches for her missing foster sister in the box cars and Safeways that dot the suburban landscape while randomly having sex with many of the other teen hobos that she meets along her journey. Even though the action of the novel is narrated by a first-person narrator, that character persistently resists readers' attempts to identify with and know her. Neither likeable nor unsympathetic, the unnamed narrator of *The Orange Eats Creeps* addresses Krilanovich's readers from a wasteland, even vacuum, that is almost entirely inaccessible to them.

At the same time, the narrative is peppered with jumps and gaps in temporality—unexplained fast forwards, abrupt rewinds and even simple quantum leaps that render the reading process at best confusing and the diegetic world virtually impenetrable. The plot runs the gamut between the banal and the nonsensical, but there is little throughline to connect one episodic scene to the next. With little sense of temporality or narrative progression to anchor the readers in the diegesis, it is difficult for those readers to gain a foothold in Krilanovich's fictional world, or to experience, without distraction, the events of the novel *as* any particular character, even the I-narrator; indeed, readers typically feel as much a nomad as the hobo, meth-head vampires who populate the suburban sameness of Krilanovich's Pacific Northwest: without guidance, without purpose and without hope. As a result, the reading experience is not immersive, not entertaining, not educational, but merely disorienting.

In this chapter, I argue that the frustration that readers experience when navigating the disorienting landscape of *The Orange Eats Creeps* mirrors the frustrations of an addict living in a world in which addiction is not simply shrouded in ignorance, but is actively misunderstood and systematically misrepresented. By not allowing readers to immerse themselves in the fictional world, but instead challenging them to remain at a critical remove from the characters and the story, *The Orange Eats Creeps* first and foremost encourages readers to engage with the text on at once an intellectual and an emotional level. Readers are forced to imagine alternative realities and ways of seeing— to consider how it feels and what it means to navigate such an unwelcoming

---

[9] Grace Krilanovich, *The Orange Eats Creeps* (Columbus, OH: Two Dollar Radio, 2010), 7.

world from such an isolated and ultimately stigmatized location. In this way, reading Krilanovich's novel constitutes an exercise in what Christopher P. Vogt, in *Patience, Compassion, Hope, and the Christian Art of Dying Well* (2004), terms "expressive compassion," meaning "the practice of restoring the voice of" those who have systematically been stripped of the privilege of self-expression and self-definition.[10]

The bulk of the frustration associated with reading *The Orange Eats Creeps* derives from the fact that Krilanovich's novel is a work of postmodern, experimental fiction, a category of literature that some critics have likened to "learning a foreign language." In "Experimental Fiction," authors from William Patterson University explain: "Experimental fiction *is* difficult—challenging in the way that foreign language learning is challenging, forcing us to come to an understanding of false cognates, to reimagine the feminine and the masculine, to expand our vocabulary and to realize that the world can be imagined in ways other than those by which we are accustomed to imagining it."[11] The analogy drawn between learning a foreign language and reading experimental fiction is an apt one given that both constitute acts of meaning-making premised precisely on the necessity of undermining the many taken-for-granteds that typically undergird representation. Learning a foreign language upends many of our shared understandings of how meaning is made, especially if the language being learned derives from a different part of the language tree than the learner's native language.

Most significant in this description is the final statement in which the authors contend that experimental fiction can pose challenges both to dominant culture and to the ideological status quo by revealing to readers unfamiliar—sometimes entirely unexpected—ways of seeing and inhabiting the world. Authors like Krilanovich initially offer readers what appears to be a conventional novel with engaging cover art, several hundred pages of printed material and so forth. But within its pages a work like *The Orange Eats Creeps* poses many challenges to readers. It "breaks rules and invents new ones,"[12] thereby reminding readers that the legal, moral and literary conventions that they regularly take for granted as ideologically neutral are not *natural*, but have, in fact, become *naturalized* through many centuries of repetition and often coercion. Such fiction also "undermines the conceptual categories by which we understand and navigate the world,"[13] throwing our sense of self-in-world

---

[10] Christopher P. Vogt, *Patience, Compassion, Hope, and the Christian Art of Dying Well* (Lanham, MD: Rowman & Littlefield, 2004).
[11] "Experimental Fiction," *Map Literary*, William Patterson University, 2017, http://www.mapliterary.org/on-experimental-fiction.html (accessed July 15, 2019).
[12] Ibid.
[13] Ibid.

into disarray, but also and simultaneously opening up myriad new and previously unimagined—perhaps unimaginable—possibilities for living in and seeing the world. Finally, such fiction "rejects the normal rhetoric of how we describe things,"[14] forcing readers to rethink not only the verbiage that is used to describe their lived experiences, but also the very representational apparatuses by which meaning is produced, including but not limited to the roles and expectations of themselves as readers.

Because the label *experimental* exists as a kind of catch-all for myriad literary movements, narrative tropes and formal techniques, it is important to establish from the onset of this chapter precisely how Krilanovich, in *The Orange Eats Creeps*, achieves the effects discussed briefly above, thereby facilitating a disorienting diegetic world and reading experience. There are two related techniques of disorientation that I want to highlight in the discussion that follows, including: (1) The language often does not mirror the vernacular, either in meaning or in function, but rather is a kind of obtuse, hauntingly poetic *ostranenie*, or "deformation of ordinary language," a technique that, as Julie Armstrong explains, "seeks to make the habitual unfamiliar, thereby making [the] reader see things differently and anew."[15] In so doing, the novel "challenges the very idea of any meaning being fixed and stable through the use of textual gaps,"[16] violently severing the cognitive and semantic links long assumed between signs and signifiers as a means of calling into question the constructedness of meaning and the polemics of the meaning-making process and (2) the narrative events are, at best, episodic and, at worst, entirely random, and there is no overarching sense of continuity or causality driving the action; instead, Krilanovich's fiction is, like postmodern experimental fiction more broadly, "fragmented, dislocated, abstract and sometimes it is simply a kaleidoscope of impressions."[17] As a result, the reading experience is defined not simply as a process of mining, or explicating, the knowable text for "oppositions and conflicts" that an ideal reader can "resolve into harmonious balance,"[18] but rather as a journey into the unknown at the start of which unpredictability, inconclusiveness and perplexity must be accepted as distinctly possible outcomes.

---

[14] Ibid.
[15] Julie Armstrong, *Experimental Fiction: An Introduction for Readers and Writers* (London: Bloomsbury Academic, 2014), 143.
[16] Ibid., 102.
[17] Ibid., 103.
[18] David H. Richter, "Formalism," *The Critical Tradition: Classic Texts and Contemporary Trends*, ed. Richter (New York: St. Martin's Press, 1989), 721–37 (729).

Deformation of Language

Throughout *The Orange Eats Creeps*, Krilanovich persistently makes the familiar strange by engaging in myriad acts of language deformation. Relatively early in the novel, for instance, the first-person narrator lapses into what she terms a "telepathy trance" after the "day's dosage" (presumably of methamphetamine) causes her to experience "a depressed shittiness." While in the throes of this trance, Krilanovich's narrator, who claims to possess powers of Extra Sensory Perception that render her especially attuned to acts of violence previously perpetuated in a given location, abruptly breaks from an increasingly vivid and vividly metaphoric stream of consciousness to offer up a catalogue of three-word items:

>   Everything satisfies precisely.
>   Engorge sticky pricks.
> Enrage secret processes.
>   Endure sexy pretense.
>   Emerge surrounded parasitically.
>   Energy sufficiently pulverized.
>   Erection scoff prevention.
>   Endorphin scream passage.
>   Ecstatic speed patriarch.
>   Embers slash plastic.
>   Embalm severe parents.
>   Epidemic seduction procedure.
>   Escape seemed possible.
>   Enormous secretion property.
>   Emergency sedative party.
>   Empire syndrome purification.
>   End species preservation.[19]

Most of the trios included in the passage above make logical sense with respect to word order when read within the context of standard US English. In fact, the bulk of the trios follow arguably the most basic of all sentence structures in the language: namely, Subject/Predicate + Action Verb + Direct Object. Despite their pared-down structures, however, many of these trios are confounding where actual meaning is concerned.

Take, for instance, "Embalm severe parents." As a process used to preserve human or animal remains in an attempt to forestall decomposition, embalming

---

[19] Krilanovich, *The Orange Eats Creeps*, 18.

presupposes that death already has occurred prior to an enactment of that process. But why, readers must question, would the implied "you" who functions as the subject of the sentence be encouraged to embalm parents who are "severe" (meaning strict? Harsh? Intense?) when that modifier implies that the parents are living, not dead? Is this sentence a call to murder issued from a young woman who has been psychologically and physically abused during her extended tenure in the foster care system, as Krilanovich's narrator repeatedly admits that she has? Is the term "embalm" used more metaphorically than literally, rendering this statement a call to safeguard protective parental figures in a world where parental neglect forces vulnerable teenagers into a dangerous and violent environment well before they are ready or able to care for themselves?

Or is the statement, indeed perhaps the entire list of trios, merely a giant middle finger to the US literati from an upstart M.F.A. who hails from a prestigious creative writing program (i.e., CalArts) and who has the backing of a well-respected, male, US author (i.e., Steve Erickson)? In interviews regarding *The Orange Eats Creeps*, Krilanovich has described her writing process for her debut novel in a manner that sounds more like a graduate student's stunt for producing a class assignment than a professional writer's approach to her chosen craft. In an online interview with her editor at Two Dollar Radio, for instance, Krilanovich admits that she "made a deck of cards to help in the writing of the novel—three 'suits' for Settings, Characters and Afflictions." She goes on in that same interview to explain that when she experienced writer's block, or sometimes just on a whim, she "would deal a 'hand' and write the scene that emerged from the juxtaposition of the three—something like 'cat-rat,' '7-Eleven,' 'sleep paralysis,' for instance."[20] In essence, what Krilanovich describes here is the construction of an almost Derridean system of signification in which "heterogeneous signifieds" are transcribed "within a system of arbitrary and common signifiers,"[21] except that the arbitrariness that Derrida, and Saussure before him, describes occurs within the relatively closed system of a living language.[22]

By contrast, Krilanovich takes a preexisting linguistic system, one admittedly premised on the arbitrariness of meaning-making, and completely

---

[20] "Grace Krilanovich: Q + A with the Editor," *Two Dollar Radio*, Blogspot, August 13, 2010, http://twodollarradio.blogspot.com/2010/08/grace-krilanovich-qa-with-editor.html (accessed July 16, 2019).

[21] Jacques Derrida, *Of Grammatology*, trans. Gayatri Chakravorty Spivak, 1974 (Baltimore, MD: Johns Hopkins University Press, 1997), Reprint.

[22] It is worthwhile here to at least mention the similarities between Krilanovich's card technique and the cut-up method, which was developed in Paris in the late 1950s by William Burroughs and Brion Gysin. This experimental technique, as A. D. Hitchin and Joe Ambrose explain in their coedited book *CUT UP!: An Anthology Inspired by the Cut-Up*

decimates it, at times juxtaposing often radically disparate items with little more reason than that supplied by a random draw of an even more randomly created deck of cards. What, for example, is an "Endorphin scream passage"? or "Erection scoff prevention"? Given how Krilanovich "crafted" much of the narrative, it should not come as much of a surprise that a similar type of ambiguity is at work within the plot of the novel. Is the Warlock that the unnamed narrator battles near the end of *The Orange Eats Creeps*,[23] for example, a true sorcerer, a metaphor (perhaps signifying the narrator's methamphetamine addiction), a figment of the narrator's waking imagination, a dream, or merely a tired character trope drawn from Krilanovich's deck of cards? Is the missing foster sister, Kim, real or imaginary? Dead or alive? A separate entity or a manifestation of the narrator's lost innocence? And how does vampirism really work in this novel? Are the hobo junkies who comprise the central cast of characters mere descendants of Vlad Țepeș? Does their "affliction"—if, indeed, it is regarded as an affliction—serve as a metaphor for addiction? Or, in 2010, when *The Orange Eats Creeps* originally was published, was vampirism merely the flavor of the month among readers of popular fiction, inserted into and drawn at random from Krilanovich's deck thanks to the overwhelming success of Stephenie Meyer's *Twilight* tetralogy, which still enjoyed enormous popularity in that historical moment?

While the novel raises these and myriad other questions both about plot points and, in a more meta fashion, about the ways in which information is constructed and presented in order to produce meaning, ultimately Krilanovich does not supply (m)any answers and, in fact, I would argue that the text actively undermines readers' attempts to decipher it. At times this undermining occurs due to the rapid pace and the fragmented nature of the narrative. In *The Orange Eats Creeps*, the narrative is peppered with abrupt jumps in time, place and situation, resisting readers' attempts to gain any sort of conventional foothold in the diegetic world and forcing readers either to discover—perhaps even invent—new points of entry into the diegesis or to acquiesce to their perpetual outsiderhood, at least during the act of reading. Furthermore, tropes and motifs regularly are presented

---

Method of William S. Burroughs & Brion Gysin (2014), "involved taking a piece of text (be it a newspaper cutting or any other segment of previously completed writing) and cutting it into pieces—then rearranging those pieces to create a new text or work of art" (5). While an exploration of the formal and thematic commonalities between Burroughs and Krilanovich falls outside of the scope of the current project, readers can learn more about the cut-up method in Joan Hawkins and Alex Wermer-Colan's comprehensive edited collection *William S. Burroughs: Cutting Up the Century* (Bloomington: Indiana University Press, 2019).

[23] Krilanovich, *The Orange Eats Creeps*, 155ff.

in rapid succession such that, before readers can even partially grasp one idea, several others, usually without any logical relationship to the former idea, are brought up.

As an example, I want to return briefly to the list of trios discussed above. Immediately following this stream of consciousness, Krilanovich reverts to fairly conventional prose and presents a scene that takes place in a generic grocery store. The initial lines of that scene read: "Knowles, Seth, and Josh were in among the potatoes and onions, in the produce section at Safeway, drinking ice beer. Hardly anybody was shopping cuz it was quarter to four a.m."[24] As with much of *The Orange Eats Creeps*, here Krilanovich makes no effort to locate the action in time and simply thrusts her readers in medias res into the narrator's first encounter with Murph, another hobo-junkie-cum-vampire. The scene that introduces Murph neither makes mention of the narrator's ESP nor draws any connection (whether explicit or implicit) to any of the concepts catalogued in the trios. Instead, the scene not only introduces a new character, one who will figure prominently throughout the remainder of the novel, but also raises new concerns, including the sexual exploitation and trafficking of homeless teens.[25]

The short scenes, coupled with abrupt shifts in subject matter, the absence of temporal and sometimes spatial cues and lengthy stream-of-consciousness paragraphs that can span anywhere between four and ten pages[26] have several significant effects on the narrative and the reading experience. In the first place, these techniques create a cognitive chasm between readers and the diegetic world, marking the reading experience as non-immersive and forcing readers simultaneously to piece together the events of the narrative (as much as is possible) and to derive from those assembled pieces some sort of thematic takeaway. However, *The Orange Eats Creeps* undermines readers' efforts to achieve these goals by repeatedly rejecting the very organizing principles and narrative strategies that would produce textual coherence, thereby lending discernible meaning to the text. As a result, readers are left to feel abandoned "in a world where meaning seems lost, or at the least ambiguous," which is a common experience within the category of experimental fiction.[27]

---

[24] Ibid., 19.

[25] Ibid., 19–20.

[26] As an example, see the section that follows the Safeway scene referenced above, which runs pp. 20–23 and is presented as a single paragraph. Many such scenes occur throughout *The Orange Eats Creeps*, including but not limited to: 64–70; 80–86; 102–5; and 107–10.

[27] Armstrong, *Experimental Fiction*, 165.

Inconsistency of Tropes

Meaning also is confounded by the fact that, while there are multiple tropes that are repeated ad infinitum throughout *The Orange Eats Creeps*, those tropes do not retain the same meanings each time they appear within the narrative. Take, for example, "The Highway That Eats People." The open highway functions as a staple metaphor for individualism, liberty and the counterculture in US fiction, with Jack Kerouac's *On the Road* (1955) standing as an exemplar of this trend. The road as metaphor also appears with some frequency in the addiction novel, most notably in Joan Didion's *Play It as It Lays* (1970),[28] Hunter S. Thompson's *Fear and Loathing in Las Vegas* (1971)[29] and Lynda Barry's *Cruddy: An Illustrated Novel* (1999).[30] For Didion's protagonist, Maria, the road represents a site for intense self-scrutiny and introspection as she confronts her waning acting career, strained familial relationships, and alcoholism. On the other hand, Thompson's novel not only equates the road with personal freedom and individualism, but also uses the protagonist's destination (i.e., Las Vegas) as a means of critiquing unfettered indulgence and consumption, which Thompson, in this novel, sees as an inherent component of mid-century US national identity. And Barry's *Cruddy* metaphorically likens the road trip that 11-year-old Roberta Rohbeson takes with her father in 1966 to that character's coming of age as a young woman who is forced too early to deal with a parent's alcoholism and violence.

In works like *Play It as It Lays*, *Fear and Loathing in Las Vegas* and *Cruddy*, the road metaphor is meticulously crafted and maintained throughout the pages of the novel, its meaning consistent with each iteration and its subject matter used in service of the novel's central thematic conceits; by contrast, Krilanovich's metaphoric road (aka "The Highway That Eats People") is kaleidoscopic in meaning, its connotations slippery, if not downright elusive, from one mention to the next. The unnamed narrator's first encounter with The Highway That Eats People is described as follows:

> We've found our way to The Highway That Eats People. Seven summers ago it ate four wasted teens who burned in a Lincoln when it wrapped around a tree while, not far away, Death sat knitting funerary lace by light of a cookstove. A crash is a rite of passage in this neighborhood, like striking the last match. They stuff themselves into their parents' big sensible cars and go for a drive. The highway is hungry. They have to

---

[28] Joan Didion, *Play It as It Lays*, 1970 (New York: Farrar, Straus, and Giroux, 2005).
[29] Hunter S. Thompson, *Fear and Loathing in Las Vegas: A Savage Journey to the Heart of the American Dream*, 1971 (New York: Vintage Books, 1971).
[30] Lynda Barry, *Cruddy: An Illustrated Novel* (New York: Scribner Paperback Fiction, 1999).

feed it. Of the four who died that night, three were jocks so it was a big deal in town. No one knows why the one non-jock was in the car but he burned anyway. Other than that there was once a girl who jumped off a cliff into the ocean and a couple of guys who took too much heroin, but usually when it happened it was all about the cars in the hills; it was a matter of the grieving teens feeding the highway with their bodies in the middle of the night.[31]

Although relatively brief, this passage is riddled with inconsistency and layered with complexity—a model for how metaphor is more broadly applied throughout *The Orange Eats Creeps*. From the onset, The Highway That Eats People is cast as dangerous, a fairly common iteration of the road metaphor that figures prominently in works as diverse as Stephen King's *Misery* (1987), E. R. Frank's *Wrecked* (2005), Richard Powers's *The Echo Maker* (2006) and Clare Mackintosh's *I Let You Go* (2011). Here, though, the road is not simply dangerous, but predatory, seeking out vulnerable teens in the dead of night to satiate its seemingly insatiable hunger while Death, cast as a kind of hobo figure, looms large over the action with knowing certainty regarding its outcome.

However, Krilanovich divests her highway of some of its predatory nature through personification. To view the highway as predatory is, in some ways, to implicitly regard it as gluttonous, as driven by the desire for excess, the desire to amass a surfeit of grieving teen bodies. At the same time, to characterize the highway as hungry, and to cast the fatal accidents that occur on that highway as a type of sustenance, is to paint Death as simply a condition that feeds and satiates an instinctual need, rather than a self-serving desire. In effect, Krilanovich crafts a mixed metaphor here and then challenges readers to hold two, three or even more competing ideas in their heads simultaneously without also offering them the possibility of achieving textual unity, coherence and reconciliation. How, readers are compelled to wonder, can a fatal car crash be a rite of passage when that phrase implies that the event both marks a significant milestone, and also fails to usher in the next phase of the lifecycle? And is the road really dangerous if, in fact, the teens willingly "[feed] the highway with their bodies in the middle of the night"?

Even more relevant to the topical focus of this volume, Krilanovich's Highway That Eats People challenges readers to consider: How can the Highway be both active and passive, both a predator that consumes its unwitting victims with relish and simply a hungry entity that willingly is fed by its self-sacrificial victims? For far too long, and at least since the Age of

---

[31] Krilanovich, *The Orange Eats Creeps*, 72–73.

Enlightenment when binary logic became vogue, Westerners have grossly oversimplified addiction. Seeing addicts either as compulsive hedons mindlessly enslaved to their weak wills or as pathetic victims of a medical condition that we dare not utter above a whisper, many Westerners still struggle to comprehend—let alone accept—that addicts can be, and, indeed, are at once active and passive in their addictions.

Perhaps Krilanovich's highway represents merely an acknowledgement and a violent undermining of the coercive pull of binary logic, although even this seemingly disruptive concept is little more than an attempt to arbitrarily impose coherence on a text that actively resists its own unification. If the highway is a metaphor for addiction—and unsurprisingly there are pieces of textual evidence that both support and undermine this interpretation—then perhaps *The Orange Eats Creeps* is attempting to draw readers' attention to the complicated interplay among agency, accountability and addiction, a relationship that is overlooked far too often in the many popular narratives that simplistically equate addiction with a lack of willpower or moral fiber.

Then again, perhaps the highway merely is a comment on the harmful effects of urbanization and industrialization on the US family.

Or perhaps it reflects the dangerous and often violent rites of passage that mark young women's sexual maturation in the twenty-first-century United States.

Or perhaps the hungry, hungry highway is just another trope drawn from Krilanovich's ridiculous deck of cards, without any significance or meaning beyond its ability to relentlessly confound the reader.

Disorientation of Readers

Finally, given the subject matter of the novel, it must be acknowledged that perhaps language use in *The Orange Eats Creeps* is not supposed to make sense—or, rather, in not making sense, the language of the novel actually makes perfect sense. After all, the main characters are addicted to methamphetamine, a substance that can so dramatically impair a user's thoughts and emotions that the user's connection with external reality is severed, in part or in toto. Indeed, in *Methamphetamine Addiction: From Basic Science to Treatment* (2009), Doris Payer and Edythe D. London report that methamphetamine use "can induce [...] psychosis, a state of paranoia, delusion, hallucination, and aggressiveness to resemble paranoid schizophrenia."[32]

---

[32] Doris Payer and Edythe D. London, "Methamphetamine and the Brain: Findings from Brain Imagining Studies," in *Methamphetamine Addiction: From Basic Science to Treatment*, ed. John M. Roll, Richard A. Rawson, Walter Ling and Steven Shoptaw (New York: Guilford Press, 2009), 61–91 (64).

This point is underscored on multiple occasions in *Methland: The Death and Life of an American Small Town* (2010), but perhaps most vividly with the example of Roland Jarvis that opens Chapter 2:

> On a cold winter night in 2001, Roland Jarvis looked out the window of his mother's house and saw that the Oelwein police had hung live human heads in the trees of the yard. Jarvis knew that police did this when they meant to spy on people suspected of being meth cooks. The heads were informants, placed like demonic ornaments to look in the windows and through the walls. As Jarvis studied them, they mumbled and squinted hard to see what was inside the house. Then the heads, satisfied that Jarvis was in fact cooking meth in the basement, conveyed the message to a black helicopter hovering over the house.[33]

In this passage, delusions (i.e., "fixed false beliefs") and hallucinations (i.e., "perceptions occurring in the absence of corresponding external or somatic stimuli")[34] co-occur, indicating a heightened state of impaired reality. Paranoia of being followed and surveilled manifest in the certainty that the trees outside of his mother's home are draped with live human heads, which is not simply a false belief, but an impossibility. The helicopter, too, is entirely a figment of Jarvis's imagination with no foundation in external reality. That these beliefs were fixed is underscored by Jarvis's subsequent dangerous actions, which included "pour[ing] down the flood drain in the floor of his mother's basement the chemicals he had stored there: anhydrous ammonia, Coleman lantern fluid, denatured alcohol, and kerosene."[35] As a long-time user and cooker of methamphetamine, Jarvis had been in and out of prison on drug-related charges for over a decade and attempted to dispose of any evidence of his wrongdoing to avoid another prison sentence—a direct effect of his firm belief that law enforcement officers were stationed just outside of his door, waiting for a signal from the live heads to force entry and arrest him.

While Reding's book provides readers with an investigative journalist's insightful exploration of the social impacts of the methamphetamine crisis on citizens of a small US town, his observations regarding methamphetamine addiction are always and only recorded at a remove from the addict. Stated

---

[33] Nick Reding, *Methland: The Death and Life of an American Small Town* (New York: Bloomsbury, 2010), 40.

[34] David B. Arciniegas, "Psychosis," *Continuum* 21, no. 3 (2015): 715–36, https://www.ncbi.nlm.nih.gov/pmc/articles/PMC4455840/#idm140046521373520title (accessed July 22, 2019).

[35] Reding, *Methland*, 41.

differently, Reding's *Methland* is a classic example of the telling model of storytelling. Positioned outside of the addict as a third-party observer, and removed from the recounted incidents by both geography and temporality, Reding merely catalogues those actions which are observable to the human eye and then simply names the emotions that motivate such actions. What Reding does not do—indeed, what Reding cannot do, at least within the traditional generic parameters of nonfiction—is provide readers any sense of what it feels like to experience the kinds of delusions, hallucinations and thought disorders that are common among methamphetamine addicts.

Krilanovich's novel, by contrast, can be seen as immersive, at least with respect to its representation of methamphetamine addiction if not, as I will discuss below, with respect to the reading process as a whole. The nonsensical plotting coupled with the evocative, if disorienting, stream-of-consciousness, invite readers into the standpoint of a character that is deep in the throes of methamphetamine-induced psychosis.

> I ran away, but you hunted for me, following me like the shadow on the glass.
>
> Whispers in the hissing rain. It needs to rain to feed what has sprung up in the wake of this generosity. Greedy, greedy forest. No end in sight, just the hissing and the moist and full cracking of its boughs breaking. They stretched their arms out so fully and too so much that they lay down and died. No—here they die standing. Their arms fell off one by one. No end in sight. Their bark curls at the edges and falls; they rot while they grow. What a sight what a sound. Their boughs hiss in the wind. They break so easily. They get soaked, wither and die. They get heavy with rain, swollen with our love, wither and die. The sound of falling boughs echoes strategically through these woods, only we are here to know it, these leaves and I, hissing leaves feeding on hissing rain [...] There is no end, only endless endings surrounding us all. Silent days, deafening nights. Hissing nights.[36]

This passage begins with one of the most common neurological manifestations of chronic methamphetamine use: that is, a delusion of persecution, whereby the I-narrator admits to feeling hunted and followed by an unidentified addressee that is simply called "you." The lack of specificity with respect to the addressee's identity, coupled with the haunting simile used to compare the "you" figure to a "shadow on the glass," reads as incredibly foreboding—an

---

[36] Krilanovich, *The Orange Eats Creeps*, 112–13.

ominous, but unnamed (perhaps unnamable) threat that looms large over the passage. This mood is reinforced throughout the passage by the repeated references to "hissing," which are, at minimum, an indication of auditory sensitivity and, at maximum, an example of auditory hallucinations, which are another common neurological manifestation of chronic methamphetamine use. Of equal interest here is the way in which the forest literally comes alive for the I-narrator—the dying of the trees, the breaking of their arms, not a simple matter of personification used to paint a more vivid picture in readers' minds, but a fixed belief that has no basis in external or somatic stimuli.

The final lines of this passage perhaps allude to the cyclic nature of an addiction—the constant seeking out of the next "fix" to the point that addiction consumes the addict's every waking moment. In *Candy*, Luke Davies describes this cycle of addiction as follows: "Only when we had virtually unlimited dope did we finally get an idea of what chasing your tail means [...] I stood back from my life and saw with horror that I'd just repeated the same day three thousand times."[37] Whether seen as "chasing your tail" or as an "endless ending," addiction constitutes a disabling process that ultimately mires the addict in the stasis of repetition and renders movement, progress and growth impossible. Perhaps this is precisely why, as Krilanovich admits in an interview with Joshua Chaplinsky, the author "wanted to keep using the same repetitive type of scenes, like déjà vu, being caught in this vortex."[38] At the very least, what Krilanovich's writing achieves is an approximation of the addict's lived experiences from within that individual's vantage point, as much as is possible. In so doing, Krilanovich crafts a novel that is perplexing. That is alienating. That is disorienting. And, at least at first, that is almost entirely foreign and virtually incomprehensible.

The initial relationship that Krilanovich cultivates between her text and her readers is not unlike the experiences that most of us already have—or, are encouraged to have—with addicts. For over two centuries, Western culture has driven a moral wedge between the sober population and addicts, stigmatizing the latter as a group of narcissistic hedons whose values (or, lack thereof) run counter to everything that the former regards as valuable, including but not limited to self-control, moderation (in all forms) and social order. In this regard, "morality" as it is socially manufactured around the stigma of addiction serves as a powerful indoctrination and coercion tool in the service of sober culture. At the same time, Western culture has fostered within addicts a strong sense of self-hatred and shame built squarely on the notion that addiction

---

[37] Luke Davies, *Candy: A Novel of Love and Addiction* (New York: Ballantine Books, 1998), 202.
[38] Joshua Chaplinsky, "Giving Birth to Creeps," *Chuck Palahniuk*, June 21, 2011, https://chuckpalahniuk.net/interviews/grace-krilanovich (accessed July 22, 2019).

is a byproduct of weak will and loose morality. The sense of Otherness that shrouds the experiences of Western addicts is similar to the sense of disorientation that readers experience when first encountering Krilanovich's band of nomadic, hobo vampire junkies, who operate within a world that is almost entirely foreign to readers.

Awakening of Compassion

While *The Orange Eats Creeps* initially presents readers with an experience marked by agitation, confusion and disorientation, as readers wend their way through the muck of Krilanovich's prose, they may come no closer to a larger takeaway for the novel, but they do begin to recognize and perhaps even make sense of some of the invisible architecture of the novel. In this way, reading *The Orange Eats Creeps* really is similar (albeit not identical) to learning a foreign language. Within this reading experience, phonology remains consistent from the reader's mother tongue, but how those sounds are organized in sentence form and how words are used to represent ideas and objects might differ, sometimes quite radically. Even the very title of the novel underscores this idea; *The Orange Eats Creeps* juxtaposes four common (at least in US English) words, but in so doing, creates a virtually incomprehensible sentence, even with the aid of personification which might imbue the moon (the most likely identity of the eponymous "orange"?) with the powers of mastication and digestion. Within the confounding reading experience that Krilanovich creates, readers cannot simply transfer knowledge between complex linguistic systems, as is typical when learning a new language, but rather they must completely reorient themselves to what constitutes a language system (here, the novel) and how meaning is produced within that language system. In other words, reading *The Orange Eats Creeps* principally involves the active creation of new cognitive frameworks.

For instance, unconventional language use, over time and with repetition, becomes not the norm, but a kind of convention in its own right, understandable within the context of its own language system, although not within the dominant language system. In this way, *The Orange Eats Creeps* does not fail to acknowledge "the mythological stereotypes that feature in public stigmatization of addiction,"[39] but rather it attempts to immerse readers into a diegetic world in which addict characters are empowered to self-author, and, as a result, those stereotypes and stigmas do not possess the same weight and power as they do in the extra-diegetic world, which, for many Western readers, would be a highly disorienting concept in its own right. Bearing witness to a

---

[39] Matthews, "Self-Stigma and Addiction," 13.

cast of addict characters that is not simply entrapped within a preexisting and toxic representational system, but that is invested with the agency to build its own representational apparatus, one in which addicts are the subjects, rather than the objects, of meaning-making, can also be incredibly empowering for addict-readers, who are used to hearing ourselves talked about in a language that does not include us and that most certainly does not reflect our lived experiences.

Readers of *The Orange Eats Creeps* also must reorient themselves to the concept of narrativity. Repeated motifs, tropes and scenes undermine the central role that a linear plot plays in literary realism, rendering "the way the story [is] told [...] as important as the story itself."[40] This emphasis on metafiction and self-reflexivity, of course, is a central concern of much experimental fiction, as illustrated in works like Julio Cortázar's *Hopscotch* (1963), John Barth's *Lost in the Funhouse* (1968) and Italo Calvino's *If on a Winter's Night a Traveler* (1979). And it is a crucial aspect of compassionate listening, as it foregrounds the ideological nature of narrative. Compassionate listening means knowingly committing to and engaging in an activity that might not lead to greater—or, for that matter, any—understanding. It can be, in other words, analogous to persisting in the reading of a novel marked by the lack of forward narrative momentum and progress, a la *The Orange Eats Creeps*. Listening typically is motivated by an empathic impulse, a desire to take the perspective and feel the emotions of another person, especially someone who has experienced trauma or/and suffering and, as a consequence, needs to share that burden as an act of emotional/psychological catharsis. The lines of communication between addict-speaker and sober-listener, however, often are interrupted by structural inequalities that compromise our abilities to genuinely grapple with the lived experiences of addiction without the imposition of morally deterministic narratives that simultaneously preexist and preempt the acts of speaking and sharing. These structural inequalities encourage us to ignore the idiosyncratic testimonials offered by individual addicts and, instead, only ever compel us to see a weak will, questionable morality and self-inflicted (and deserved) suffering. (This type of seeing is reinforced powerfully by the Twelve-Step industry, which levels out differences among addicts and regards them as a sea of sameness.) In this respect, we commit to hearing, rather than listening, engaging our sense of sound not with the intent to lend attention to a fellow human's pain, but with the intent to confirm what we already think we know about addiction.

By contrast, compassionate listening is forward looking and hopeful, even if it never enables the listener to gain purchase in cultivating a more accurate and

---

[40] Armstrong, *Experimental Fiction*, 19.

thorough understanding of addiction. To engage in compassionate listening is to enter into a compact that, at least for the listener, is chiefly benevolent in nature. To listen with the primary intent of paying attention to someone in need, and without the expectation of increased awareness, appreciation or comprehension, constitutes an act of generosity that affirms the integrity of the speaker and the value of her/his/their lived experiences. It is an act of acknowledgement whereby the listener commits, as much as is possible, to sharing in the pain of addiction, not for the purposes of co-optation, exploitation or shaming, but simply in the hope that such an acknowledgement perhaps can alleviate some of the trauma and pain that has resulted from a substance use disorder. Compassionate listening is fueled by optimism—an attitude that sadly is in short supply in most conversations around addiction—and it pursues, and invests hope in, a future that is uncertain precisely because its potential pay-off (i.e., greater understanding, compassion, connection among human beings) is regarded as more valuable than its potential failure.

Reading *The Orange Eats Creeps* demands that readers engage in acts of compassionate listening, not only with respect to the hobo junkie vampire characters, but also with respect to the author. As I already have noted, Krilanovich's novel is, at best, difficult to navigate, even for readers who are fairly well versed in the peculiarities of the postmodern novel. From its very first sentence, *The Orange Eats Creeps* thrusts readers into a diegetic world that is absent nearly every formal feature that would facilitate comprehension and, more importantly, understanding, and then actively disrupts the reading process with both formal and topical motifs that confound readers. Further, the prose quite frequently is impossible, neither conveying important plot points and character details, nor advancing the narrative forward. There is only ever a crippling sense of sameness, even stasis, that looms large over the diegetic world and, indeed, the reading experience.

In this way, the novel provides a compelling illustration of the kind of postmodern fiction that David Lodge describes in *The Modes of Modern Writing: Metaphor, Metonymy, and the Typology of Modern Literature* (1977)—that is, writing that is characterized by "its efforts to deploy both metaphoric and metonymic devices in radically new ways, and to defy (even if such defiance is ultimately in vain) the obligation to choose between"[41] "either of the poles of metaphor (modernist) or metonymic (antimodernist) writing."[42] *The Orange Eats Creeps*, in short, constitutes a novel that is marked by Lodge's five strategies of postmodern writing: contradiction, discontinuity, randomness, excess and

---

[41] David Lodge, *The Modes of Modern Writing: Metaphor, Metonymy, and the Typology of Modern Literature* (London: Bloomsbury Publishing, 2015), 280.

[42] Brian McHale, *Postmodernist Fiction* (London: Routledge, 1987), 7.

short circuit, and it is precisely these kinds of narrative strategies that demand readers to exercise hypervigilance with respect to the reading experience—not only to pay attention but also to avoid being defensive when the reading experience becomes difficult and to offer an interested eye to prose that may or may not ever really make sense.

The episodic, even piecemeal, nature of Krilanovich's narrative makes visible the normally unseen operations of ideology, which functions as the invisible glue that cements the many pieces of a linear narrative together. This kind of narrative structure forces readers to be cognizant of the ways in which any narrative—be it a personal anecdote, a "mythological stereotype," a realist novel or even an anti-narrative like the one at work in *The Orange Eats Creeps*—constitutes an invested framing of experience which benefits some parties while handicapping or/and injuring certain Others. When we accept that there are many ways to tell a story, then the who and why of authorship (and of readership) become equally important, if not more so, than the what of narrative. We begin to invest our attention and our energies in the individual's truth, which we may or may not "understand" in a conventional sense of reconciling all the various parts to a single, unified whole, but which we must respect as reflective of that individual's lived experience and as central to that individual's sense of self and well-being. What I am describing is a profoundly compassionate reading practice that is premised on a deep and abiding respect for the specificity and uniqueness of lived experience. This is something that has been denied to addicts at least since the nineteenth century when "addict" became a collective identity built on the unsteady foundations of stereotype and stigma—that is, a representation of what a group of people inherently were rather than a reflection of an individual's behavior and lived experience.[43]

Finally, the gaps in time, the radical shifts in location and the inconsistencies in character that liberally pepper the pages of *The Orange Eats Creeps* mark the reading experience as non-immersive and demand that readers adopt an active, critical mindset with respect to the subject matter, the narrative and the representational apparatus. For over two centuries, Western readers have assumed that they understand who addicts are, how addiction works and how addicts navigate the world with a substance use disorder, even when these assumptions ran counter to publicly available knowledge, medical or otherwise. A novel like *The Orange Eats Creeps* forces readers to pose critical, and sometimes uncomfortable, questions that they are not used to asking, at least

---

[43] This topic is very thoughtfully discussed by Susan Zieger in her seminal text *Inventing the Addict: Drugs, Race, and Sexuality in Nineteenth-Century British and American Literature* (Amherst: University of Massachusetts Press, 2008).

where addiction is concerned. *What do I need to know that I am not being told? And why is this vital information being withheld from me? What do I not question and what biases drive my inability or unwillingness to question these things? What, in short, is missing and why?* At the heart of these and related questions is the kind of self-inflicted ignorance that has allowed narratives like *The Lost Weekend* and *A Star Is Born* to dominate conversations regarding addiction for far too long and to dictate what is True, what is Good and what is Right with respect to how addicts see and are seen. When we become aware of our ignorance, we gain the ability (if not the willingness) to relinquish the biases, the bigotry, the fear and even sometimes the hatred that we might feel toward those who are different from us. We take on a more complex understanding of what constitutes truth, and with it an added responsibility to exercise more compassion in the crafting of our self-truths and in our engagement with the self-truths of others. We come to understand that the agitation and frustration that are born out of ignorance can be overcome (or, at the very least, mitigated) with simple patience. We realize that confusion can be undercut by a willingness to listen and an openness to new ideas and knowledge. And we begin to accept that disorientation just might be a necessary step in the process of forging deep and meaningful human connections, especially with individuals who are (or, initially are depicted to be) radically different than ourselves. By the close of *The Orange Eats Creeps*, readers may still be scrambling to discern a clear takeaway, but if they have accepted and moved through their disorientation, then they very well may have come a shade closer to grasping what it feels like to walk among the living in a state of living death, a state that those who are addicts living in a manically sober world know only too well. And that shade of understanding just might be where genuine compassion takes root.

CONCLUSION

> I believe that fiction writing is the guardian of the moral and ethical sense of the community. Especially now that organized religion is scattered and in disarray, and politicians have, Lord knows, lost their credibility, fiction is one of the few forms left through which we may examine our society not in its particular but in its typical aspects; through which we can see ourselves and the ways in which we behave towards each other, through which we can see others and judge them and ourselves.
> —Margaret Atwood, *Second Words*[1]

For as long as there have been addicts, there have been metaphors of brokenness that have dictated how we are supposed to see addicts, whether those addicts are ourselves or Others. To be broken is to be damaged goods—no longer whole or in working condition or both. Addiction, we are told, is responsible for breaking addicts, a state of being that can refer to anything and everything from physiological damage inflicted on the material body, neurological damage inflicted on the brain, emotional damage inflicted on the psyche, financial damage inflicted on the bank account, professional damage inflicted on the career, social damage inflicted on relationships with intimates and so on. For addicts, again we are told, this state of brokenness is a natural, even inevitable state of being—the rock bottom toward which all addicts are presumably always and already headed, perhaps from even before those addicts take their first drink or acquire their first fix.

Brokenness as a metaphor also can refer to a psychological state of being marked by hopelessness and despair. This particular iteration of the metaphor of brokenness is especially ubiquitous within Judeo Christianity, and, more broadly, Western spiritualism where it has spawned a wealth of self-help books, including but not limited to Charles Stanley's *The Blessings of Brokenness: Why*

---

[1] Margaret Atwood, *Second Words: Selected Critical Prose 1960–1982* (Toronto: House of Anansi Press, 1982), 346.

God Allows Us To Go through Hard Times (1997); Nancy Leigh DeMoss's *Brokenness: The Heart God Revives* (2002); Lon Solomon's *Brokenness: How God Redeems Pain and Suffering* (2005); Tunde Bolanta's *Spiritual Brokenness: The Key to Becoming More Like Christ* (2011); and Alan E. Nelson's *Embracing Brokenness: How God Refines Us through Life's Disappointments* (2016). Within such tomes, brokenness typically is seen as a precondition to eternal salvation: a "shattering of […] self-will—the absolute surrender of [the individual's] will to the will of God. It is saying 'Yes, Lord!'—no resistance, no chafing, no stubbornness—simply submitting [the self] to His direction and will."[2]

While brokenness circulates as a metaphor within discourses of both spirituality and addiction, the metaphor ultimately has radically different connotations for each. Within both, brokenness is a state of being characterized by hardship, struggle, frustration and defeat. Within both, brokenness is regarded as an "original" state of being—the starting point for self-identity. However, in the former, acknowledging one's brokenness constitutes an act of faith: a freefall into the (metaphoric) arms of Christ and into the (again, metaphoric) community of God. This acknowledgement is the central conceit of Carrie Underwood's "Jesus, Take the Wheel." It is simultaneously a cry for help (e.g., "Jesus, take the wheel/Take it from my hands/'Cause I can't do this on my own") and a relinquishment of control in the face of overwhelming suffering, privation or/and sin (e.g., "I'm letting go/So give me one more chance/And save me from this road I'm on"). Further, within the Judeo Christian tradition, this acknowledgement, which signifies a person's profound humility, is met with grace and mercy.

By contrast, for addicts, an acknowledgment of our brokenness constitutes merely an affirmation of our lack of self-worth within a culture that would prefer to shame and blame, rather than actually help. During the writing of this volume, for instance, Elton John celebrated 29 years of sobriety by sharing on social media a photograph of an Alcoholics Anonymous sobriety coin that was captioned: "Twenty-nine years ago today, I was a broken man. I finally summoned the courage to say 3 words that would change my life: 'I need help.' Thank you to the selfless people who have helped me on my journey through sobriety. I am eternally grateful."[3] On the surface, statements like this seem celebratory and affirmative, and likely to some degree they are. But statements like this also perpetuate a problematic and false binary by linking addiction to brokenness and implicitly linking sobriety to wholeness—a conceit that also

---

[2] Nancy Leigh DeMoss, *Brokenness: The Heart God Revives* (Chicago, IL: Moody, 2002), 51.
[3] Dave Quinn, "Elton John Celebrates 29 Years of Sobriety in Touching Post: 'I Was a Broken Man,'" *Yahoo! Entertainment,* July 29, 2019, https://www.yahoo.com/entertainment/elton-john-celebrates-29-years-131507016.html (accessed July 31, 2019).

runs through the 2019 biopic about John's rise to fame and concomitant struggles with addiction, *Rocketman*. John's statement is especially noteworthy because, in his deep internalization of the illusory wholeness, he demonstrates just how ubiquitous and how compelling these metaphors really can be for addicts. Additionally, his decades of sobriety—sadly, the exception, rather than the rule where the Twelve Steps are concerned[4]—legitimizes the wholeness/brokenness binary, conferring upon it a heightened degree of authority and truthfulness that even actual evidence (aside from the occasional anecdote) could never approximate.

This particular iteration of brokenness derives much of its meaning and force from the ways in which illness and disease are constituted within Western discourse. In *Disease and Representation: Images of Illness from Madness to AIDS* (1988), Sander L. Gilman writes, "Disease, with its seeming randomness, is one aspect of the indeterminable universe that we wish to distance from ourselves. To do so we must construct boundaries between ourselves and those categories of individuals whom we believe (or hope) to be more at risk than ourselves."[5] The boundaries to which Gilman makes reference, while at times literal (as, e.g., with the physical quarantining of plague victims), often are discursive and ideological in nature and serve as a "means of social control."[6] Such boundaries identify "the diseased" as, in some way, broken, as in need of a fix, which is a double-edged turn of phrase with respect to addicts whose endless quest for a high (more colloquially known as a "fix") is seen as the root of their brokenness and, thus, the raison d'être of their difference; in so doing, such boundaries also manufacture clear (albeit often arbitrary) lines of demarcation between "the healthy," whose bodies are perceived to be unified, whole and inviolable, and "the diseased," whose bodies are always and only perceived as broken, as damaged.

While I do not deny the myriad damages that addiction inflicts on individuals, I do take issue with the brokenness metaphor, and, in particular, the ways in which that metaphor is mobilized and weaponized against addicts, used as a tool to undermine a person's self-esteem, credibility, social value and self-worth. What this metaphor suggests is that wholeness, with respect to self-identity, is not only possible, but also is the goal, despite the fact that that particular holy grail is entirely illusory, even for those who maintain sobriety across the lifecycle.[7]

---

[4] For more on this topic, see Charles Bufe, *Alcoholics Anonymous: Cult or Cure?*, 2nd ed. (Tucson, AZ: See Sharp Press, 1998).

[5] Sander L. Gilman, *Disease and Representation: Images of Illness from Madness to AIDS* (Ithaca, NY: Cornell University Press, 1988), 4.

[6] Ibid., 10.

[7] In *Simians, Cyborgs, and Women: The Reinvention of Nature* (1991), Donna J. Haraway explains the historical origins of this idea as follows: "From the eighteenth to the mid-twentieth centuries, the great historical constructions of gender, race, and class were embedded in the organically marked bodies of woman, the colonized or enslaved, and the worker.

If identity is always and only fragmented, and if self-identity therefore constitutes an ongoing and incomplete quest, then we set addicts up not simply for disappointment, but most certainly for failure, when we tell them that wholeness is the prize awaiting them on the other side of their rock bottom.

One of the most obvious ways that the metaphor of brokenness has been weaponized is through the creation and dissemination of a complementary metaphor: that is, the medical model of addiction. Although not identical, the medical model of addiction draws heavily on its sister metaphor, the medical model of disability, which, in *Key Concepts in Health Studies* (2010), is explained as follows:

> The medical model [...] understands disability in the context of the biological and physical aspects amenable only to the intervention of the expert. Disability is located here in the impaired body of the individual where limbs and organs do not function in accordance with "normal" expectations. It is those malfunctioning limbs and organs that are the cause of disability. As a consequence [...] people with a disability are therefore deemed to be dependent on the expertise of the medical profession in order to either "cure" or minimize their problems [...] In this model, a person with a disability is held to be a passive social actor, who is either incapable or not expert enough to make decisions concerning how they lead their lives and is denied access to the decision-making processes that may govern their medical or social care.[8]

Whereas the medical model of disability focuses on perceived deficiencies (i.e., brokenness) in the material body, the medical model of addiction emphasizes perceived deficiencies in willpower and morality, which manifest themselves in bodies and minds that presumably do not function in the same way as other, nonaddict bodies and minds function. In both, the goal—not unlike the goal of wholeness—is to normalize what is regarded as abnormal, even abject, by rendering that abnormality an object, rather than the subject, of its "treatment" and by subjecting said abnormality to the gaze and the authority of experts. With respect to those who are disabled, the experts in question are physicians and medical specialists; with respect to addicts, the experts often are anyone who can lay claim to sobriety, but especially individuals with some foothold in the treatment industry or legal profession.

Those inhabiting these marked bodies have been symbolically other to the fictive rational self of the universal, and so unmarked, species man, a coherent subject" (210).

[8] Chris Yuill, Iain Crinson and Eilidh Duncan, *Key Concepts in Health Studies* (Los Angeles, CA: Sage, 2010), 16.

CONCLUSION 141

The desire to normalize what is perceived to be abnormal is, in effect, a compulsion to fix, or repair, what is perceived to be broken. The assumption, of course, is that addiction is an affliction that can be healed—this despite the wealth of medical research that confirms that addiction is an ongoing condition marked by multiple relapses and recurrences across time. This book began, at least in part, as a response to the toxic notion that addicts are damaged goods who need to be altered, healed and fixed. As an addict, I take issue with the idea that my medical condition infantilizes me, rendering me incapable of self-authorship and impotent with respect to the "decision-making processes that govern" my health care and social being. Never was my intention to suggest that addicts should be enabled in their addictions, or discouraged from seeking treatment. With the current volume, I "merely" wanted to shed a clinical light on the heavy-handed paternalism that dominates the rhetoric around and the lived experiences of addiction, and, as an addict, scholar and global citizen, to search for alternative discourses about and, of equal importance, relationships to addiction. In short, I sought to unfix (read detach) the addict from harmful representational histories that have, for far too long, dictated how the addict is "treated" (or, more aptly, mistreated) in the extra-diegetic world.

My quest took me immediately to literature because, as Lauren Gunderson so astutely articulates in her play *The Revolutionists* (2018), "story is the heartbeat of humanity and humanity gets really dark when the wrong stories are leading the people."[9] Stated differently, our responses to literature—how it is conceived, how it is produced, how it is consumed—are irreducibly relational and historical in nature. Stories told become repositories for how groups of people understand themselves and one another at a given point in time and space. Those stories are (re-)produced, or not, given what Atwood, in the epigraph that opens this chapter, terms the "moral and ethical sense of the community" that exists in/around their creation and reception. As those stories are heard/read, they invite readers into worlds and psyches that are not their own and they encourage those readers to forge connections with individuals, places and even ideas that might once have seemed entirely foreign. Even as those stories look to the past or the present, they also are always and already looking forward, allowing writers and readers to imagine selves that are more compassionate, mindful, wise, and to envision worlds that are kinder and more habitable, especially for those who, in the present moment of creation/reception, might be regarded as outsiders, as morally- or/and socially objectionable Others.

The five novels that I discuss within the body of this volume suggest first and foremost that as writers, as readers and, indeed, as human beings, we

---

[9] Lauren Gunderson, *The Revolutionists* (New York: Dramatists Play Service, 2018), 16.

must resist the rhetoric of repair that dominates discussions of addiction precisely because that rhetoric is, at best, indifferent and, at worst, cruel. In their own ways, each of the novels included in the table of contents rejects the idea that its addict characters are subhuman without ignoring the myriad damages that addiction inflicts upon those characters. In *Leaving Las Vegas*, Ben's physical decline, catalogued with such microscopic attention to verisimilitude, is harrowing to witness, as are Rachel's many denials and self-deceptions in *The Girl on the Train* and Clay's indifference, in *Less Than Zero*, to the overdoses and deaths that plague his peer group. But in the end O'Brien, Hawkins and Ellis refuse to compare these characters to an arbitrary standard of normality that ultimately would saddle those characters with pathos and castigate them for failing to achieve an impossible and illusory goal.

In *Dope*, by contrast, Gran's supporting characters repeatedly hold her protagonist up to toxic standards of normality and decency that were operative in the mid-century United States, not to underscore Joe's brokenness (although Gran insists that Joe is broken in many ways), but rather to critique the standards of normality and decency themselves, which is precisely what is at stake in the novel's surprising climactic conflict between Shelley and Joe. And both Ellis and Krilanovich imagine worlds in which those standards, in part or in toto, are absent, a move that reveals much about readers' reliance on those standards to maintain a modicum of order and "control" over a broken, chaotic extra-diegetic world. In rejecting the rhetoric of repair, these five novels work subtly to unsettle the notion that addicts are damaged goods—a notion that has very real and very harmful material consequences for addicts in the everyday. This notion, for instance, which systematically undercuts the integrity and value of addicts as human beings, is at least partially responsible for the dearth of effective treatment models, as well as the virtual inaccessibility of the most "successful" among existing approaches to treatment. It also, again at least partially, is responsible for increasingly draconian drug legislation, which, since the early 1970s in the United States, has over time virtually bankrupted addicts' rights before the law.

In place of a rhetoric of repair imposed from outside by a maniacally sober culture, the five novels discussed in this volume insist on the importance of self-authorship as a means of empowerment, as well as an act of political dissent. None of the five novels included in the table of contents merely reiterates one of the two by-now all-too-familiar narratives of addiction that have been, and still widely are championed and disseminated within Western publishing industries and Western reading cultures, which is why they, rather than the other 300-plus novels that I read while researching this book, were selected for inclusion. Even the most seemingly familiar and conventional of the lot—O'Brien's *Leaving Las Vegas*—calls this representational legacy into question through the unconventional and often uncomfortable relationships that he creates between readers, text and characters. Yes, O'Brien seems to say through this highly original novel, Ben eventually does die by the bottle; but he does so on his own terms, and without the kinds of gross and cruel scopophilia that the Western novel historically has afforded its readers with respect to the subject of addiction. By rejecting his own codification and objectification in a prepackaged, one-size-fits-all narrative that has nothing to do with his lived experience, and instead adopting an active voice that insists on being listened to—that is, by reminding readers that addiction is "not what the story is about"—Ben also and simultaneously lays claim to the power and privilege of self-authorship. He insists on defining what he believes, who he is and how he exists in relation to others both within and outside of O'Brien's diegesis, which is an incredibly significant display of self-empowerment when the subject in question is an addict.

These five novels, though, do not only issue a call to "construct our own visions, make informed decisions [...], act appropriately, and take responsibility for those actions,"[10] which is how self-authorship generally is defined, especially within the field of education where it originates. Additionally, these five novels acknowledge that self-authorship, especially when seized by someone who typically functions (or, is forced to function) outside of the bounds of "normal" society, constitutes an act of political dissent. In his Foreword to Nancy Chang's *Silencing Political Dissent: How Post-September 11 Anti-Terrorism Measures Threaten Our Civil Liberties* (2002), noted historian Howard Zinn defines *political dissent* as "the freedom to speak, to resist the power of the state when it demands unity and slavish obedience to the arbitrary decisions of" ideology.[11] For writers, for addict characters and for readers, experimental fiction constitutes an act of political dissent when such writing questions, critiques or/and pushes against a monolithic (representational) apparatus (e.g., literary realism) that ensures its dominance, authority and control through the stigmatization and ostracization of historically underrepresented or/and marginalized groups. Such an apparatus demands slavish obedience, attempting to impose a standardized "way of seeing" on its readers, despite the many subtle and not-so-subtle, as well as subconscious and conscious ways in which readers can and do impose their own ways of seeing on a text.

---

[10] Marcia B. Baxter Magolda, *Creating Contexts for Learning and Self-Authorship: Constructive-Developmental Pedagogy* (Nashville, TN: Vanderbilt University Press, 1999), 10.

[11] Howard Zinn, "Foreword," *Silencing Political Dissent: How Post-September 11 Anti-Terrorism Measures Threaten Our Civil Liberties*, edited by Nancy Chang (New York: Seven Stories Press, 2002), Kindle.

Political dissent typically constitutes a more overt form of resistance. It begins with an acknowledgment of disenfranchisement and oppression. It involves giving voice to discontent at that state of being, saying, "This is unfair and I won't accept it any longer." It is fueled by equal parts anger, integrity and compassion. It seeks only justice. In various ways, and through the employment of varied experimental narrative techniques, the novels examined throughout this volume look to the monolith of dominant (sober) culture and say, "No more." No more ideological slights. No more misrepresentations or outright lies. No more speaking for or about or as addicts. Political dissent is crucial, both Zinn and Chang aver, in light of violations of civil liberties and human rights, which addicts regularly experience around employment, public assistance, housing, education and child custody, to name only a few arenas of public life where such violations are witnessed. When addicts— whether writers, characters or readers—give voice to such discontent, when they speak the words "I dissent," they also and simultaneously assert their belonging within a culture that systematically and unequivocally rejects them. This dissent can happen in virtually any type of literary text and reading experience, but is especially common with respect to postmodern, experimental fiction which takes as a point of departure the project of "challeng[ing] the grand narratives on which conventional […] ideologies rely."[12]

To assert belonging to a group that actively, at times violently, insists on one's outsiderhood, if not subhumanity, is an act of brave self-authorship and self-empowerment that demands nothing less than compassion from both self and others. Lauren Berlant, in her introductory chapter to *Compassion: The Culture and Politics of an Emotion*, regards compassion not as "an organic emotion" but as "a social and aesthetic technology of belonging."[13] She goes on to suggest that compassion is "a particularly modern topic, because members of mass society witness suffering not just in concretely local spaces but in the elsewheres brought home and made intimate by sensationalist media, where documentary realness about the pain of strangers is increasingly at the center of both fictional and nonfictional events."[14] From A&E's *Intervention* (2005–present) to popular films like *A Star Is Born* (2018) and *Rocketman* (2019) to news media coverage of all ideological stripes and popular fiction like Zadie Smith's *NW* (2012) and Ruth Ware's *The Woman in Cabin 10* (2016), Western culture exploits the pain of addicts for the visual pleasure of its sober spectators, but in

---

[12] Len Platt and Sara Upstone, "Introduction," in *Postmodern Literature and Race*, ed. Platt and Upstone, 1–12 (New York: Cambridge University Press, 2015), 1.

[13] Lauren Berlant, "Compassion (and Withholding)," in *Compassion: The Culture and Politics of an Emotion*, ed. Berlant, 1–14 (New York: Routledge, 2004), 5.

[14] Ibid.

so doing, it evacuates that pain of its visceral quality, and it renders the subject of that pain an object to be visually and ideologically trafficked as a spectacle of degradation.

Through the employment of experimental narrative techniques like witnessing, betraying, gaslighting, transgressing and disorienting, the novels discussed within the pages of *Addiction, Representation and the Experimental Novel, 1985–2015* insist that readers "look at [representations] that record great cruelties and crimes [...] [and] think about what it means to look at"[15] those representations. With novels that shift the balance of power between readers and characters (like *Leaving Las Vegas* and *The Girl on the Train*), that disrupt readerly expectations regarding generic and narrative conventions (like *Dope* and *The Orange Eats Creeps*) and that push at—sometimes completely annihilate—the boundaries of normality and acceptability (like *Less Than Zero*), experimental fiction forces readers to be accountable for what they read and for how they read. It acknowledges that no act of reading, even of popular genre fiction which often is erroneously written off as mere escapist literature, is ideologically neutral. It demands accountability to self and to others, which is one of the foundational tenets of compassion. And it insists that we resist the urge to speak for or about or even with the addict, and that, in the end, we simply listen to the unique voices and experiences that are emerging from the margins of Western culture broadly, and the Western novel more specifically.

There is great privilege and responsibility associated with the act of listening, just as there is great privilege and responsibility associated with the act of reading. Both typically presuppose agency and access to a vantage point from which we can see without necessarily being seen, and we can look with the intent to consume and possess, but not necessarily engage or comprehend. Experimental fiction requires readers to adopt a very different relationship to listening and reading than Western readers in particular are used to adopting. Often such fiction positions readers well outside of the diegetic world, prohibiting them from immersing themselves in the narrative action and forcing them to first acknowledge and then come to terms with their marginality. By stripping readers of their privileged vantage point, by disallowing them the option of seeing without necessarily being seen, experimental fiction can forge meaningful affective relationships between readers and addicts that allow the former to understand better the latter's lived experiences without co-opting or judging those experiences. By crafting diegetic worlds and reading experiences that are, at best, unfamiliar and, at worst, disorienting, writers of experimental fiction force readers to pay attention, to carefully listen, to

---

[15] Susan Sontag, *Regarding the Pain of Others* (New York: Farrar, Straus and Giroux, 2003), 95.

actively engage—reactions that, sadly, many readers are not used to affording addicts because addicts have for so long been codified and contained within highly familiar metaphors of brokenness, moral decrepitude and waste.

In the end, experimental fiction manufactures situations "through which we can see ourselves and the ways in which we behave toward each other" more clearly.[16] Such fiction forces us to bear witness to the trauma of addiction, when our basest "instincts" are screaming at us either to exploit, thereby rendering that trauma less traumatic and, therefore, more palatable to consume, or simply to look away. Such fiction betrays readerly expectations regarding what constitutes genre, textuality, narrativity and authority, and, in so doing, encourages its readers to extend such challenges to the everyday, where we might also begin to question the how and why of social categories and identities (e.g., "addict") that exclude, that silence and that kill. Such fiction gaslights its readers, thereby forcing readers to acknowledge the harmful cultural scripts that they have slavishly obeyed and accepted—whether willingly or not—regarding who addicts are and how they navigate the world with a substance use disorder. Such fiction engages in acts of transgression that shock readers out of the complacency of tradition and compel readers to imagine worlds—both diegetic and extra-diegetic—that are more welcoming, more inclusive, kinder than the worlds that we currently know. And such fiction disorients us, denying us the kinds of footholds that might otherwise anchor us to the familiar worlds that we commonly inhabit, not as an act of base cruelty, but as a means to greater understanding of and compassion toward of those who are forced to walk in the world as winos, as junkies, as waste.

Ultimately, experimental fiction, at its best, invites an interpretive process that is, in a word, liberating. In the Foreword to Louise M. Rosenblatt's *Literature as Exploration* (1995), Wayne Booth recognizes that "many postmodernists talk as if they had invented liberated reading—'resistant' reading, 'reading against the grain,' reading that invigorates and transforms readers by freeing them from critical constraints."[17] Yet, throughout the book, Rosenblatt insists (rightly so) that the idea that reading can have "a liberating and fortifying effect in the ongoing life of the reader"[18] predates both postmodernity and postmodern fiction and might very well be a precondition of imaginative writing. We look to literature to recall what was, to grapple with what is, and to imagine what might be. In this way, the diegetic worlds about which we

---

[16] Atwood, *Second Words*, 346.

[17] Wayne Booth, "Foreword," *Literature as Exploration*, by Louise M. Rosenblatt (New York: Modern Language Association of America, 1995), Kindle.

[18] Louise M. Rosenblatt, *Literature as Exploration* (New York: Modern Language Association of America, 1995), 277.

read can quite profoundly shape the extra-diegetic worlds within which we read, we live, we love, we become addicted, we work and we die. When we read literature with an eye toward liberation, we see the practice of interpretation, to quote Susan Sontag's seminal *Against Interpretation and Other Essays* (1961), as "a means of revising, of transvaluing, of escaping the dead past."[19] For addicts, this interpretive practice of liberating, of unfixing ourselves from a dead representational past is not simply a matter of revising or escaping, although it absolutely implicates both outcomes, but it can quite frankly be the difference between compassion and indifference, between hope and despair, between living and dying.

---

[19] Susan Sontag, *Against Interpretation and Other Essays*, 1961 (New York: Picador, 2001), 4.

BIBLIOGRAPHY

9 to 5. Directed by Colin Hughes. Performed by Lily Tomlin, Jane Fonda and Dolly Parton. United States: 20th Century Fox, 1980. DVD.
"120 Years of American Education: A Statistical Portrait." *National Center for Education Statistics*. U.S. Department of Education, January 1993. https://nces.ed.gov/pubs93/93442.pdf (accessed February 27, 2019).
Abani, Chris. *GraceLand*. New York: Farrar, Straus and Giroux, 2004.
"About Us." *Compassionate Listening Project*, n.d. https://www.compassionatelistening.org/about-us (accessed June 25, 2019).
Acker, Kathy. *Blood and Guts in High School*. New York: Grove, 1978.
"addiction, n." *OED Online*, December 2018, http://www.oed.com.ezproxy.bgsu.edu/view/Entry/2179?redirectedFrom=addiction (accessed January 10, 2019).
Alexander, Anna, and Mark S. Roberts, eds. *high culture: reflections on addiction and modernity*. Albany: State University of New York Press, 2003.
Allende, Isabel. *Maya's Notebook*. New York: HarperCollins, 2013.
Altman, Rick. *A Theory of Narrative*. New York: Columbia University Press, 2008.
Anderson, Miranda, ed. *The Book of the Mirror: An Interdisciplinary Collection Exploring the Cultural Story of the Mirror*. Newcastle upon Tyne: Cambridge Scholars, 2007.
Anker, Justin J., and Marilyn E. Carroll. "Females Are More Vulnerable to Drug Abuse Than Males: Evidence from Preclinical Studies and the Role of Ovarian Hormones." In *Biological Basis of Sex Differences in Psychopharmacology*, edited by Jo C. Neill and Jayashri Kulkarni, 73–96. New York: Springer-Verlag, 2011.
Arciniegas, David B. "Psychosis." *Continuum* 21, no. 3 (2015): 715–36. https://www.ncbi.nlm.nih.gov/pmc/articles/PMC4455840/#idm140046521373520title (accessed July 22, 2019).
Armstrong, Julie. *Experimental Fiction: An Introduction for Readers and Writers*. London: Bloomsbury Academic, 2014.
Armstrong, Nancy. *Desire and Domestic Fiction: A Political History of the Novel*. Oxford: Oxford University Press, 1987.
Atwood, Margaret. *Second Words: Selected Critical Prose 1960–1982*. Toronto: House of Anansi Press, 1982.
Azarian, Bobby. "Trump Is Gaslighting America Again—Here's How to Fight It." *Psychology Today*, August 31, 2018. https://www.psychologytoday.com/us/blog/mind-in-the-machine/201808/trump-is-gaslighting-america-again-here-s-how-fight-it (accessed May 29, 2019).
Barnes, Julian. *The Only Story*. New York: Alfred A. Knopf, 2018.
Barry, Lynda. *Cruddy: An Illustrated Novel*. New York: Scribner, 1999.
Barth, John. *Lost in the Funhouse*. New York: Doubleday, 1968.

Barthes, Roland. *S/Z: An Essay*, translated by Richard Miller. New York: Hill and Wang, 1974.
Beaver, Frank Eugene. *Dictionary of Film Terms: The Aesthetic Companion to Film Art*. New York: Peter Lang, 2007.
Beck, Koa. "Female Characters Don't Have to Be Likeable." *The Atlantic*, December 31, 2015. https://www.theatlantic.com/entertainment/archive/2015/12/in-praise-of-fictions-unlikable-women-in-2015/421698/ (accessed March 19, 2020).
Becker, Jill B., Michele L. McClellan and Beth Glover Reed. "Sex Differences, Gender and Addiction." *Journal of Neuroscience Research* 95, nos. 1–2 (2017): 136–47.
Belsey, Catherine. *Critical Practice*. London: Routledge, 1980.
Ben-Amots, Zach. "The Rise of 'Soft' Holocaust Denial." *The Tower*, October 2016, http://www.thetower.org/article/the-rise-of-soft-holocaust-denial/ (accessed June 21, 2019).
Berlant, Lauren. "Compassion (and Withholding)." In *Compassion: The Culture and Politics of an Emotion*, edited by Berlant, 1–14. New York: Routledge, 2004.
Berry, Ellen E. *Women's Experimental Writing: Negative Aesthetics and Feminist Critique*. London: Bloomsbury Academic, 2016.
Berry, R. M. "Metafiction." In *The Routledge Companion to Experimental Literature*, edited by Joe Bray, Alison Gibbons and Brian McHale, 128–40. London: Routledge, 2012.
Bolanta, Tunde. *Spiritual Brokenness: The Key to Becoming More Like Christ*. Lake Mary, FL: Creation House Books, 2011.
Booth, Wayne. "Foreword." *Literature as Exploration*, by Louise M. Rosenblatt, New York: Modern Language Association of America, 1995. Kindle.
———. *The Rhetoric of Fiction*, 2nd ed. Chicago, IL: University of Chicago Press, 1983.
Brodie, Janet Farrell, and Mark Redfield, eds. *High Anxieties: Cultural Studies in Addiction*. Berkeley: University of California Press, 2002.
Bronfen, Elisabeth. *Over Her Dead Body: Death, Femininity, and the Aesthetic*. New York: Routledge, 1992.
Bufe, Charles. *Alcoholics Anonymous: Cult or Cure?*, 2nd ed. Tucson, AZ: See Sharp Press, 1998.
Bukowski, Charles. *Women*. New York: Ecco, 2014.
Cain, James M. *The Postman Always Rings Twice*. New York: Vintage, 1989.
Calvino, Italo. *If on a Winter's Night a Traveler*, translated by William Weaver. New York: Everyman's Library, (1979) 1993.
Cameron, Colin. "The Medical Model." In *Disability Studies: A Student's Guide*, edited by Cameron, 98–100. Los Angeles, CA: Sage, 2014.
Carpenter, Amanda. *Gaslighting America: Why We Love It When Trump Lies to Us*. New York: Broadside Books, 2018.
Castillo, Debra A. *Easy Women: Sex and Gender in Modern Mexican Fiction*. Minneapolis: University of Minnesota Press, 1998.
Chang, Nancy. *Silencing Political Dissent: How Post-September 11 Anti-Terrorism Measures Threaten Our Civil Liberties*. New York: Seven Stories Press, 2002. Kindle.
Chaplinsky, Joshua. "Giving Birth to Creeps." *Chuck Palahniuk*, June 21, 2011. https://chuckpalahniuk.net/interviews/grace-krilanovich (accessed July 22, 2019).
Cheever, John. *The Stories of John Cheever*. New York: Alfred A. Knopf, 2000.
Cinnamon, Lynn. "The Story behind *Leaving Las Vegas*." *Lynn Cinnamon*, August 2014, http://lynncinnamon.com/2014/08/leaving-las-vegas/ (accessed August 12, 2018).
Clark, Robert C. *American Literary Minimalism*. Tuscaloosa: University of Alabama Press, 2014.

Cobley, Paul. "Objectivity and Immanence in Genre Theory." In *Genre Matters: Essays in Theory and Criticism*, edited by Garin Dowd, Lesley Stevenson and Jeremy Strong, 41–54. Bristol: Intellect, 2006.

Cohen, Michael. *Murder Most Fair: The Appeal of Mystery Fiction*. Madison, WI: Fairleigh Dickinson University Press, 2000.

"confession, n." *OED Online*, June 2018, http://www.oed.com.ezproxy.bgsu.edu:8080/view/Entry/38779?redirectedFrom=confession (accessed July 24, 2018).

Conlin, Christy Ann. *Heave*. Toronto: Anchor Canada, 2003.

Cooper, Dennis. *Frisk*. New York: Grove, 1991.

Cortázar, Julio. *Hopscotch*, translated by Gregory Rabassa. New York: Pantheon, (1963) 1987.

Culler, Jonathan. "Literary Competence." In *Reader-Response Criticism: From Formalism to Post-Structuralism*, edited by Jane P. Tompkins, 101–17. Baltimore, MD: Johns Hopkins University Press, 1980.

Dardis, Tom. *The Thirsty Muse: Alcohol and the American Writer*. London: Abacus, 1989.

David, Anna. *Party Girl*. New York: HarperCollins, 2007.

Davies, Luke. *Candy: A Novel of Love and Addiction*. New York: Ballantine Books, 1998.

DeMoss, Nancy Leigh. *Brokenness: The Heart God Revives*. Chicago, IL: Moody, 2002.

Derrida, Jacques. *Of Grammatology*, translated by Gayatri Chakravorty Spivak, 1974. Reprint, Baltimore, MD: Johns Hopkins University Press, 1997.

Dickos, Andrew. *Street with No Name: A History of the Classic American Film Noir*. Lexington: University of Kentucky Press, 2002.

Didion, Joan. *Play It as It Lays.*. New York: Farrar, Straus, and Giroux, (1970) 2005.

Diehl, Heath A. "'Listen to the Silence': Dismantling the Myth of a Classless Society in the Fiction of Marcia Muller and Sara Paretsky." In *Class and Culture in Crime Fiction: Essays on Works in English since the 1970s*, edited by Julie H. Kim, 49–68. Jefferson, NC: McFarland, 2014.

———. "'There Are Times When an Old Rule Should Be Abandoned, or a Current Rule Should Not Be Applied': Narration, Innovation, and the Hardboiled Mystery in Sue Grafton's '*T*' *Is for Trespass*." *TEXT: Journal of Writing and Writing Courses* 37 (October 2016), http://www.textjournal.com.au/speciss/issue37/Diehl.pdf (accessed February 14, 2019).

———. "'W' Is for 'Woman': Deconstructing the Private Dick in Sue Grafton's Alphabet Series." In *Murdering Miss Marple: Essays on Gender and Sexuality in the New Golden Age of Women's Crime Fiction*, edited by Julie H. Kim, 120–141. Jefferson, NC: McFarland 2012.

———. *Wasted: Performing Addiction in America*. London: Routledge, 2016.

Dilley, Kimberly J. *Busybodies, Meddlers, and Snoops: The Female Hero in Contemporary Women's Mysteries*. Westport, CT: Greenwood, 1998.

Dodes, Lance, and Zachary Dodes. *The Sober Truth: Debunking the Bad Science Behind 12-Step Programs and the Rehab Industry*. Boston, MA: Beacon Press, 2014.

Dolan, Jill. *Presence & Desire: Essays on Gender, Sexuality, Performance*. Ann Arbor: University of Michigan Press, 1993.

Donoghue, Emma. *Room*. New York: Little, Brown, 2010.

Doughty, Louise. *Apple Tree Yard*. New York: Faber & Faber, 2013.

Douglass, Ryan. "More Men Should Learn the Difference Between Masculinity and Toxic Masculinity." *HuffPost*, August 4, 2017. https://www.huffpost.com/entry/the-difference-between-masculinity-and-toxic-masculinity_b_59842e3ce4b0f2c7d93f54ce (accessed June 6, 2020).

Duca, Lauren. "Donald Trump Is Gaslighting America." *Teen Vogue*, December 10, 2016. https://www.teenvogue.com/story/donald-trump-is-gaslighting-america (accessed May 29, 2019).
Earle, Steve. *I'll Never Get Out of This World Alive*. Boston, MA: Mariner Books, 2011.
Eco, Umberto. *The Role of the Reader: Explorations in the Semiotics of Texts*. Bloomington: Indiana University Press, 1979.
Ellis, Bret Easton. *Imperial Bedrooms*. New York: Vintage, 2010.
———. *Less than Zero*. New York: Vintage Contemporaries, 1998.
"The End of Alice—A. M. Homes." *Books, Time, and Silence*, April 10, 2009, http://bookstimeandsilence.blogspot.com/2009/04/end-of-alice-am-homes.html (accessed June 9, 2019).
Entin, Joseph B. *Sensational Modernism: Experimental Fiction and Photography in Thirties America*. Chapel Hill: University of North Carolina Press, 2007.
"Experimental Fiction." *Map Literary*. William Patterson University, 2017, http://www.mapliterary.org/on-experimental-fiction.html (accessed July 15, 2019).
Fabre, Cara. *Challenging Addiction in Canadian Literature and Classrooms*. Toronto: University of Toronto Press, 2016.
Fante, Dan. *86'ed*. New York: Harper Perennial, 2009.
Felski, Rita. *The Limits of Critique*. Chicago, IL: University of Chicago Press, 2015.
Felten, Eric. "After the Shock Is Gone: Postmodern Times." *Wall Street Journal*, December 3, 2010. https://www.wsj.com/articles/SB10001424052748703377504575650882413327998 (accessed June 9, 2019).
Fitzgerald, F. Scott. *The Beautiful and Damned*. New York: Signet, 2007.
Fletcher, Anne M. *Inside Rehab: The Surprising Truth about Addiction Treatment—and How to Get Help That Works*. New York: Viking, 2013.
Flynn, Gillian. *Gone Girl*. New York: Crown, 2012.
Frank, E. R. *Wrecked*. 2005. New York: Atheneum Books for Young Readers, 2015.
Freeden, Michael. *Ideology: A Very Short Introduction*. Oxford: Oxford University Press, 2003.
Friedan, Betty. *The Feminine Mystique*. New York: W. W. Norton, 1997.
Fusco, Coco. *The Bodies That Were Not Ours: And Other Writings*. London: Routledge, 2001.
Gardner, James. "Naked Breakfast, Lunch and Dinner." *New York Times*. April 23, 1995, p. 49.
Gaslight. Directed by George Cukor. Performed by Ingrid Bergman and Charles Boyer. United States: Metro-Goldwyn-Mayer, 1944. DVD.
Gelder, Ken. "The Fields of Popular Fiction." In *New Directions in Popular Fiction: Genre, Distribution, Reproduction*, edited by Ken Gelder, 1–20. London: Palgrave Macmillan, 2016.
Gilman, Sander L. *Disease and Representation: Images of Illness from Madness to AIDS*. Ithaca, NY: Cornell University Press, 1988.
Gilmore, Thomas B. *Equivocal Spirits: Alcoholism and Drinking in Twentieth-Century Literature*. Chapel Hill: University of North Carolina Press, 1987.
Goines, Donald. *Dopefiend*. New York: Kensington, 1999.
Goldberg, Benjamin. *The Mirror and Man*. Charlottesville: University of Virginia Press, 1985.
Gomberg, Edith S. Lisansky. "Shame and Guilt Issues among Women Alcoholics." *Alcoholism Treatment Quarterly* 4, no. 2 (1988): 139–55.
Gorrara, Claire. *The Roman Noir in Post-war French Culture*. Oxford: Oxford University Press, 2003.
"Grace Krilanovich: Q + A with the Editor." *Two Dollar Radio*, Blogspot, August 13, 2010, http://twodollarradio.blogspot.com/2010/08/grace-krilanovich-qa-with-editor.html (accessed July 16, 2019).

Gran, Sara. *Dope*. New York: Berkley Books, 2006.
Gregg, Melissa, and Gregory J. Seigworth. "An Inventory of Shimmers." In *The Affect Theory Reader*, edited by Gregg and Seigworth, 1–25. Durham, NC: Duke University Press, 2010.
Greiner, Rae. *Sympathetic Realism in Nineteenth-Century British Fiction*. Baltimore, MD: Johns Hopkins University Press, 2012.
Gunderson, Lauren. *The Revolutionists: A Comedy/A Quartet/A Revolutionary Dream Fugue/A True Story*. New York: Dramatists Play Service, 2018.
Hall, Clayton R., Jr., *Becoming Whole after Addiction*. Morrisville, NC: Lulu, 2017.
Hamid, Mohsin. *The Reluctant Fundamentalist*. Orlando, FL: Harcourt, 2007.
Hamilton, Patrick. *Gaslight*. New York: Samuel French, 2015.
Hammett, Dashiell. *The Maltese Falcon, the Thin Man, Red Harvest*. New York: Alfred A. Knopf, 2000.
Hannaham, James. *Delicious Foods*. New York: Back Bay Books, 2016.
Hapke, Laura. *Girls Who Went Wrong: Prostitutes in American Fiction, 1885–1917*. Bowling Green, OH: Bowling Green State University Popular Press, 1989.
Haraway, Donna J. *Simians, Cyborgs, and Women: The Reinvention of Nature*. New York: Routledge, 1991.
Harrison, A. S. A. *The Silent Wife*. New York: Penguin, 2013.
Hawkins, Joan, and Alex Wermer-Colan, eds. *William S. Burroughs: Cutting Up the Century*. Bloomington: Indiana University Press, 2019.
Hawkins, Paula. *The Girl on the Train*. New York: Riverhead Books, 2015.
Highsmith, Patricia. *Strangers on a Train*. New York: W. W. Norton, 2001.
Hilton, Frank. *Baudelaire in Chains: A Portrait of the Artist as a Drug Addict*. London: Peter Owen, 2003.
Hitchin, A. D., and Joe Ambrose. "Introduction." In *CUT UP!: An Anthology Inspired by the Cut-Up Method of William S. Burroughs & Brion Gysin*, edited by Hitchin and Ambrose, 5. Oneiros Books, 2014. http://www.paraphiliamagazine.com/books/oneirosbooks.
Holman, C. Hugh, and William Harmon. *A Handbook to Literature*, 6th ed. New York: Macmillan, 1992.
Holub, Robert C. *Reception Theory: A Critical Introduction*. London: Methuen, 1984.
Homes, A. M. *The End of Alice*. New York: Scribner, 1996.
Hser, Yih-ing, M. Douglas Anglin and Mary W. Booth, "Sex Differences in Addict Careers: III. Addiction." *The American Journal of Drug and Alcohol Abuse* 13, no. 3 (1987): 231–51.
Huber, Werner, Martin Middeke and Hubert Zapf. "Introduction." In *Self-Reflexivity in Literature*, edited by Huber, Middeke and Zapf, 7–12. Würzburg, Germany: Königshausen & Neumann, 2005.
Jackson, Charles. *The Lost Weekend*. New York: Vintage Books, 2013.
Jaffe, Adi. "Want to Beat Addiction? Stop Blaming Addicts." *Psychology Today*, April 23, 2018. https://www.psychologytoday.com/us/blog/all-about-addiction/201804/want-beat-addiction-stop-blaming-addicts (accessed January 24, 2019).
Janowitz, Tama. *Slaves of New York*. New York: Bloomsbury, 1986.
Johnson, Bankole A., ed. *Addiction Medicine*. New York: Springer, 2010.
Johnston, Ann Dowsett. *Drink: The Intimate Relationship between Women and Alcohol*. New York: Harper Wave, 2013.
Kandall, Stephen R. *Substance and Shadow: Women and Addiction in the United States*. Cambridge, MA: Harvard University Press, 1996.

Kaslik, Ibi. *Skinny.* New York: HarperCollins, 2004.
Kerouac, Jack. *On the Road.* New York: Penguin, (1955) 1999.
Keyes, Marian. *Rachel's Holiday.* New York: HarperCollins, 1998.
King, Stephen. *Misery.* New York: Viking, 1987.
———. *'Salem's Lot.* New York: Anchor Books, 2011.
———. *The Shining.* New York: Anchor Books, 2013.
Krilanovich, Grace. *The Orange Eats Creeps.* Columbus, OH: Two Dollar Radio, 2010.
Laing, Olivia. *The Trip to Echo Springs: On Writers and Drinking.* New York: Picador, 2014.
Laub, Dori. "Truth and Testimony: The Process and the Struggle." In *Trauma: Explorations in Memory*, edited by Cathy Caruth, 61–75. Baltimore, MD: Johns Hopkins University Press, 1995.
Leone, Ryan. *Wasting Talent.* United States: Catharsis Fiction, 2014.
Less Than Zero. Directed by Marek Kanievska. Performed by Andrew McCarthy, Jami Gertz and Robert Downey Jr. United States: 20th Century Fox, 1987. DVD.
Levant, Ronald F., and Shana Pryor. *The Tough Standard: The Hard Truths about Masculinity and Violence.* New York: Oxford University Press, 2020.
Lilienfeld, Jane. "Introduction." In *The Languages of Addiction*, edited by Lilienfeld and Jeffrey Oxford, xiii–xxvii. New York: St. Martin's Press, 1999.
Lilienfeld, Jane, and Jeffrey Oxford, eds. *The Languages of Addiction.* New York: St. Martin's Press, 1999.
Lindquist, Mark. *The King of Methlehem.* New York: Simon and Schuster, 2007.
Linnemann, Travis, and Tyler Wall. "'This Is Your Face on Meth': The Punitive Spectacle of 'White Trash' in the Rural War on Drugs." *Theoretical Criminology* 17, no. 3 (2013): 315–34.
Little, Eddie. *Another Day in Paradise.* New York: Penguin, 1997.
Lloyd-Smith, Allan. "Abjection/Abjectivism." *European Journal of American Culture* 24, no. 3 (December 2005): 191–203.
Lodge, David. *The Modes of Modern Writing: Metaphor, Metonymy, and the Typology of Modern Literature.* London: Bloomsbury, 2015.
Mackintosh, Clare. *I Let You Go.* New York: Berkeley, (2011) 2016.
Macy, Beth. *Dopesick: Dealers, Doctors, and the Drug Company That Addicted America.* New York: Little, Brown, 2018.
Magolda, Marcia B. Baxter. *Creating Contexts for Learning and Self-Authorship: Constructive-Developmental Pedagogy.* Nashville, TN: Vanderbilt University Press, 1999.
Maillet, Arnaud. *The Claude Glass: Use and Meaning of the Black Mirror in Western Art*, translated by Jeff Fort. New York: Zone Books, 2004.
Marling, William. *The American Roman Noir: Hammett, Cain, and Chandler.* Athens, GA: University of Georgia Press, 1995.
Martin, Greg. *Crime, Media and Culture.* New York: Routledge, 2019.
Martin, Peter R., Bennett Alan Weinberg and Bonnie K. Bealer. *Healing Addiction: An Integrated Pharmacopsychosocial Approach to Treatment.* Hoboken, NJ: John Wiley 2007.
Matthews, Steve. "Self-Stigma and Addiction." In *The Stigma of Addiction: An Essential Guide*, edited by Jonathan D. Avery and Joseph J. Avery, 5–32. Basingstoke, UK: Springer, 2019.
McCarthy, Larry. "Less Than Zero." *Saturday Review* July/August 1985: 80.
McClellan, Michelle L. *Lady Lushes: Gender, Alcoholism, and Medicine in Modern America.* New Brunswick, NJ: Rutgers University Press, 2017.
McEwan, Ian. *Atonement.* London: Jonathan Cape, 2001.

McHale, *Postmodernist Fiction*. London: Routledge, 1987.
McInerney, Jay. *Bright Lights, Big City*. New York: Vintage, 1984.
Meigs, James B. "A Gaslight unto the Nations: How a Word Became the Cliché of the Trump Years." *Commentary Magazine*. December 2018. https://www.commentarymagazine.com/articles/gaslight-unto-nations/ (accessed May 29, 2019).
Melchoir-Bonnet, Sabine. *The Mirror: A History*. New York: Routledge, 2000.
Mian, Mian. *Candy*, translated by Andrea Lingenfelter. New York: Back Bay Books, 2003.
Mookerjee, Robin. *Transgressive Fiction: The New Satiric Tradition*. New York: Palgrave Macmillan, 2013.
Moore, Brian. *The Lonely Passion of Judith Hearne*. New York: New York Review Books Classics, 2010.
Moore, Lewis D. *Connecting Detectives: The Influence of the 19th Century Sleuth Fiction on the Early Hard-Boileds*. Jefferson, NC: McFarland, 2015.
Moshfegh, Ottessa. *Eileen: A Novel*. New York: Penguin, 2015.
Mosionier, Beatrice Culleton. *In Search of April Raintree*. Reprint, Winnipeg: HighWater Press, (1983) 1999.
Muller, Mark. "The Importance of Taking and Bearing Witness: Reflections on Twenty Years as a Human Rights Lawyer." In *We Shall Bear Witness: Life Narratives and Human Rights*, edited by Meg Jensen and Margaretta Jolly, 257–63. Madison: University of Wisconsin Press, 2014.
Nashawaty, Chris. "John O'Brien's Bittersweet Departure." *Entertainment Weekly*, November 10, 1995. https://ew.com/article/1995/11/10/john-obriens-bittersweet-departure/ (accessed January 30, 2019).
Nelson, Alan E., EdD. *Embracing Brokenness: How God Refines Us through Life's Disappointments*. Scotts Valley, CA: CreateSpace Independent, 2016.
Nünning, Vera. "Conceptualising (Un)reliable Narration and (Un)trustworthiness." In *Unreliable Narration and Trustworthiness: Intermedial and Interdisciplinary Perspectives*, edited by Nünning, 1–30. Berlin: Walter de Gruyter, 2015.
Nussbaum, Martha C. "Compassion: The Basic Social Emotion." *Social Philosophy and Policy* 13, no. 1 (1996): 27–58.
———. *Cultivating Humanity: A Classical Defense of Reform in Liberal Education*. Cambridge, MA: Harvard University Press, 1998.
Nyman, Jopi. *Men Alone: Masculinity, Individualism, and Hard-Boiled Fiction*. Amsterdam: Rodopi B.V., 1997.
Oates, Joyce Carol. "The Domestic Thriller Is Having a Moment." *The New Yorker*, February 19, 2018. https://www.newyorker.com/magazine/2018/02/26/the-domestic-thriller-is-having-a-moment (accessed May 31, 2019).
"objective narration." *Oxford Dictionary of Media and Communication*, 2011, Oxford University Press. http://www.oxfordreference.com/view/10.1093/oi/authority.20110803100243605 (accessed February 2, 2019).
O'Brien, John. *Leaving Las Vegas*. New York: Grove Press, 1995.
O'Neill, Heather. *lullabies for little criminals*. New York: Harper Perennial, 2006.
O'Neill, Tony. *Black Neon*. West Yorkshire: Bluemoose Books, 2014. Kindle.
———. *Digging the Vein*. Hull: Wrecking Ball Press, 2007.
———. *Down and Out on Murder Mile*. New York: Harper Perennial, 2008.
Palahniuk, Chuck. *Haunted*. New York: Anchor, 2005.
Patterson, Kevin. *Consumption*. New York: Anchor, (1967) 2008. Reprint.

Payer, Doris, and Edythe D. London. "Methamphetamine and the Brain: Findings from Brain Imagining Studies." In *Methamphetamine Addiction: From Basic Science to Treatment*, edited by John M. Roll, Richard A. Rawson, Walter Ling and Steven Shoptaw, 61–91. New York: Guilford Press, 2009.

Pendergrast, Mark. "Introduction: Mirror Mirror: A Historical and Psychological Overview." *The Book of the Mirror: An Interdisciplinary Collection Exploring the Cultural Story of the Mirror*, edited by Miranda Anderson, 1–14. Newcastle upon Tyne: Cambridge Scholars, 2007.

———. *Mirror, Mirror: A History of the Human Love Affair with Reflection*. New York: Basic Books, 2004.

Penn, Farrah. *Twelve Steps to Normal*. New York: Little, Brown, 2018.

Peterson, Jeffery Chaichana, Aline Gubrium and Alice Fiddian-Green. "Meth Mouth, White Trash, and the Pseudo-Racialization of Methamphetamine Use in the U.S." *Health Communication* 34, no. 10 (2018): 1–10.

Piazza, Jo. *Love Rehab: A Novel in Twelve Steps*. New York: Open Road, 2013.

Platt, Len, and Sara Upstone. "Introduction." *Postmodern Literature and Race*, edited by Platt and Upstone, 1–12. New York: Cambridge University Press, 2015.

Powers, John. "The MTV Novel Arrives." *Film Comment* 21, no. 6 (November–December 1985): 44–46.

Powers, Richard. *The Echo Maker*. New York: Farrar, Straus and Giroux, 2006.

Punter, David. *Literature of Pity*. Edinburgh: Edinburgh University Press, 2014.

Quinn, Dave. "Elton John Celebrates 29 Years of Sobriety in Touching Post: 'I Was a Broken Man.'" *Yahoo! Entertainment*, July 29, 2019. https://www.yahoo.com/entertainment/elton-john-celebrates-29-years-131507016.html (accessed July 31, 2019).

Radway, Janice A. *Reading the Romance: Women, Patriarchy, and Popular Literature*. Chapel Hill: University of North Carolina Press, 1984.

Reding, Nick. *Methland: The Death and Life of an American Small Town*. New York: Bloomsbury, 2010.

"Retirement and the Demon Drink." *The Summerhouse Years*, May 3, 2017. http://thesummerhouseyears.com/retirement-and-the-demon-drink/ (accessed January 30, 2019).

Richter, David H. "Formalism." *The Critical Tradition: Classic Texts and Contemporary Trends*, edited by Richter, 721–37. New York: St. Martin's Press, 1989.

Rivkin, Julie, and Michael Ryan. "Introduction: 'The Politics of Culture.'" In *Literary Theory: An Anthology*, edited by Rivkin and Ryan, 1025–27. Malden, MA: Blackwell, 1998.

Robinson, Eden. *Monkey Beach*. New York: Houghton Mifflin Harcourt, 2000.

Rocketman. Directed by Dexter Fletcher. Performed by Taron Egerton. United States: Paramount Pictures, 2019. Film.

Rolls, Alistair, and Deborah Walker. *French and American Noir: Dark Crossings*. New York: Palgrave Macmillan, 2009.

Ronell, Avital. *Crack Wars: Literature Addiction Mania*. Urbana: University of Illinois Press, 2004.

Rosenberg, Paul. "Lies, Bulls**t and Gaslighting: A Field Guide to Trump's Reality-Warping Mendacity." *Salon*, February 24, 2019. https://www.salon.com/2019/02/24/lies-bullst-and-gaslighting-a-field-guide-to-trumps-reality-warping-mendacity/ (accessed May 29, 2019).

Rosenblatt, Louise M. *Literature as Exploration*. New York: Modern Language Association of America, 1995.

Roth, Megan E., Kelly P. Cosgrove and Marilyn E. Carroll. "Sex Differences in the Vulnerability to Drug Abuse: A Review of Preclinical Studies." *Neuroscience and Biobehavioral Reviews* 28, no. 6 (2004): 533–46.
Roxworthy, Emily. *The Spectacle of Japanese American Trauma: Racial Performativity and World War II*. Honolulu: University of Hawai'i Press, 2008.
Rzepka, Charles J. *Detective Fiction*. Cambridge, MA: Polity Press, 2005.
SaFranko, Mark. *Hating Olivia*. New York: Harper Perennial, 2010.
Salter, Mary Jo. "In Short: Fiction." Review of *Less Than Zero*, by Bret Easton Ellis. *New York Times*, June 16, 1985. https://www.nytimes.com/1985/06/16/books/in-short-fiction-050756.html (accessed June 24, 2019).
Sarkis, Stephanie. "Donald Trump Is a Classic Gaslighter in an Abusive Relationship with America." *USA Today*, October 3, 2018. https://www.usatoday.com/story/opinion/2018/10/03/trump-classic-gaslighter-abusive-relationship-america-column/1445050002/ (accessed May 29, 2019).
Scarry, Elaine. *The Body in Pain: The Making and Unmaking of the World*. Oxford: Oxford University Press, 1985.
Science Daily. *Confirmation Bias*. https://www.sciencedaily.com/terms/confirmation_bias.htm (accessed March 30, 2019).
Sedgwick, Eve Kosofsky. *Epistemology of the Closet*. Berkeley: University of California Press, 1990.
Shaffer, David. Review of *The Girl on the Train*, by Paula Hawkins. *Star Tribune*, January 8, 2015. http://www.startribune.com/review-the-girl-on-the-train-by-paula-hawkins/287991531/ (accessed March 19, 2020).
Shaw, Janice Marion. "P.D. James's Discontinuous Narrative: A Suitable Job for a Reader." In *New Perspectives on Detective Fiction: Mystery Magnified*, edited by Casey Cothran and Mercy Cannon, 96–112. New York: Routledge, 2016.
Shea, Victor. "Culler, Jonathan Dwight." In *Encyclopedia of Contemporary Literary Theory: Approaches, Scholars, Terms*, edited by Irene Rima Makaryk, 283–84. Toronto: University of Toronto Press, 1993.
Shriver, Lionel. *We Need to Talk about Kevin*. New York: Harper Perennial, 2004.
Silverblatt, Michael. "Shock Appeal/ Who Are These Writers, and Why Do They Want to Hurt Us: The New Fiction of Transgression." *Los Angeles Times*, August 1, 1993. https://www.latimes.com/archives/la-xpm-1993-08-01-bk-21466-story.html (accessed June 9, 2019).
Smith, Murray. "Just What Is It That Makes Tony Soprano Such an Appealing, Attractive Murderer?" *Ethics at the Cinema*, edited by Ward E. Jones and Samantha Vice, 67–88. Oxford: Oxford University Press, 2011.
Smith, Zadie. "Now More Than Ever." *The New Yorker*, July 16, 2018. https://www.newyorker.com/magazine/2018/07/23/now-more-than-ever (accessed July 29, 2019).
———. *NW*. New York: Penguin, 2012.
Solomon, Lon. *Brokenness: How God Redeems Pain and Suffering*. Potomac, MD: Red Door Press, 2005.
Sontag, Susan. *Against Interpretation and Other Essays*. New York: Picador, (1961) 2001.
———. *Regarding the Pain of Others*. New York: Farrar, Straus and Giroux, 2003.
Southgate, Martha. *The Taste of Salt*. Chapel Hill, NC: Algonquin Books, 2011.
Spicer, Andrew. *Historical Dictionary of Film Noir*. Lanham, MD: Scarecrow Press, 2010.
Stanley, Charles. *The Blessings of Brokenness: Why God Allows Us to Go Through Hard Times*. Grand Rapids, MI: Zondervan, 1997.

A Star Is Born. Directed by William A. Wellman. Performed by Janet Gaynor and Fredric March. United States: Selznick International Pictures, 1937. DVD.

A Star Is Born. Directed by George Cukor. Performed by Judy Garland and James Mason. United States: Transcona Enterprises, 1954. DVD.

A Star Is Born. Directed by Frank Pierson. Performed by Barbara Streisand and Kris Kristofferson. United States: Warner Brothers, 1976. DVD.

A Star Is Born. Directed by Bradley Cooper. Performed by Lady Gaga and Bradley Cooper. United States: Warner Brothers, 2018. DVD.

Stern, Robin. *The Gaslight Effect: How to Spot and Survive the Hidden Manipulation Others Use to Control Your Life*. New York: Harmony Books, 2007.

Stevenson, Robert Louis. *The Strange Case of Dr. Jekyll and Mr. Hyde*. Ware, Hertfordshire: Wordsworth Editions Limited, (1886) 1993. Reprint.

Stoker, Bram. *Dracula*. 1897. London: Wordsworth, 2000. Reprint.

Stowe, Harriet Beecher. *Uncle Tom's Cabin*. Mineola, NY: Dover Thrift, (1852) 1972. Reprint.

Stratton, Kimberly B., and Dayna S. Kalleres, eds. *Daughters of Hecate: Women & Magic in the Ancient World*. New York: Oxford University Press, 2014.

Strong, Bryan, and Theodore F. Cohen. *The Marriage and Family Experience: Intimate Relationships in a Changing Society*, 13th ed. Boston, MA: Cengage Learning, 2017.

Sturken, Marita. *Tangled Memories: The Vietnam War, the AIDS Epidemic, and the Politics of Remembering*. Berkeley: University of California Press, 1997.

Susann, Jacqueline. *Valley of the Dolls*. New York: Grove Press, 1966.

Tartt, Donna. Review of *Less Than Zero*, by Bret Easton Ellis. *Amazon.com*. n.d. https://www.amazon.com/Imperial-Bedrooms-Vintage-Contemporaries-Easton-ebook/dp/B0036S49VY (accessed June 27, 2019).

"Temperance—History." *Ohio History Connection*. http://www.ohiopix.org/contentdm-search-results/?cdm-keywords=Temperance--History&cdm-mode=all&cdm-field=subjec (accessed January 30, 2019).

Thomas, Scot, MD. "12 Step Drug Rehab and Alcohol Treatment Programs." *American Addiction Centers*, June 11, 2019. https://americanaddictioncenters.org/rehab-guide/12-step (July 24, 2019).

Thompson, Hunter S. *Fear and Loathing in Las Vegas: A Savage Journey to the Heart of the American Dream*. New York: Vintage Books, 1971.

Thompson, Jim. *The Killer Inside Me*. New York: Mulholland Books, 2014.

Todorov, Tzvetan. *The Poetics of Prose*, translated by Richard Howard. New York: Cornell University Press, 1977.

Tompkins, Jane P. "An Introduction to Reader-Response Criticism." In *Reader-Response Criticism: From Formalism to Post-Structuralism*, edited by Tompkins, ix–xxvi. Baltimore, MD: Johns Hopkins University Press, 1980.

"transgress, v." *OED Online*, June 2019, Oxford University Press. http://www.oed.com.ezproxy.bgsu.edu/view/Entry/204775?rskey=BFADjt&result=2 (accessed June 9, 2019).

Tumanov, Vladimir. *Mind Reading: Unframed Interior Monologue in European Fiction*. Amsterdam: Rodopi, 1997.

The Twelve Steps of Alcoholics Anonymous. Hazelden Betty Ford Foundation. https://www.hazeldenbettyford.org/articles/twelve-steps-of-alcoholics-anonymous (accessed May 23, 2019).

Ulas, Ekin. "Outrageous Insights: The Ethical Value of Transgressive Literature." Master's Thesis, University of Hong Kong, 2014.

Ulman, Richard B., and Harry Paul. *The Self Psychology of Addiction and Its Treatment: Narcissus in Wonderland.* New York: Routledge, 2006.
Underwood, Carrie. "Jesus, Take the Wheel." By Hillary Lindsey, Gordie Sampson, and Brett James. Recorded 2005. Track 4 on *Some Hearts.* Arista Nashville. Compact disc.
Vaage, Margrethe Bruun. *The Antihero in American Television.* New York: Routledge, 2016. Kindle.
Vogt, Christopher P. *Patience, Compassion, Hope, and the Christian Art of Dying Well.* Lanham: Rowman & Littlefield, 2004.
"voyeur, n." *OED Online*, June 2018, Oxford University Press. http://www.oedo/com.ezproxy.bgsu.edu:8080/view/Entry/224799?rskey=homfrS&result=1 (accessed July 2, 2018).
Waldman, Katy. "From Theater to Therapy to Twitter, the Eerie History of Gaslighting." *Slate.* April 18, 2016. https://slate.com/human-interest/2016/04/the-history-of-gaslighting-from-films-to-psychoanalysis-to-politics.html (accessed May 29, 2019).
Walker-Morrison, Deborah. *Classic French Noir: Gender and the Cinema of Fatal Desire.* London: I. B. Tauris, 2019.
Wallace, David Foster. *Infinite Jest.* New York: Back Bay Books, 2006.
Ware, Ruth. *The Lying Game.* New York: Scout Press, 2017.
———. *The Woman in Cabin 10.* New York: Scout Press, 2016.
Watson, S. J. *Before I Go to Sleep.* New York: HarperCollins, 2011.
Welsh, Irvine. *Trainspotting.* New York: W. W. Norton, 1996.
Werness, Hope B. *The Symbolism of Mirrors in Art from Ancient Times to the Present.* Lewiston, NY: Edwin Mellen Press, 1999.
White, Aaron M. "What Happened?: Alcohol, Memory Blackouts, and the Brain." *Alcohol Research & Health* 27, no. 2 (2003): 186–96. *National Institute on Alcohol Abuse and Alcoholism.* https://pubs.niaaa.nih.gov/publications/arh27-2/186-196.htm (accessed April 1, 2019).
Whitlock, Gillian. "Protection." In *We Shall Bear Witness: Life Narratives and Human Rights*, edited by Meg Jensen and Margaretta Jolly, 80–99. Madison, WI: University of Wisconsin Press, 2014.
Wilde, Oscar. *The Picture of Dorian Gray.* Mineola, NY: Dover Publications, 1993.
Wilder, Thornton. *Our Town: A Play in Three Acts.* New York: HarperCollins, 2003.
Woodward, Kathleen. "Calculating Compassion." In *Compassion: The Culture and Politics of an Emotion*, edited by Lauren Berlant, 59–86. New York: Routledge, 2004.
Yandow, Valery. "Alcoholism in Women." *Psychiatric Annals* 19, no. 5 (1989): 243–47.
Youssef, Essam. *A 1/4 Gram*, translated by Loubna A. Youssef. Cairo, Egypt: Montana Studios, 2008.
Yuill, Chris, Iain Crinson and Eilidh Duncan. *Key Concepts in Health Studies.* Los Angeles, CA: Sage, 2010.
Zahed, Hyder. "Compassionate Listening." *HuffPost* July 11, 2017. https://www.huffpost.com/entry/compassionate-listening_b_10921036 (accessed June 25, 2019).
Zieger, Susan. *Inventing the Addict: Drugs, Race, and Sexuality in Nineteenth-Century British and American Literature.* Amherst: University of Massachusetts Press, 2008.
Zinn, Howard. "Foreword." *Silencing Political Dissent: How Post-September 11 Anti-Terrorism Measures Threaten Our Civil Liberties*, edited by Nancy Chang. New York: Seven Stories Press, 2002. Kindle.
Zweig, Michael. *The Working Class Majority: America's Best Kept Secret.* Ithaca, NY: Cornell University Press, 2012.

INDEX

9 to 5 27

Abani, Chris 6
Acker, Kathy 98
addict, as identity 1n3, 15–16, 18, 21, 24, 36, 44–45, 91, 134
Addiction Medicine (Johnson) 94n2
addiction novel
  ideology of 26, 29, 47, 93, 94–95
  and *The Lost Weekend* 2, 41n65
  reception of 42, 56
  and road metaphor 125
  as testimony 23
The Adventures of Ozzie and Harriet 52–53
affect theory 13
Against Interpretation and Other Essays (Sontag) 147
Alcoholics Anonymous 31n34, 53, 78, 138–39
Alcoholics Anonymous: Cult or Cure? (Bufe) 139n4
alcoholism
  and blackouts 38–41, 78–83
  in *The Girl on the Train* 69, 71–72, 76–83, 84–85, 87, 90–91
  in *Leaving Las Vegas* 19–20, 22, 24–25, 29–30, 35, 37, 45–46
  liar, stereotype of 107n46
  treatment in addiction novel 2–3, 41n65, 125
  treatment in literary criticism 14, 16
  and women 71–72
Alexander, Anna 13–14
Allende, Isabel 6
Altman, Rick 4, 87–88
American Literary Minimalism (Clark) 110

The American Roman Noir: Hammett, Cain, and Chandler (Marling) 57
Anderson, Miranda 105n44
The Andy Griffith Show 27
Another Day in Paradise (Little) 65
Apple Tree Yard (Doughty) 81–82n50
Armstrong, Julie 7–8, 51, 120, 124, 132
Armstrong, Nancy 28
Atonement (McEwan) 70
Atwood, Margaret 137, 141, 146
aversion, rhetoric of 115–17

Ballard, J. G. 98
Barnes, Julian 5
Barry, Lynda 125
Barth, John 132
Barthes, Roland 67, 82–83
Baudelaire in Chains: A Portrait of the Artist as a Drug Addict (Hilton) 14–15
Bealer, Bonnie K. 90
The Beautiful and Damned (Fitzgerald) 20
Beaver, Frank Eugene 60–61
Becoming Whole After Addiction (Hall) 79n40
Before I Go To Sleep (Watson) 70
Belsey, Catherine 8, 10, 17
Ben-Amots, Zach 95
Berlant, Lauren 6, 115–16, 144–45
Berry, Ellen E. 117
Berry, R. M. 117
The Big Book of Alcoholics Anonymous 31n34, 107n46
Black Neon (Tony O'Neill) 94–98
blackouts
  in *The Girl on the Train* 69, 78–83, 84–85
  in *Leaving Las Vegas* 19, 23, 38–41
Blood and Guts in High School (Acker) 98

The Bodies That Were Not Ours: And Other
  Writings (Fusco) 4–5
The Body in Pain: The Making and Unmaking
  of the World (Scarry) 46n82
The Book of the Mirror: An Interdisciplinary
  Collection Exploring the Cultural Story of
  the Mirror (Anderson) 105n44
Booth, Wayne C. 9, 69, 146
Bright Lights, Big City (McInerney) 6, 29,
  65, 100
brokenness, metaphor of 137–42, 146
Bronfen, Elisabeth 43–44
Bufe, Charles 139n4
Burroughs, William 98, 122n22
Busybodies, Meddlers, and Snoops: The Female
  Hero in Contemporary Women's Mysteries
  (Dilley) 70

Cain, James M. 47, 50
Calvino, Italo 132
Candy (Mian) 6
Candy: A Novel of Love and Addiction (Davies)
  6, 34n45, 65, 130
Carter, Angela 98
Castillo, Debra A. 25n18
Chang, Nancy 143–45
Cheever, John 20
Classic French Noir: Gender and the Cinema of
  Fatal Desire (Walker-Morrison) 64
Clark, Robert C. 110
The Claude Glass: Use and Meaning of the Black
  Mirror in Western Art (Maillet) 105n44
Cobley, Paul 49
Cohen, Michael 48, 68
Cohen, Theodore F. 55
compassion
  absence in addiction novel 1, 3, 4
  definition of 6, 115–16, 119
  in *Dope* 51, 64, 66
  in *The Girl on the Train* 88–89, 91
  in *Leaving Las Vegas* 30, 43, 46
  in *Less Than Zero* 103
  as listening practice 108–13
  in *The Orange Eats Creeps* 131–35
  and political dissent 142–47
  as reading practice 8, 11, 12–13,
    18, 141
  relationship to literary imagination 12

Compassion: The Culture and Politics
  of an Emotion (ed. Berlant) 6,
  115–16, 144–45
"Compassion (and Withholding)" (Berlant)
  115–16, 144–45
compassionate listening 108–13, 132–33
Compassionate Listening Project 111
compassionate reading 12–13, 103, 134
Connecting Detectives: The Influence of the 19th
  Century Sleuth Fiction on the Early Hard-
  Boileds (Lewis D. Moore) 54–56
Cooper, Dennis 98, 99
Cortázar, Julio 132
Crack Wars: Literature Addiction Mania
  (Ronell) 13–14
Creating Contexts for Learning and Self-
  Authorship: Constructive-Developmental
  Pedagogy (Magolda) 143
Crime, Media and Culture (Greg Martin) 57
Critical Practice (Belsey) 8, 10, 17
Cruddy: An Illustrated Novel (Barry) 125
Cukor, George 85–86
Culler, Jonathan 10–11, 10n31, 109
Cultivating Humanity: A Classical Defense of
  Reform in Liberal Education (Nussbaum)
  7, 12–13
cut-up method 122n22

Dardis, Tom 14–15
Daughters of Hecate: Women & Magic in
  the Ancient World (Stratton and
  Kalleres) 25n18
David, Anna 85
Davies, Luke 6, 34n45, 65, 130
Delicious Foods (Hannaham) 6, 65
Derrida, Jacques 122
Desire and Domestic Fiction: A Political History
  of the Novel (Nancy Armstrong) 28
Detective Fiction (Rzepka) 48, 68
Dickos, Andrew 51, 65
Dictionary of Film Terms: The Aesthetic
  Companion to Film Art (Beaver) 60–61
Didion, Joan 125
Digging the Vein (Tony O'Neill) 95
Dilley, Kimberly J. 70
disease model of addiction 109
Disease and Representation: Images of Illness
  from Madness to AIDS (Gilman) 139

INDEX

Dodes, Lance 107n46
Dodes, Zachary 107n46
Dolan, Jill 91
Donoghue, Emma 69
Dope (Gran) 8, 16, 47–66, 67, 93, 142, 145
Dopefiend (Goines) 43–44
Dopesick: Dealers, Doctors, and The Drug Company That Addicted America (Macy) 94n2
Doughty, Louise 81–82n50
Down and Out on Murder Mile (Tony O'Neill) 20, 85
Drink: The Intimate Relationship Between Women and Alcohol (Johnston) 71n13

Earle, Steve 29, 65
Easy Women: Sex and Gender in Modern Mexican Fiction (Castillo) 25n18
The Echo Maker (Powers) 126
Eco, Umberto 10
Eileen (Moshfegh) 78
Ellis, Bret Easton 16, 30, 93–113, 142, 145
The End of Alice (Homes) 99
Entin, Joseph B. 117
Epistemology of the Closet (Sedgwick) 91
Equivocal Spirits: Alcoholism and Drinking in Twentieth-Century Literature (Gilmore) 1, 16
experimental fiction
  definition of 7–9, 11, 117, 132
  deformation of language 121–24
  disorientation of readers 127–31
  Dope, as example 51, 65–66
  The Girl on the Train, as example 69, 88–91
  inconsistency of tropes 125–27
  Leaving Las Vegas, as example 31, 34–36, 40–41
  Less Than Zero, as example 102
  as political dissent 142–47
Experimental Fiction: An Introduction for Readers and Writers (Julie Armstrong) 7–8, 51, 120, 124, 132
exploitation 43–44, 62–63, 68–69, 94–97, 133, 144–46
expressive compassion 119

Farley, Chris 97n11
Farrell, Brodie 13–14
Fear and Loathing in Las Vegas (Hunter S. Thompson) 125
Felski, Rita 67–68
Felten, Eric 99–100
The Feminine Mystique (Friedan) 59–60
femme fatale 50n15, 64
Fitzgerald, F. Scott 20
Fletcher, Anne M. 107n46
Flynn, Gillian 70
formalism 120
Frank, E. R. 126
Freeden, Michael 75–76
French and American Noir: Dark Crossings (Rolls and Deborah Walker) 48
Friedan, Betty 59–60
Frisk (Cooper) 99
Fusco, Coco 4–5

Gardner, James 98
Gaslight (Cukor) 85–86
Gaslight (Hamilton) 85–86
The Gaslight Effect: How to Spot and Survive the Hidden Manipulation Others Use to Control Your Life (Stern) 86
gaslighting 8, 85–91, 145, 146
gaze theory 2, 4, 33–35, 43, 143
Gelder, Ken 49
genre fiction 48–49
Gilman, Sander L. 139
Gilmore, Thomas B. 1, 16
The Girl on the Train (Hawkins) 7, 8, 16, 67–91, 93, 142, 145
Girls Who Went Wrong: Prostitutes in American Fiction, 1885–1917 (Hapke) 25n18
Goines, Donald 43–44
Goldberg, Benjamin 105n44
Gone Girl (Flynn) 70
Gorrara, Claire 48, 50
GraceLand (Abani) 6
Grafton, Sue 49n12
Gran, Sara 8, 16, 47–66, 67, 93, 142, 145
Gregg, Melissa 13
Greiner, Rae 116–17
Gunderson, Lauren 141

Hall, Clayton R., Jr. 79n40
Hamid, Mohsin 69–70
Hamilton, Patrick 85–86
Hammett, Dashiell 48, 57
Hannaham, James 6, 65
Hapke, Laura 25n18
Haraway, Donna 139–40n7
Harmon, William 52
Harrison, A. S. A. 81–82n50
Haunted (Palahniuk) 98
Hawkins, Paula 7, 8, 16, 67–91, 93, 142, 145
Healing Addiction: An Integrated Pharmacopsychosocial Approach to Treatment (Peter R. Martin, Weinberg, and Bealer) 90
High Anxieties: Cultural Studies in Addiction (Farrell Brodie and Redfield) 13–14
high culture: reflections on addiction and modernity (Alexander and Roberts) 13–14
Highsmith, Patricia 47, 50
The Highway That Eats People 125–27
Hilton, Frank 14–15
Historical Dictionary of Film Noir (Spicer) 50n15
Hoffman, Gene Knudsen 111–12
Holman, C. Hugh 52
Holmes, Sherlock 68
Holub, Robert C. 9–10, 16
Homes, A. M. 98, 99
Hopscotch (Cortázar) 132
Huber, Werner 88–89

Ideology: A Very Short Introduction (Freeden) 75–76
If on a Winter's Night a Traveler (Calvino) 132
I Let You Go (Mackintosh) 126
I'll Never Get Out of This World Alive (Earle) 29, 65
Imperial Bedrooms (Ellis) 107–8
Infinite Jest (Wallace) 31n34
Inside Rehab: The Surprising Truth About Addiction Treatment—and How to Get Help That Works (Fletcher) 107n46
Intervention 2n6, 144–45

Jackson, Charles 2–5, 7, 41n65, 51, 63, 65, 85, 135
Jaffe, Dr. Adi 12
James, P. D. 68
Janowitz, Tama 31–2
"Jesus, Take the Wheel" (Underwood) 138
John, Elton 138–39
Johnson, Bankole A. 94n2
Johnston, Ann Dowsett 71n13
Judith Hearne (Brian Moore) 20

Kalleres, Dayna S. 25n18
Kandall, Stephen R. 55, 62–63
Keyes, Marian 85
The Killer Inside Me (Jim Thompson) 47, 50
King, Stephen 6, 27, 126
The King of Methlehem (Lindquist) 20
Krilanovich, Grace 8, 39, 93, 115–35, 142

Lady Lushes: Gender, Alcoholism, and Medicine in Modern America (McClellan) 71n13
Laing, Olivia 14–15
The Languages of Addiction (Lilienfeld and Oxford) 14
Leaving Las Vegas (O'Brien) 8, 19–46, 110, 142–43
Less Than Zero (Ellis) 16, 30, 93–113, 142, 145
Less Than Zero (film) 109
Lilienfeld, Jane 14
The Limits of Critique (Felski) 67–68
Lindquist, Mark 20
Lisansky Gomberg, Edith S. 71n13
literary competence 10–11, 10n31, 109
Literature as Exploration (Rosenblatt) 146–47
Literature of Pity (Punter) 5
literature qua literature 16
Little, Eddie 65
Lloyd-Smith, Allan 99
Lodge, David 133–34
London, Edythe D. 127
Lost in the Funhouse (Barth) 132
The Lost Weekend (Jackson) 2–5, 7, 41n65, 51, 63, 65, 85, 135
Love Rehab (Piazza) 94n2
Lullabies for Little Criminals (Heather O'Neill) 15, 20, 21, 65
The Lying Game (Ware) 81–2n50

INDEX

MacGuffin 60–63
Mackintosh, Clare 126
Macy, Beth 94n2
Magolda, Marcia B. Baxter 143
Maillet, Arnaud 105n44
The Maltese Falcon (Hammett) 48
Marling, William 57
The Marriage and Family Experience: Intimate Relationships in a Changing Society (Strong and Cohen) 55
Martin, Greg 57
Martin, Peter R. 90
Matthews, Steve 116, 131
Maya's Notebook (Allende) 6
McClellan, Michelle L. 71n13
McEwan, Ian 70
McHale, Brian 117, 133
McInerney, Jay 6, 29, 65, 100
medical model of addiction 140
medical model of disability 11n36, 140
Meigs, James B. 86–87
Melchoir-Bonnet, Sabine 105n44
Men Alone: Masculinity, Individualism, and Hard-Boiled Fiction (Nyman) 47–48, 64
Metafiction 5, 117, 132
Methamphetamine addiction 127–31
Methamphetamine Addiction: From Basic Science to Treatment (Payer and London) 127
Methland: The Death and Life of an American Small Town (Reding) 128–29
Mian, Mian 6
Middeke, Martin 88–89
Mind Reading: Unframed Interior Monologue in European Fiction (Tumanov) 35
minimalism 110
mirror 29–36, 42, 84, 103–8
The Mirror: A History (Melchoir-Bonnet) 105n44
The Mirror and Man (Goldberg) 105n44
Mirror, Mirror: A History of the Human Love Affair with Reflection (Pendergrast) 105n44
Misery (King) 126
Modernism 1–2, 51, 133–34
The Modes of Modern Writing: Metaphor, Metonymy, and the Typology of Modern Literature (Lodge) 133–34

Mookerjee, Robin 99–100
Moore, Brian 20
Moore, Lewis D. 54–56
moral model of addiction 1n3
   in *Black Neon* 96
   in *Dope* 54, 64
   in *The Girl on the Train* 76–77, 89, 91
   in *Leaving Las Vegas* 21–22, 24–25, 40–41
   in *Less Than Zero* 102–4, 108, 109–10
   in *The Orange Eats Creeps* 130–31, 140
Moshfegh, Ottessa 78
Muller, Mark 30
Murder Most Fair: The Appeal of Mystery Fiction (Cohen) 48, 68

NAMES Project AIDS Quilt 21
Nünning, Vera 69, 89
Nussbaum, Martha 6, 12–13
NW (Smith) 144–45
Nyman, Jopi 47–48, 64

Oates, Joyce Carol 81n50
O'Brien, John 8, 19–46, 110, 142–43
Of Grammatology (Derrida) 122
O'Neill, Heather 15, 20, 21, 65
O'Neill, Tony 20, 85, 94–98
A 1/4 Gram (Youssef) 6
The Only Story (Barnes) 5
The Orange Eats Creeps (Krilanovich) 8, 39, 93, 115–35, 142
Our Town (Wilder) 28
"Outrageous Insights: The Ethical Value of Transgressive Literature" (Ulas) 102–3
Over Her Dead Body: Death, Femininity, and the Aesthetic (Bronfen) 43–44
Oxford, Jeffrey 14

Palahniuk, Chuck 98
Party Girl (David) 85
pathos
   in *Candy: A Novel of Love and Addiction* 34n45
   in *Less Than Zero* 22, 34, 36, 41
   in *The Lost Weekend* 41n65
   and narrative resolution 8, 94, 117, 142
   relationship to morality 20
   relationship to trauma 2–4

Patience, Compassion, Hope, and the Christian Art of Dying Well (Vogt) 119
Paul, Harry 26n21
Payer, Doris 127
Pendergrast, Mark 105n44, 106
Penn, Farrah 94n2
Piazza, Jo 94n2
The Picture of Dorian Gray (Wilde) 5
pity 1–2, 5, 41, 69
Platt, Len 144
Play It As It Lays (Didion) 125
The Poetics of Prose (Todorov) 67–68
political dissent 142–44
The Postman Always Rings Twice (Cain) 47
postmodern fiction 7, 119–20, 133–34, 144, 146–47; *see also* experimental fiction
Postmodernist Fiction (McHale) 133
Postmodern Literature and Race (ed. Platt and Upstone) 144
Powers, Richard 126
Presence & Desire: Essays on Gender, Sexuality, Performance (Dolan) 91
Prostitution
  in *Black Neon* 93
  and Chris Farley 97n11
  in *Dope* 47, 52, 54, 56–59, 62–63
  in *Leaving Las Vegas* 20, 23–25, 37–38, 45
  in *Less Than Zero* 103
  in *lullabies for little criminals* 21
  in *Slaves of New York* 32
psychosis 127–30
Punter, David 5

Rachel's Holiday (Keyes) 85
Radway, Janice A. 117
Reader-Response Theory 9–12, 9n27, 16, 18, 141
Reading the Romance: Women, Patriarchy, and Popular Literature (Radway) 117
realism
  contrast to experimental fiction 7–9, 102, 104–5
  ideological authority of 17, 21, 91, 94, 143
  in *Less Than Zero* 93
  linear plotting in 132
  protagonist, role of 3–4, 116–17
  readerly history 109n51

Reception Theory: A Critical Introduction (Holub) 9–10, 16
Redfield, Mark 13–14
Reding, Nick 128–29
Regarding the Pain of Others (Sontag) 1, 5, 33, 45–46, 145
The Reluctant Fundamentalist (Hamid) 69–70
The Revolutionists (Gunderson) 141
The Rhetoric of Fiction (Booth) 69
Rivkin, Julie 13–14
road, as metaphor 125–27
Roberts, Mark S. 13–14
Rocketman 138–39, 144–45
The Role of the Reader: Explorations in the Semiotics of Texts (Eco) 10
Rolls, Alistair 48
roman noir 47–51, 57, 64–65, 87
The Roman Noir in Post-war French Culture (Gorrara) 48, 50
Ronell, Avital 13–14
Room (Donoghue) 69
Rosenblatt, Louise M. 9, 146
Roxworthy, Emily 2
Rushdie, Salman 100
Ryan, Michael 13–14
Rzepka, Charles J. 48, 68

'Salem's Lot (King) 27
Salter, Mary Jo 108
Scarry, Elaine 46n82
Second Words: Selected Critical Prose 1960–1982 (Atwood) 137, 141, 146
Sedgwick, Eve Kosofsky 91
Seigworth, Gregory J. 13
self-authorship 141–44
The Self Psychology of Addiction and Its Treatment: Narcissus in Wonderland (Ulman and Paul) 26n21
Self-Reflexivity in Literature (Huber, Middeke and Zapf) 88–89
Sensational Modernism: Experimental Fiction and Photography in Thirties America (Entin) 117
"Shame and Guilt Issues Among Women Alcoholics" (Lisansky Gomberg) 71n13
Shaw, Janice Marion 68
The Shining (King) 6

Shriver, Lionel 78
Silencing Political Dissent: How Post-September 11 Anti-Terrorism Measures Threaten Our Civil Liberties (Chang) 143–45
The Silent Wife (Harrison) 81–82n50
Silverblatt, Michael 98
Simians, Cyborgs, and Women: The Reinvention of Nature (Haraway) 139–40n7
The Simpsons 27
Slaves of New York (Janowitz) 31–32
Smith, Zadie 46, 144–45
The Sober Truth: Debunking the Bad Science Behind 12-Step Programs and the Rehab Industry (Dodes and Dodes) 107n46
soft Holocaust denial 95
Sontag, Susan 1, 5, 33, 45–46, 145, 147
Southgate, Martha 85
spectacle of degradation 2–3, 20, 36, 42–43, 53, 97n11, 145
The Spectacle of Japanese American Trauma: Racial Performativity and World War II (Roxworthy) 2
Spicer, Andrew 50n15
A Star Is Born 63, 65, 135, 144–45
Stern, Robin 86
Stevenson, Robert Louis 5, 15
The Strange Case of Dr. Jekyll and Mr. Hyde (Stevenson) 5, 15
Strangers on a Train (Highsmith) 47
Stratton, Kimberly B. 25n18
stream of consciousness 104–5, 121, 124, 129–30
Street with No Name: A History of the Classic American Film Noir (Dickos) 51, 65
Strong, Bryan 55
Sturken, Marita 21, 43
Substance and Shadow: Women and Addiction in the United States (Kandall) 55, 62–63
suicide 20, 24, 40, 43–45, 65
Susann, Jacqueline 5–6
"The Swimmer" (Cheever) 20
The Symbolism of Mirrors in Art from Ancient Times to The Present (Werness) 105
Sympathetic Realism in Nineteenth-Century British Fiction (Greiner) 116–17
S/Z: An Essay (Barthes) 67, 82–83

Tangled Memories: The Vietnam War, The AIDS Epidemic, and the Politics of Remembering (Sturken) 21, 43
Tartt, Donna 107–8
The Taste of Salt (Southgate) 85
tavern fool/town drunk 27–30
Temperance Movement 24, 63, 76
testimony 22–3
A Theory of Narrative (Altman) 4, 87–88
The Thirsty Muse: Alcohol and the American Writer (Dardis) 14–15
Thomas, Scot 116
Thompson, Hunter S. 125
Thompson, Jim 47, 50
Todorov, Tzvetan 67–68
Tompkins, Jane P. 10–11, 18
Trainspotting (Welsh) 6
transgressive fiction 94, 98–100, 100–108, 109–13
Transgressive Fiction: The New Satiric Tradition (Mookerjee) 99–100
The Trip to Echo Springs: On Writers and Drinking (Laing) 14–15
Tumanov, Vladimir 35
Twelve-Steps
  critiques of 94n2, 111, 116, 139
  in *Dope* 53–54
  in *The Girl on the Train* 78
  in *Infinite Jest* 31n34
  philosophy of 132
  relationship to narrative structure 85, 108
  talk therapy 31
Twelve Steps to Normal (Penn) 94n2

Ulas, Ekin 102–3
Ulman, Richard B. 26n21
Underwood, Carrie 138
Unreliable Narration and Trustworthiness: Intermedial and Interdisciplinary Perspectives (Nünning) 69, 89
unreliable narrator 69, 78–83, 88–91, 97
Upstone, Sara 144

Valley of the Dolls (Susann) 5–6
Vogt, Christopher P. 119

Walker, Deborah 48
Walker, Kara 4

Walker-Morrison, Deborah 64
Wallace, David Foster 31n34
Ware, Ruth 81–82n50, 144–45
waste metaphor 28–29, 41, 63, 108, 116, 146
Wasted: Performing Addiction in America (Diehl) 2n6, 108, 116
Watson, S. J. 70
Weinberg, Bennett Alan 90
Welsh, Irvine 6
We Need to Talk About Kevin (Shriver) 78
Werness, Hope B. 105
White, Aaron M. 81
Whitlock, Gillian 22
Wilde, Oscar 5
Wilder, Thornton 28
witnessing 2, 8, 144–46
　in *Dope* 69
　in *Leaving Las Vegas* 22–23, 29–30, 36–37, 40, 41–46
　in *The Orange Eats Creeps* 115, 131–32
The Woman in Cabin 10 (Ware) 144–45
Women's Experimental Writing: Negative Aesthetics and Feminist Critique (Ellen E. Berry) 117
Woodward, Kathleen 6
Wrecked (Frank) 126

Yandow, Dr. Valery 71
Youssef, Essam 6

Zahed, Hyder 111
Zapf, Hubert 88–89
Zinn, Howard 143–44

www.ingramcontent.com/pod-product-compliance
Lightning Source LLC
Chambersburg PA
CBHW021830300426
44114CB00009BA/398